CHILDREN OF THE ROOJME

CHILDREN OF THE ROOJME

A Family's Journey

ELMAZ ABINADER

W·W·NORTON & COMPANY·NEW YORK·LONDON

These stories are based on letters, diaries, interviews, and personal memories. The major events are true. Some of the names have been changed and the activities enhanced.

Copyright © 1991 by Elmaz Abinader
All rights reserved.

Printed in the United States of America.

The text of this book is composed in Bodoni Book,
Composition and manufacturing by
The Maple-Vail Book Manufacturing Group.
Book design by Guenet Abraham

First Edition.

Library of Congress Cataloging in Publication Data

Abinader, Elmaz.
Children of the roojme : a family's journey / Elmaz
Abinader.
p.   cm.
1. Lebanese Americans—Biography.   2. Abinader
family.
3. Abinader, Elmaz—Family.   I. Title.
E184.L34A25   1991
973'.049275692022—dc20
[B]   90–41136

ISBN 0-393-02952-2

W.W. Norton & Company, Inc.
500 Fifth Avenue, New York, N.Y. 10110
W.W. Norton & Company, Ltd.
10 Coptic Street, London WC1A 1PU

1 2 3 4 5 6 7 8 9 0

ACKNOWLEDGMENTS

My father is eighty years old this year. He has spent the last ten years working with me on this book, translating his father's diaries, writing his memoirs, answering the telephone in the middle of the day to answer questions, and giving me his love. I thank him, and my mother for taking the arduous journey into her past and sharing her secrets with me. I am glad she raised intelligent women.

Before her death, Azzizy, my mother's sister, also shared her life with me. I thank her and her daughter Jeannette Abi-Nader, H.M.

My sisters and brothers shared their love and supported my work in special ways. I thank Selma for remembering with me our trip to Lebanon, Jean for promoting the book, Roger for lending me his computers, Geralyn for listening more than once, and Elias for sharing his wisdom. My oldest friend, Peter Monahon, often ran to New York to breathe life into my computer.

The bulk of this book was written under the Schweitzer Fellowship for the Humanities at the State University of New York at Albany. I am grateful to Toni Morrison for that time and more.

A creative incentive grant through the Research Foundation of the City University of New York helped me take time for the final touches. Mary Cunnane and Lizzie Grossman have remarkable faith in and patience for this project.

And finally, I thank Alan Lemke, for his love and for living in all the right places.

I hope for peace.

C O N T E N T S

Contents

PART TWO

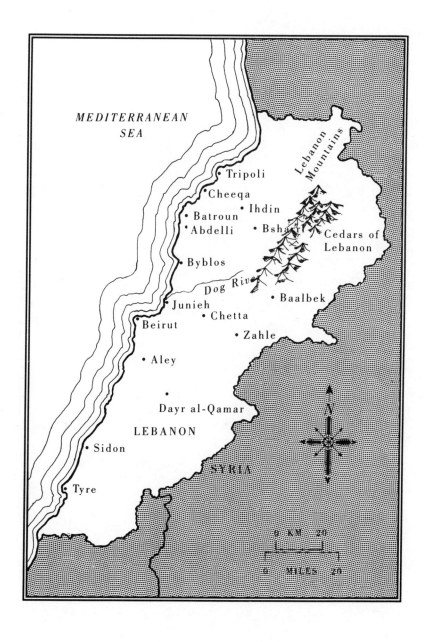

F A M I L Y
T R E E

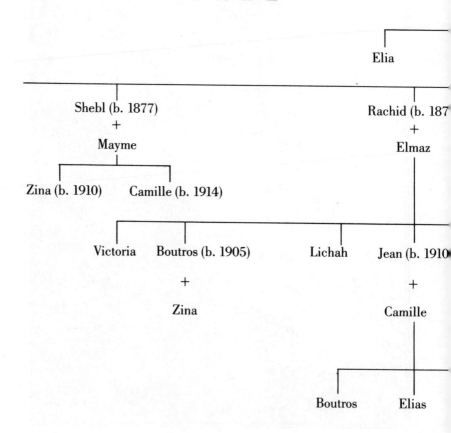

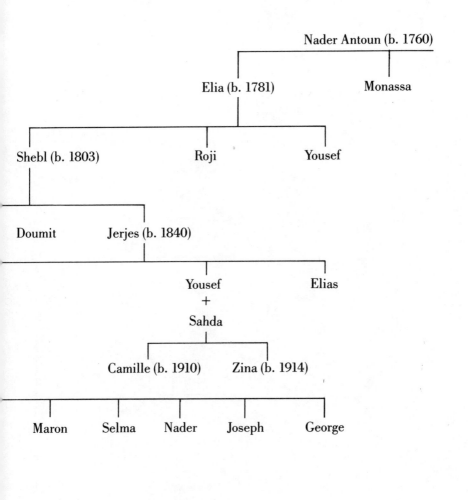

CHILDREN OF THE ROOJME

◆

The

Poetry

of

Men

◆

M y f a t h e r l a i d his jacket on the fence and rolled up his sleeves. His nephews were already in the garden collecting the fallen limbs and branches. They stepped up to the road and piled the wood onto the wheelbarrow. With my father leading, the boys steered the load to the edge of the cliff. My father sorted the wood into piles according to size. The children watched and wondered what their uncle was going to do. He carried the stack of branches onto the *roojme* and dropped them onto the stones. Lifting one large

stick after another, he held them upright in a row. He then selected
a forked branch and stood it against the ground, allowing the structure to lean against it.

Although the sun was directly overhead and the few cows in the
village huddled in the shade of the border trees, my father continued to work. He wiped his brow with his recently pressed handkerchief and started adding sides to his structure. During his time
on the *roojme*, his brothers, nieces, and nephews wandered down.
My father declined their prompting to rest and their offers to
help. He kept to his task, pausing only to drink a glass of lemonade.

My sister Selma and I stayed inside, out of the August sun. We
would go down to the *roojme* later, when evening was near and the
winds rose and cooled the white roads of Abdelli, Lebanon. We
lay in our mother's childhood bedroom in Beit Shebl, her father's
house, which we called the harra. The walls and shutters were
painted green, and the ceilings rose twenty feet above the marble
floors. From this room we could see in the distance my father on
the *roojme* behind his uncle's house, Beit Yousef. The only change,
since he was last here in 1937, was the placement of an electrical
pole that held two wires stretched out to the north and south. A
small buzz accompanied my father's labor.

His father's house, Beit Rachid, stood nearby as well, for the
houses of the three brothers were built at the same time, and were
responsible for the existence of the *roojme*. I had heard stories of
the place since I was a child. My mother and father's courtship
had taken place there, under a sky chalky with stars. My father
had stood on the *roojme* when he decided that he, my mother, and
my grandmother, Sittie Marwa, should go to America. I once asked
a Lebanese cousin visiting our home in Pennsylvania about it. He

shrugged and responded, "It's just a bunch of rocks." How could it be just a bunch of rocks, I wondered, positioned as it was on the mountainside, providing a view of Mount Lebanon, the Mediterranean, and on clear days Cyprus.

The *roojme* was built during the time my grandfather, Jiddi Shebl, was sheik of the village. After dinner, the men gathered atop its stones, drinking arak and smoking their hookahs. Someone would start a poem about the harvest, asking God, in rhyme, for figs the size of his fist. Another celebrated the sea; others glorified a woman's beauty or praised God. Eventually a word would trigger a song, and the men's voices bounced in the canyon.

Very little was hidden from the visitors to the *roojme*. All the sounds from the towns in the valley rose up to the men on the cliff. At six, when the monks at the monastery Dayr Kefifan recited their prayers in the courtyard, my father and his brothers knelt and prayed with them. The shouts and bets of a Saturday-night poker game in the village below punctuated their talk. Eventually they could identify the voice of the winner, and of the player who would go home to be scolded by his wife.

When I first walked down the path toward it, the wind was blowing the electric cable back and forth. The *roojme* did look like a pile of rocks that seemed to extend from the mountainside. Could my father's longing for his home have distorted his memory? He had been accurate about everything else on the journey so far. Beirut was magnificent—hotels dotted the seaside, glassy blue water splashed on the white beach, and European tourists filled the street. In the souq, miles of vendors sold their wares from tables, slaughtering sheep and goats to the buyer's specifications, cutting leather forms around feet for sandals. In the *bourj*, the downtown district, Beirutis in galabiyas, burnooses, fezzes, and European suits mingled at the bus stops and cafés. Veiled women sat next to the French tourists in their skimpy beach clothes.

When we left the city to come to Abdelli and we took the road north, palm trees lined the roads along the sea to Junieh and Byblos, the ancient port cities. At Batroun the small roads climbed and switched back through the mountains. We drove slowly, but other cars sped around the curves, the drivers beeping and calling to one another. I could see Druze shepherds marching their sheep to the pasture, and jackasses teetering with their loads as they were led down to a village. The hills were covered with sandstone, limestone, and rock. Pomegranate, oak, olive, cypress, and mulberry trees broke through the hard land and twisted toward the sun. Yellow grass sprouted intermittently, and little wild flowers congregated near the shallow streams. The hillsides were terraced with rocks to make small ledges where once coffee, wheat, and vegetables grew. In the valleys, fig orchards bordered tobacco fields and vineyards.

The apricots were as big as oranges, the oranges as big as grapefruit. My parent hadn't exaggerated. However, as I approached the *roojme,* I guessed it had looked different thirty-six years before. I tried to imagine the September day of the birds' migration when the boys stood ready to shoot the passing birds. They would kill hundreds for the feast that night. This was no longer done. The boys did not hunt and they did not gather the bushes, for the building of the bonfire on the Feast of the Cross had been discontinued. Since my parents lived here, Abdelli had become a summer home without harvests, haflat, the celebrations, or roasting birds.

When I actually stepped onto the *roojme* that first day, I finally saw what my parents had described—the mountainside villages, the lush valley below, and the pale sea with its ships tiny in the distance. What I stood on, this pile of rocks, was my foundation, and although its existence was unintentional, it had held over the years.

During our visit, my father and mother most often visited the *roojme* late at night, after we had sleepily rinsed out our coffee cups and gone to bed. As first cousins, my parents shared a family history, and the stones that held them were put there by their fathers and their uncle Yousef.

Early in the century, the three brothers had returned to Lebanon from Brazil with profits from their rubber trade. Their first order of business was to build homes, a harra for each family. My father's parents, Rachid and Elmaz, already had two children, but Yousef and Sahda, and my mother's parents, Marwa and Shebl, had none. Their three large lots were located on the edge of the town. All the ground in Abdelli was rocky, and to put in a foundation, the three brothers had to cut into boulders. As they unearthed large rocks, the area was soon filled with heaps. There was no room on the building site to dispose of them. Rachid searched until he found a spot behind Yousef's lot forty feet below the mountain. The workers built a three-sided fence extending from the ground to the cliff. It formed a box against the mountainside. As they excavated, they tossed the debris over the cliff. In no time the discarded stones had reached to the height of the cliff. The brothers walked out onto it and surveyed the sights. They were reminded of the large plazas overlooking the sea in Rio de Janeiro. Each night they met there to discuss their progress and plan for the days ahead. Soon the *roojme* became the center of family activity. Over the seven years of building the harras, the brothers used the *roojme* as their headquarters.

When I visited Lebanon that summer in 1973, all three brothers were dead, but their houses towered before me like palaces of stone, and the *roojme* held its position in command of the sea. That evening when my father finished his job, he came into the harra and washed for dinner. My mother and aunt had prepared large dishes of lamb and rice, and we all ate heartily. During dinner my father reminded us of an Arabic saying: *Breakfast and work, lunch and a nap, supper and a walk.* After the dishes were cleared, we headed down the road toward Beit Yousef. The night was clear and cool and the sky was full of stars. As we approached the *roojme*, I could see my father's structure balanced against its limb. It was about four feet high and reminded me of a shelter I had seen on the Appalachian Trail. Enclosed on three sides, its open end faced the sea and north. My father put his hand out. "What do you think?"

Mother smiled and nodded. "That's exactly how you used to build them. Did you do it yourself?"

"I wanted to," my father replied.

"What did you do in it?" Selma asked.

"We sat out of the wind or the sun and looked at the sea."

The four of us stood for a moment. The wind was mild and welcome after the hot day. Some voices rose from a village below as if some people were arguing. A door slammed. Then we heard nothing but the buzz from the electrical pole. My mother bent under the wooden roof of my father's shelter. She sat down and then we joined her. We spent the night watching the sky.

PART ONE

♦

Fathers

and

Sons

♦

J e a n

1973

Jean expects to smell onions. As he walks from Beit Shebl to the garden behind his mother's old house, he remembers that the onions were always the first vegetable to sprout in the spring. Their hollow stems poked through the soil like thick blades of grass. No matter how high the beans grew, how long the squash vines ran, how heavy the tomatoes hung, the aroma of the onions always filled the air.

In 1937, his last spring in Lebanon, Jean broke the frozen ground with a rusty spade and planted two rows each of onions, tomatoes, and green beans, one row each of eggplant, squash, cucumbers, lettuce, and peppers. Each morning, he inspected his vegetables and found some tomato stakes had fallen or some new bugs had invaded. Jean rubbed the leaves between his fingers, pulled the weeds from the ground, and secured the tomato vines. He roamed through the garden facing the cliff that overlooked the Mediterranean Sea miles below. Behind him, his mother's harra opened up with the morning. Joseph, George, and Nader, three of his younger brothers, prepared the wagons to go to the fig orchards and the tobacco fields. When his mother, Elmaz, shouted from the French doors over the back balcony for them to take their lunches, Jean plucked a brown leaf from a bean plant and ran up to the gravel road.

Now the principal roads in Abdelli are tarred, and every family has more than one automobile. From Beit Shebl, Jean passes the three Abi-Nader homes built by his father and his uncles. They sit on the north end of the village with their new electric lights glowing in the second-floor parlor, the salon, the bedrooms and dining rooms. Below, the stables have been closed off and are used for storage; the firewood stoves are covered with old newspapers, and the flat stone his mother once pounded bread on holds his brother's tools. All three houses need work. The paint on wooden shutters over the wrought-iron window frames is peeling on Nader's home, some of the stones of Lichah's foundation are crumbling, and his mother's old house, now occupied by Joseph and his family, is losing its red-tiled roof, piece by piece.

Jean steps down to the south side of the house. Two bicycles lie against a pomegranate tree whose leaves once brushed his bedroom window. He climbs down the hill and walks west and immediately feels the breeze from the sea. Empty clotheslines cross over his head, and he angles around the back past the *roojme*. Down the last small decline sits the plateau where the garden once lay. Small white stones still surround the plot around the edges, but nothing else is the same. There are no vegetables. High thorny bushes tangle together, and the whole garden is a jungle of unruly brown weeds. Jean steps in. The ground is soft from the damp morning. Stalks rise to his waist and burrs cling to the arm of his light brown suit jacket. When he pulls his foot from the loop of vines, a field mouse jumps up and runs off.

Jean's jaw tightens as he pushes aside the thistle and turns to leave. His feet are stuck in the mud, and he begins to sink until his patent-leather loafers are swallowed up to the gold buckles. It was ridiculous for him to come here dressed for church. He lifts a foot up and lets the dirt drop. He wobbles, then stomps from the garden into the yard.

Jean shakes his head. His trousers are hemmed with dirt and his jacket is pricked with tiny burrs. He must run back to the house before mass begins. Since he came to Lebanon two weeks before, he and his wife, Camille, have attended mass every day.

As Jean changes his clothes, he thinks, *This is what it is like to return.* When he left Lebanon thirty-six years before, the lands were producing at their maximum yield: figs, coffee, tobacco, olives, everything. The crops sustained the village. The smell of cooking figs sifted through the air, the *bydre* ground wheat on Saturday mornings, and olive presses clanged below the houses. Now the village has no crops. Not just the Abi-Nader lands lie thick with overgrowth, so do the pistachio fields of Abi-Deeb, and the pomegranate grove of Elian.

Lebanon's is a service economy, not an agricultural one, his older brother Lichah has explained. He, Joseph, and Nader work for the government. Abdelli has become what his brothers call their summer home. When Lichah and Jean toured the arbors the day before, Jean pulled away at the woven grapevines. Lichah offered his arm to his brother. "You're wasting your time, Jean. You haven't been here for thirty-six years; you cannot fix everything in a few weeks." Jean stopped and stared. Lichah led him from the garden. "Listen, my children have jobs in the city. What would they want with this tiny mountain village?" The men returned to the house arm in arm.

Jean puts a gold cedar pin onto his tie. He is like the village, slack and wasteful. Once he rose over six feet, bulged with sun-baked muscles, carried stones up and down the steep village slopes; now gray streaks his dark hair, which he brushes straight off his forehead. His brown eyes are circled with lines, and he needs glasses when he reads. He brushes down his peppery mustache. Camille tells him he is the handsomest of his brothers. It's true, they have become stout men, very broad, like his father, except none of them is as tall as he was. Nader and Lichah carry stomachs, which Jean is glad he hasn't developed. He pats his blue jacket pockets for a handkerchief and pulls at the creases in his suit pants, which are a little too long.

This is not how he planned to return to Lebanon. Like his father, Rachid, he wanted to come back rich and successful; to buy things for his mother, his family, and their children. He wipes his shoes with a rag. What would his father think if he saw the garden now? Jean imagines Rachid with an extended arm shouting, "Down to the garden and pull those weeds, *by the roots.*" Perhaps if he had come sooner, Jean could have done something. He waited until his six children were grown, and one of them could take care of the family store. The years have passed so quickly. The two daughters, Selma and Elmaz, who were able to come are already in their twenties, almost the age he was when he left.

Perhaps he should have stayed in Lebanon, but it seemed then that all the men from Jean's generation were leaving for the Americas, many to Brazil and Bolivia, others to Detroit and Cleveland, and some to western Pennsylvania, where Jean and his family moved from coal town to farm village setting up a dry-goods business. In America, Jean sold clothes from the back of a truck, off the seats of cars, out of a small rented corner shop, until finally he bought his own store in Carmichaels where he sold socks to miners' wives.

There his house is big, but his garden is small. He keeps a garden, as he has at every house they have lived in. When he returns from the store or while Sunday dinner is being cooked, Jean puts on old trousers, a threadbare shirt, and a large overcoat. On his feet he slips his worn dress shoes. Cast-off wing-tips, old black oxfords, shoes he once polished diligently before mass on Sundays, sit by the cellar door with their toes curled and their sides spread beyond the soles. When Jean goes down to pick up the fallen tomatoes, to reroute the squash vines, and to drop beans into a metal pail, he wears these dress shoes instead of boots.

In Carmichaels, Jean watches the flowers and the fruits in his garden, he stoops beneath his grape trellis behind the garage and walks toward the orchard; he steps between the bare peony bushes and crosses herb patches. The sun is mild and the pears ripen slowly. All summer long they hang, first small and round, then they form their long skinny necks; by autumn, some turn gold and fall into the yard. Jean picks one from the ground and squeezes it. The veins in his hand rise when his palm meets the pear's firmness. Jean keeps his fist wrapped around the dark green skin—his arm tenses and then his shoulder aches. He slips the pear into his pocket.

The vegetable garden is surrounded by orange border marigolds. As he strolls along the edge, Jean presses soil into his fist. It is not like the ground in Abdelli, dry and cold. The dirt sifts through his fingers easily, leaving its dark brown stain on his large hand. As Jean turns back toward the orchards, his father's ghost appears. Rachid stands under the pear tree wearing a suit Jean recognizes from their days together in Brazil. Rachid waves a cane at his son. Jean squints his eyes. His father's ghost has joined him before. Rachid has emerged from between the cornstalks, has stood in the light of the sun as Jean tilled the spring ground, and has plucked some peppermint while Jean picked leaves for the evening salad.

Rachid holds a pear, too, slashes it with his pocketknife, then slips his piece off with the blade. Jean drops the dirt in his hand and crosses the garden. He tramps through the marigolds, keeping his eyes on his father. When Jean reaches him, Rachid offers Jean a section of the pear. He does not take it; instead he whispers to Rachid, puts his hand on his father's shoulder. They begin to stroll and they talk, of course, of Lebanon. Rachid wants to know why Jean is not there. Jean raises his hands, his empty arms to the sky.

Jean knows his family watches him from the house, sees him talking to himself, they think, but he continues to chat with his father's ghost, smiling and gesturing. They discuss Abdelli and the smell of the pears in the orchard by the church.

Jean remembers them. The branches bent and pears hung green and golden, not too soft. Bees did not favor the pears as much as they did the grapes or figs. A fig bursts from the outer shell in ripeness. The juice, milky and white, coats the fruit. The orchards were cool, without disturbances.

His father's ghost has traveled with him all through Pennsylvania: to behind the McClellandtown store, north to the New Castle apartments, south again to Masontown, and then across the Monongahela River to Carmichaels. Father and son tread easily between rows of staked tomatoes, green beans, vines of white squash. Rachid's shiny shoes gather the dry clay of late summer. Jean fans out his feet when he walks; his legs are leaner and longer than his father's, but when they stop, Jean sees his father as young as himself. Both men are tall and dark. Rachid's hair, like his son's, is combed back; his forehead is square and unwrinkled. Jean glances at his father's pockets stuffed with letters he has written to him. Year after year he explained: *We cannot visit, a new baby; We cannot visit, another business; We cannot visit, a sickness inside.*

Were those explanations ever any good? In 1949 Rachid had actually visited Jean in Pennsylvania. The three girls were not yet born; the three boys were quite small and looked up at their *jiddi*'s large stature in awe. His hair had grayed completely and his tanned face had thinned, but Jean could see his muscles poke through his pressed white shirts and bulge on the back of his neck. At the table they talked about their nine years in Brazil, about home, about his mother.

On Sunday nights Jean heard more stories of Lebanon from his friends who had already gone to visit. At his Uncle Elias's parish, St. George's Maronite Catholic Church, the men congregated at the Lebanese Club. They who had left Abdelli, Tula, Zahle, and Batroun peered at their poker hands or stood at the bar. Namey dealt the cards around the table, telling his tale. "You can't believe it, Jean, it's so changed."

"I stood on the spot where I was born," added John George. "I thought, 'What a beautiful place,' but my house was gone, my favorite oak tree was pulled up when they put in an apartment house."

"Trees, what trees? There are hardly any cedars left," Hanna snorted at the bar.

Jean held the cards rigidly. "My mother is there, that's all I care about. That is where my home is. This is not my home, this place." Jean waved his hands toward the dull-green walls of the lounge. His friends did not stay in Lebanon. "I will go back to live," Jean said, "I will go back to die." Rachid died five years before Jean had a chance to return to Lebanon for the first time.

Now in Abdelli, all that remains for Jean is the glimpses of himself from long ago. When he walks to church, he checks to see if he's holding his cassock as he did as a young altar boy. After he sits to eat, he wiggles to look out the window so he can see the sunrise on Mount Sannin.

There had been nine children in a row, oldest to youngest. Easter. Jean was the fourth, standing straight, as his father had told him to do. "There was a time we thought we would lose you, but by the grace of God, you survived," Elmaz whispered. Holding his posture, he told her, *I am fine, Mother,* but she wept all the same.

When he fell from the roof, at age five, his body thudded like a wounded animal keeling over. It was a loud sound. The other children screamed, their voices rising up far away from him. Jean's back cracked and the pain shot up to his head and down through his legs. His mother lifted him and placed him in something warm. Her face pressed closely to Jean's, a handkerchief hiding her nose and mouth, a white blur. "Be well, be well, my son." *I am fine, Mother.*

A strong smell enveloped him, but he didn't know what it was until he saw the sheepskin hanging on the line. The wool was long

and tangled and the half-legs pointed to the sea and to the mountains. They had wrapped him inside of it, and the smell of new
meat gagged him. Jean became the sheep. "Do you think he'll ever
walk again?" A voice outside the door. Perhaps on all fours, Jean
thought.

A sick child becomes a mama's boy, standing precariously at
her waist in the kitchen while the steam gathers in droplets on her
face. He becomes a witness to her mumbled thoughts—thoughts
that are not very loud and not directed. Or perhaps to the conversation with the pot that will not scald the milk quickly enough or
the shadow of a father away on a trip, gone too long. Two weeks
later, Jean walked ably from the bedroom to the kitchen. His mother
spun in his direction, seeing him on the threshold in his long white
nightgown. "Jean, your shoes! Don't leave your feet uncovered!"
Elmaz knelt and kissed his face, rose, and ordered, "Go put something on your feet."

After mass Jean leaves Camille to wake up the girls and goes to
his mother's house. He watches as Camille climbs the steps to Beit
Shebl. Although new houses are scattered everywhere, Jean recognizes all the roads from each of the three churches to the town
square. Abdelli rises and falls with small hills. Tufts of grass push
through the sandy rocks that nearly cover Mount Lebanon. The
trees are not large, but they snake, turn, and twist. Across from
his family harra sits the cemetery of St. George's Church, and the
road that curves around it turns off and goes to Dayr Kefifan.

Most of the houses in Abdelli are large but not imposing. As
Jean looks up at his mother's shuttered windows, he thinks of how
they placed the stones without mortar, how they put in tiny arched

windows above the casements and hung large crystal chandeliers from the high ceilings. Elmaz will not be awake yet, but Jean has something he must do. He passes by the large stone porch and turns toward the basement. Grabbing the ring on the door, he twists it; the door nearly dislodges itself as it cranks open. Jean takes one step in.

Somewhere down here among the broken furniture may be a notebook that once belonged to Jean. In 1935 he wrote an essay, "The Life of a Stranger" and nailed it to the back of a desk in his uncle's harra. "The Life of a Stranger"—what did he have to say at twenty-five? Did he feel more a stranger than he does in Carmichaels?

The United States is dark. In western Pennsylvania, the families live beneath rich green hills and slate houses. The brown land on top is turned over and over by farmers who sow circles of crops around the hills. The miners work underneath the town. Jean sees them after their shift wearing coal dust on their faces. Even the houses are built in darkness—each in the shadow of its neighbor. From his house he sees only the neighbor's garden and garage.

Lebanon is white. The limestone roads, the terraced hillsides, the rocky mountainside; even the cities, with their bleached hotels and apartments dotting the seaside, extend from the sky. From the tops of Mount Sannin and Mount Lebanon, the villages lie like heaps of stone, a stray rock here and there lying on the outskirts. The hills and the sea, the earth and the sky; nothing interrupts these natural links.

Now in his mother's basement, a shaft of light coming through the slightly opened door, angles across the wall by the stairs. Some furniture lies on its side. Jean doesn't know where to begin. He wants to recognize something, to find a dresser that held his father's shirts, or a bookcase where the leather-bound holy books fell against the language primers.

As Jean pulls a large secretary desk upright, the smell of wood is sweet. Papers and books are scattered on the floor where the desk was lying. As he raises his arms to hang the lantern on a bent nail, the lamp swings back and forth, and Jean nearly drops it. He sits on a backless chair and stares into the pile. Envelopes, letters, tablets, papers, books, and magazines, some damp at the corners, others yellow, mix in the heap. Jean spreads them out with his foot, then reaches for a batch. Receipts and school papers, written in Arabic and French, fill the first pile. He pulls out a drawer and stacks them inside. Underneath the second pile lies a large manuscript with a black cover. Jean drops to his knees, allowing the papers to cascade from his hands. He lifts the folder. The binding is leather and the front is blank. He positions himself directly under the light, opening the book from the back, and finds in faded fountain-pen ink Rachid's writing. The Arabic script reads, "The ignorant says in his heart, there is no God." Jean has seen this before. His father wrote it when he was absorbed in thought, wherever he could: scrawled on napkins, carved into trees, cut on a table, and in this book. Jean opens to the next page. Instead of Arabic, he sees English type—it is an ending of something. Jean turns the book over to the front. A white label curls on the cover. He rolls it back but finds the title has faded away. Inside the first page, the words are very clear: *A History of the Druze* by Elias Abi-Nader, a play written in the forties by his uncle.

Jean blows out the lantern. Outside, cars and trucks rumble along the village roads to Beirut and Batroun. When he was young, during the day Abdelli was noisy. Villagers called to each other on their way to the fields, to the well, and to work at the public ovens.

Oxen-pulled carts kicked stones from the roads onto the grass, and women's voices filtered through the tobacco fields, jackasses clopped through the rocks, bullets from young boys' rifles rang through the air. Not even half of those two thousand people of his youth live in Abdelli now. His father predicted it one night when they sat on the *roojme*. He looked in the direction of the Mediterranean, the black line of the unknown: "That is the way to our friends, and our friends' way to us." The boys thought that like the Phoenicians, their ancestors, they would leave Lebanon and return with knowledge and fame. They dreamed of this aloud together.

Footsteps cross the ceiling and stop at the basement door. Jean rises and goes to the steps; he hears the feet move on. His mother is awake now. He climbs the stairs.

In his mother's living room, the sunlight spills on the furniture, reddening the rosewood coffee table. Gold threads glint in a shawl hanging over the back of the couch; every window, open now, shows something: the flat roofs of their neighboring town, Tula, a cluster of trees below the mountain, all the hills of Lebanon.

The front door opens and the maid enters. "Good morning." She bows her head and her black hair hangs along her face. Her thin body barely fills her cotton dress; it is belted at the waist and falls near her shins.

"Are you Muntaha's girl?" Jean asks, seeing the face of his childhood friend, but this girl couldn't be more than fourteen.

"I am her granddaughter." She enunciates her Arabic carefully, as if Jean might not understand.

"Has my mother had breakfast?"

"No, she is waiting for you; she is washing." The girl steps

away. Jean wants to speak with her, tell her that her grandmother
and he were friends as children. His daughters are older than she,
but perhaps she would like to meet them. The other village girls
stand in the churchyard at night, wearing blue jeans and smoking
cigarettes.

"Are you going to eat?" His mother holds herself up in the doorway of the dining room. Her hair is pulled back from her face,
exposing her round cheeks and dark eyes. Her skin has lost the
rosy color Jean remembers; age has left it thick and gray. She
places an arm at the bottom of her curved back as she walks into
the dining room.

"Are you in pain?" he asks her.

"I fell last month." She sits slowly. "It makes it hard to sleep."
Her eyes are so beautiful, deeply, deeply brown.

They linger over breakfast as they have every day for the last
week. He tells her of his children: this one is in school, a writer,
this one is taking care of the store during his visit, and the little
one, Geralyn, is an artist. His mother stares. Perhaps his words
are a blur. What do you make of my life, Mother? Should I apologize? Repeat everything? Are we beautiful to you, Mother? Smart?
Do you see your eyes in my daughter who was named after you? *I
am fine, Mother.* His mother reaches her hand to his face. They are
suddenly old—mother and son.

"We are going to the caves today." Jean holds up the coffee pot
in an offer.

She waves a no. "In Gheta?"

Jean nods. "Saleem is driving us. Selma and Elmaz don't feel
well. Too many apricots." His daughters had listened to his stories
of the fruit in Lebanon. They ate every one in the bowl on their
aunt's table the night they arrived. Now they have dysentery.

Jean watches Camille during their tour of the caves at Gheta. Golden dust falls from the stalactites into her black hair and nestles in the curls. Saleem, their driver, is chattering, and other tourists flash pictures. Camille stands and walks to the edge of an underground pool.

When Jean raises his camera to photograph her, she does not smile, but gazes toward the water. He stares at his wife's face. "Lily, do you want to go into the city?" The first week in Lebanon, over the protests of his brothers, Jean rented a suite in the Hotel Florida in Beirut. The owner himself carried the bags to the room.

Camille leads the way to the car. "Yes, it's time to go back to Beirut. Let's go this weekend. The girls like it better there."

So does Lily, Jean thinks as she folds herself into the backseat of the Mercedes. Saleem leans against the fender. Jean looks up to the cross fixed in the dirt above the opening. The caves at Gheta are large and cavernous, not like the ones of his childhood. He nods—the cross is appropriate. Protection and prayer. Many elders have a great fear of caves. When the Turks invaded Lebanon, tunnels and caves were dug around the village so that people could escape from their homes. One tunnel wound from Mar Elias, their church, all the way to Dayr Kefifan, the monastery some eleven miles away. Stories of caves were told in muted voices. Jean's Uncle Naum died while walking with his sister, Mayme, in a cave nearby. Mayme, his wife's mother, lived with Jean's family the last twenty years of her life. She called to Naum in the night. She had seen the earth pull him down and bury him.

Jean first discovered one of the village caves when he was five. His Aunt Anna married a man Jean's father considered lower-class. In protest, Rachid moved the family away from their house to their vineyard on their land near Mar Simon Church. He mounted a tent divided like a house into four large rooms over a ground-floor foundation about three hundred feet from the church.

One warm dry day in the summer, Jean and Lichah were playing under the oaks that formed a circle for half a mile around the churchyard. Some leaves had fallen but the trees were large and still full and shaded them. The boys held a throwing contest. Jean weighed his rock up and down in his hand before launching it in an arc. The rock fell into the shrubs out of sight. The boys ran to a grove where it had landed, Jean searching through the bushes, Lichah crawling on the ground, but they couldn't find it. Jean felt around with his hands until his arm sank into a hole. He shot straight up. "Lichah, look." Lichah ran to Jean. They pulled at the vines surrounding the hole. Inside, steps descended into darkness.

"Let's see what's down there," Lichah said. Jean wiped his hands on the legs of his pants, then put one foot carefully on the first step. It was sturdy. Jean released his brother's grasp and walked down a few more steps, supporting himself by holding the walls. The stairs softened and the wall crumbled. Jean stopped. "It's too dark."

Lichah stared into the cave. "We could get a candle. Maybe there's something good down there." They ran over to the house and tiptoed into the kitchen. They grabbed matches and a candle from the drawer, then fled back to the cave.

At the opening Jean held the candle while Lichah lit it. Jean walked into the dark again; the light flickered against the muddy walls and went out. Lichah struck another match. The sulfur hissed inside the cave, but before the light reached the candle, it died. Soon he was out of matches. Jean stuck the candle inside his pocket and they went home.

As they approached the kitchen door, they discussed a new

strategy. They would take an oil lamp and explore the whole cave. Suddenly their mother charged toward them screaming, "Boys, where have you been?" She was holding a basket of clothes and staring at their feet.

Jean looked down at his shoes covered with dirt. "We found a cave by Mar Elias; we didn't walk far, though," he said.

Elmaz dropped her basket. "What?" Holding him by the arms, she felt his forehead with her wet hand. When she placed her palm on Lichah's face, he wiggled.

"What's the matter?" Lichah asked. "I'm okay."

She pulled the boys inside and washed them down and put them to bed. They were astonished into silence. She covered them in flannel nightshirts. Pulling a blanket up to Jean's chin, she mumbled prayers. Jean lay stiffly. "If you feel anything, call me," she warned.

I feel fine, Mother.

After she left, Lichah rose and opened the shutters. Jean swung around and dangled his legs off the edge of the mattress. They spoke in whispers until they heard Rachid arrive. He came in and sat on the bed. He placed his open hand on their foreheads and then examined their eyes. "You're okay," he said. "You can go outside."

The boys jumped down and put their clothes on. As they reached the door, Rachid shouted, "Don't play in the cave. Go weed the garden. You should have done it this morning."

In a small vegetable patch behind the house, they bent over the beans and pulled at the stray growth. Their mother's voice reached them in the yard. "Don't you remember what they say about people who went into the caves? Some disappeared; one came out blind and crazy."

"I've been there myself," Rachid said. "It's nothing but mud and water."

"I was worried," Elmaz sobbed.

Lichah and Jean did not speak to each other. They quietly cleared the garden until dinnertime. That night their father blocked the entrance to the cave.

The car spins through the mountains toward the village. Camille rests her head against the car seat. She has been quiet for days. This is her first trip back to the old country too. On the first day when she stood on the threshold of her father's house, she quivered, not stepping forward, not retreating. Jean followed her eyes; tried to imagine what she was seeing. The ceiling was more than twenty feet high. When the house was built, a mural was painted on it—like a coat of arms, representations of the family history framing a larger picture, but Jean couldn't remember what it was. Someone painted over it—tried to follow its lines and left a double image. A man on horseback, the Blessed Virgin, mountains—a child's scrawl.

Jean watches the valley disappear and reappear. He has two more days to explore the basement before they return to Beirut. He hopes he can convince Camille to walk with him on the old paths down and up the mountains to the villages they can see across the valley.

The basement's coolness sends a chill across the tops of Jean's shoulders. He sets up the lantern and sifts quickly through the papers on the floor. No time to collect what he needs. Rolling

Ummi Elias's play, he puts it in his pocket. He reads the inventory from his Uncle Shebl's old store from 1922; he smooths pages of his brother's Aramaic prayer book; he examines the signature on letters that crack in his hands.

The door leading to the main floor creaks open, but Jean doesn't look up. In his hand is a book—the pages laced together at the leather binding. He presses the book against his cheek, trembling. His eyes fill with tears. His father's writing fills the pages from margin to margin.

> I am writing what I have heard from the people and what my father and grandfather told me—what has happened in our time. My father was a tall man: blond hair, blue eyes, reddish-brown mustache, intelligent, honest; he despised wheeling and dealing. He loved to work and help his countrymen. He was blessed with an excellent memory and a sense of humor.
>
> In the winter after supper, he would sit by the fire cross-legged and we sat around him, roasting nuts and popping corn. He would tell them what his grandfather Elia told him about his father, Nader Antoun. . . .

Jean rocks back and forth, holding the book against himself. *Remember who you are, you told me, Father.* Jean tells the stories to his children, too, just as his father told him. Their college friends, who fill the house over the holidays, drink coffee without saucers and laugh as Jean retells the story of the time he stopped the angry bull. They try to pronounce the names of food as they pick up the stuffed grape leaf and dip it in the yogurt—*mishee warak areesh, laban.* "Mr. Abinader . . ." "No, call me Uncle John."

∴ *26* ∴

Is it not enough? His home in Carmichaels does not overlook the sea. The curtains are always drawn and a single chandelier hangs near the centerpiece on the large dining-room table.

1916

. . . A man from Beirut took the petition and interpreted it to Jamal. Jamal Pasha got furious and angry and said, "Who is this man from Abdelli? Bring him to me with his books, the club records, and the sheik's transactions. And when he comes here, I will show him who the Turks are." And the pasha sent orders to Kaymakam Zuine to send me to him in irons.

When the kaymakam received the order, he got bewildered and started looking for ways to help me. He told Touma el Chidac to write me a letter and to tell me of the danger I am in and to make my last will because the accusations against me were too strong and it would cause my hanging. Especially since they accused me of saying, 'To hell with the Turks; soon France will send a warship and destroy them and the Turk's name will be erased forever.' Touma sent me the letter and a copy of the petition and accusations. He insisted I make my last will because there is no hope of my being saved or of returning to Abdelli.

When I read the letter, my color changed and I started sweating terribly—not because I feared death. I was facing death every day, but what would happen to my family? I saw them starving to death one by one.

Jean carries the diary with him the whole day. It lies beside him on the table as he eats; he pores over it as he sits on the edge of the bed before sleeping. "What are you reading?" Camille presses on her suitcase.

Jean wipes his eyes and helps snap the case shut. "My father's diary. I found it in my mother's basement."

"Why was it there?" She slides under the blanket and pulls her rosary off the night table.

Jean takes the book and slips in beside her. "They save nothing. They have little respect for the past. Look at the orchards and the fields. My mother can't find many of her treasures. I have started to sort out the junk in the basement, but it is a big job. I'll go back in the morning."

She puts out her light. His daughters' voices travel from across the hall. But Jean hears only his father: "I saw them starving to death one by one."

♦

T h e

B l a c k

R o o s t e r

♦

J e a n

1916

W h e n   t h e i r   m o t h e r called them to dinner, Jean, six, and Lichah, eight, ran up the stairs. Pulling on the French doors, they entered the dining room and took their places behind their seats. They could hear their mother singing a lullaby to their new baby sister. The servant, a girl of twelve, put a plate of kibbee into their sister Victoria's hands. The meat steamed on its way to the table. While Rachid was hiding from the Turks, the family had been on a steady diet of what could be grown or bought on the

black market. Running his fingers along the scalloped edge of the
china plate before him, Jean surveyed the room to see what had
been sold or bartered to get this precious meat. Victoria dropped
a flat loaf of bread in front of each child. They always had bread
but often only with yogurt and onions or figs.

Elmaz came to the table quietly, blessed herself, and watched
as each of them prayed with her. The servant crossed the hall and
closed the wooden shutters on the windows. The house felt foreign
with Father away and Boutros in the fields; their empty chairs loomed
like large thrones. The children spoke in whispers.

"Jean, take some food down to Boutros tonight," Elmaz instructed.
Boutros was guarding the fig orchards throughout the summer. When
the war started and many people lost their land, the hills became
their homes. Some called them refugees; others said they lived like
nomads. Rachid mumbled "thieves," and no other name. With
nothing left to trade, they stole whatever they could get—even figs.
Each morsel became precious. Rachid had his children guard the
larders well, even from the people in their own village. Even from
their cousins.

After dinner Jean ran through the village to get to Boutros in the
valley. The moon dipped up and down. Jean didn't stop for the low
breathing of the livestock. He ran, sweating and breathing in short
spurts.

At the orchards, Boutros sat in his open tent. A lantern glowed
beside him, casting light only on his crossed legs and on the shotgun that lay on them. As Jean jumped off the road into the valley,
the crossed legs unfolded, leaving only the boots visible.

"Boutros, it's me." Jean stood for a moment, then stuck out the
towel with the bread and kibbee. Boutros frightened him, although

Jean was nearly as tall as his brother and his shoulders and chest were broad.

Boutros ate silently. Jean sat on a rock and asked, "Will you sleep here again?"

"I think I should." He took a bite from the bread.

Jean left Boutros in the orchards as soon he was finished eating. He walked up the slope quickly. He wanted to turn and wave good-bye to his brother, but something inside of him quivered. He quickened his pace, allowing himself to trip over the stones in the path. Jean thought of his father and somehow expected him home when he returned. He walked to the terrace and looked out. Lichah was resting against the wall of the house, staring at the sky. Jean slid down beside him.

Elmaz and Victoria brought chairs out and sat with the boys. His mother sang a song in Aramaic while she braided Victoria's long brown hair. Suddenly a light in the sky flashed toward the earth. "Oh," Victoria whispered.

"What's happening, Mother?" Jean turned and saw on her face a half-smile.

"That was a falling star. The legend says that everyone on this earth has his own star, and it comes to be when he is born, and the star dies when he dies."

They looked into the sky. The stars were thick and they seemed fused together in clouds. Jean could hardly distinguish one from the other. "Which is mine?" he asked her.

"You'll find out for yourself," she answered.

Jean squinted at the sky.

"Some say all the stars are in love with the moon," she told them. "Look at the one near the moon," she whispered. "It tells the future. The others are guarding the moon, so it won't be mobbed by lovers." She held the brush up motionless, as if with one movement she could bring them down to sit around her as her children did.

"Then they all die?"

"Some stars die from despair; others in their excitement stumble on each other and die." Her voice rose and she shifted her legs beneath her long skirts. "Since I was a little girl, I have heard so many stories about the moon and her relation to our lives and our weather and crops—lots of things about the moon puzzle me. You are too young to understand."

Jean examined the sky, wishing he knew his father's star. If he could see it . . .

The others went inside.

The next morning, Jean carried the feed to the jackasses wandering below the harra. Spreading the hay on the rocky ground, he looked into the valley. The terraces bordered the mountains—both Sannin and Lebanon; the roofs on the houses in Tula and Batroun fell like folds on a paper fan, slanting one way and the other. Elmaz stood on the terrace. Her hair was wrapped in a white scarf embroidered with black threads, and little strands of her dark brown hair scattered across her forehead. Sometimes she looked holy—like those soft pictures of saints and apostles with their steady eyes. Jean watched her.

"Jean, go down to Boutros and send him here. You and Lichah pick the figs today, then Boutros will return at supper."

Jean walked into the cellar and placed the rake against the white chalky wall. "Jean," Lichah's voice called. "We have to go to the orchards."

"I know. Is Victoria already gone?" Jean walked back into the sun. This day would be hot. Already the stones of the road shone like the surface of the sea and the day wasn't yellow but bright white.

At Hroussa, the wrapped heads of old women bobbed as they worked in the tobacco fields. They filled their aprons with leaves and carried them over to the tables. The village grandmothers spread the leaves to dry them. They worked slowly, their voices singing back and forth to each other as they crossed between the tables. They placed the leaves down carefully, one by one, holding them lightly with two fingers as if they were layering filo dough for baklava.

"Mahraba!" the boys greeted them. The women paused and yelled to the brothers, calling them by the name of their harra, Beit Shebl.

They passed the orchards and descended between shrubs. Below, Victoria's head moved in and out of the trees. They raced down the hill and stopped quickly as they noticed Boutros standing with his rifle in front of a tree. He looked up, then back to the tree, to the small thin man who was tied to it. The man's head bent toward his chest and his hair fell forward.

"Boutros, what happened?" Lichah raced over.

Boutros ignored him and said to the man, "You may take the things you picked with you, and the next time you're hungry for figs, come during the day and ask." He handed his shotgun to Lichah and untied the man. When the rope fell away from his chest and arms, he reached for his basket and ran without saying a word.

"I caught him stealing figs." Boutros put out his hand to receive his shotgun from Lichah. From the bottom of the hill Jean watched as his brother described his adventure. He talked like a man, like his father, echoing his father's words. "You can't shoot people because they are hungry. And so I told him to come back and ask."

While Jean picked figs that day, he envisioned the thief's body pulled against the tree with rope. His father might have been caught. He would be subject to the anger of men, not the righteousness of a boy.

It was more than one hundred degrees. "Oh, my hands," Lichah moaned. The milk of the figs burned into their skin, and their fingers felt as if a million tiny splinters had lodged in them. Through the crooked branches, Jean could see his mother accepting a bamboo tray from Victoria. She emptied the figs onto a large sheet. Her skirts pushed the dust into a cloud as she moved between the table and the tray.

At lunch they sat together under the tent and ate bread rolled with fig paste. Jean rubbed lemon on his hands, wincing as the juice entered his pores. "Why don't the French help us?" Victoria asked.

As Elmaz squatted, she folded napkins and placed them into the basket. "They have a war of their own. My uncle says all of Europe is fighting."

"When's Father coming back?" Jean gazed at the juice as it ran down his red hand.

"I don't know." Elmaz rose and folded the sheet they had eaten on. "That depends on the governor."

Each summer day and each summer night they picked figs. No rest would come until the grapes, pears, and olives had been picked, pared, dried, canned, pressed, marinated, mashed, or stewed. The locusts did not come as they had in 1915. Perhaps they and the

other families of the village, other fatherless homes, would survive
after all. The children took turns staying in the orchard. Sometimes
Lichah spent the nights with Jean, but often Jean had to stay alone.
When Boutros had to go to Batroun for his mother, he left Jean the
gun. Tucking it under his arm, Jean paced. When the stars rose,
he sat cross-legged in the entrance of the tent and talked to them,
retelling the old stories with himself as the hero: he found the
treasure for the king, he released the prisoners from the pagan
ruler. Eventually, he fell asleep; the shotgun lay on the ground.

Jean couldn't stand to cry in those days. He trembled and felt
his tears crystallizing and surrounding him. He would weep that
night. Lying across his bed, he watched a star through the window,
blinking his eyes to blur it and scatter its image. Sleep brought
only more silence. Just as his eyes were closing, something knocked
against another window—a knock, two quick knocks. The latch
scraped open, and Elmaz released a tiny shriek.

It was Rachid. Finally. Jean was sure of it. Suddenly the door
flung open and Elmaz came in. "Jean, Boutros, Lichah, come up,
come." She shook their arms. Her hair was down, covering her
shoulders.

Rachid was in the dark family room, his back arched against
the wall. Holding her children's shoulders, Elmaz arranged them
in a line across from him. She lit a lantern. Victoria's white gown
fell like an angel's dress as she held the baby. Jean wanted to leap
and grab his father's legs, but waited as Rachid stared blankly at
them—at Victoria, Boutros, Lichah, Jean, the babies, Maron and
Selma. Boutros watched Rachid carefully, Lichah swayed sleepily,
and Jean stared, waiting for his chance to speak. But it didn't
come. Rachid placed his hand over his face and waved everyone
from the room. The boys went back to their bedroom, Boutros and

Lichah climbing under the sheets without speaking. Jean returned
to the hall. He crept up to the door and stood just outside. His
father was crying and shaking.

"I was hiding in Jabal Libnan. Lord Governor Zuine told me to
stay out of sight until he could think of a way to pacify the pasha.
The Patriarch Elias Huwayyik was there." He lowered his head.
Elmaz knelt beside him. He continued, "I thought we could get
some help, from a friend."

"What did he say?"

Rachid looked at her and then at the door. Jean shrank back.
"He said, 'Son, I am hiding too. Father Boulous just came back
from Rhodes with the news that the Germans may take Paris, and
I don't know how we are going to survive. I pray to God to show
the way, and he will, with every difficulty.'

"We knelt and prayed together; then he shared some food with
me. Before I left, I took him aside and asked him if he knew what
I could do to save my family."

Rachid put his hand on the window as he looked out. "This is
what he said: 'Son, I know this is cruel, but the only advice I have
now is this: pick the best child of your children and try to save him
and let the others go.' " Rachid leaned his head against the window, his body stiffening. Jean slunk to the ground. He felt as if he
were sitting on a raft on a river and it were taking him away. Elmaz
sat there with her face uplifted to Rachid, and Jean floated backward, his hands held out. He couldn't cry.

His father's face was pale; his mouth and his chin quivered.
"That is what he said. I couldn't believe I heard this from a holy

man." Elmaz knelt like a statue, except her face was on fire and her hair fell like a nun's veil.

"We live together or we perish together," Rachid said. Elmaz gasped and put her head into her arms.

Father!

"Are you sick, son?" Jean felt his mother's chilly hand on his forehead the next morning.

"No." Jean sat up. Her eyes examined him.

"Get up," his mother said. "I have an errand for you." In the kitchen she gave him some yogurt and some bread.

"I dreamed Father came home." He held his bread tightly without taking a bite.

"Jean." She crouched down beside him. "Forget you ever saw him."

"Where is he now?"

"I am going to send you to him, but you must tell no one." His heart jumped as he listened. "Go chase the birds with your slingshot until your father finds you. Don't call him or tell anybody where you are going."

She spread cooked figs and olives on some bread and tied them in a bandanna. "Stand." She fastened the bundle around his waist. "Now go."

Jean ran down the terraced walls into Hroussa in no time. The fields were filled with workers, but he did not pause. In the valley, the houses and trees fused into spots of green. The bushes rustled and a stick cracked behind him. Jean turned quickly. Silently, his father approached, and embraced his son so tightly his bones seemed

to crush. Rachid's body was cold. They moved back into the shadow
of the mountain. Rachid untied the bundle from Jean's waist and
put the food into a cloth bag on the ground. His wide brown face
had thinned along the cheeks, and his mouth was cracked dry.
"Go back the way you came, and tell Mother I'll visit again at
midnight. I'll knock on the window."

Jean gave Elmaz his father's message. She looked down at the
baby and said very seriously, "This is our secret, Jean, forever."

On his last morning in Abdelli, Jean arrives at his mother's house.
The shutters are still latched when he arrives. He enters the basement, and he goes to the remaining drawers and bookcases. Soft
footsteps creak on the stairs and then stop. Jean turns and sees
Elmaz standing with her robe sashed around her thick waist. Her
hair falls on her shoulders, black with silvery wisps spraying her
face.

"Son, do you want to tell me what you are looking for? You have
searched this place many times. Maybe I can help."

Jean goes to her. "I am looking for an essay I wrote once, many
years ago, 'The Life of a Stranger.' "

Without a word, she leads him to a bench across the room. "Was
that you who wrote 'Hyatt al Gareeb'?" She uses the Arabic title,
although the title was also written in Portuguese. "You, my son,
felt like a stranger? You are the dearest to our hearts. Your father
and I always loved you and praised you." She squeezes his hand.
"Your father expected you to lead the family. Everybody loved you
and loves you now, and you feel like a stranger."

Jean lowers his eyes and stares at the stone floor. "I spent the
best years of my life far away from home, from my mother, sisters,

brothers. I felt guilty when I wrote it. I feel guiltier now." Elmaz's tears drop on his sleeve. Jean can hardly speak. At her side again, he's a boy in the kitchen.

His mother's hands are small and rough. "Son, let at least one of your children come and reside here to keep your name and commemorate your roots in your homeland, the land of your heart. As the Bible says, we shed blood, sweat, and tears to preserve it."

Jean thinks of his children sitting around the canning stove, reciting Arabic with their mother. The children's game, a tap on each hand, *"Hroonkus, broonkus, tal en, nazy, ouñie, oonkus,"* recited until only one hand is left, the winner. They do not know about the *blood.* "Mother, nothing will interest my children here, once you are gone. They love you and know that I never passed a moment without thinking of you."

Elmaz smiles, taking a tissue from her pocket, wipes her face. She looks off into the room. "We moved the library and everything from the big house to here. We fixed this place to live in during the winter; it is warm and we can burn charcoal and wood. We spent the summers upstairs.

"The book was nailed to the back of the desk. Someone pulled it and tore it. One day when I was cleaning, I found the papers on the floor; I took them to your father and told him where I had found them. He took it and read aloud, 'Hyatt al Gareeb.' The words were written in heavy letters, and below the title was something in French or Portuguese."

" 'La Vida d'Estajeiro,' " Jean tells her.

"Yes." She shifts and crosses her legs. "Those words stayed in my mind and bothered me for a long time. Your father, most of the time, after lunch used to lie down, and more than once I saw the book lying on the blanket on his chest. One time I heard a noise and looked in. He held the book in both hands and was crying. He dried his eyes on a towel."

Jean missed his father's aging. He was told Rachid never weakened, his back never bent; he dressed in a suit every day and walked to church with Elmaz beside him.

Jean is now sixty-three, a father, and strong, as a man should be, like the son of Rachid.

"I asked your father what the book was about. He never gave me a good answer, and it had no name on it. One day while I was fixing the bed, I found the book under the pillows. That day he had left early to be with the workers who were trimming the grapevines in Haghy. I sat in the sun in front of the house and read what I could. I felt lonely and sad. I put the book under the pillows and never asked your father about it again. He kept reading and rereading it. I was used to it. I forgot about it until you mentioned it to me." She rises. "He didn't say anything about the book, but he talked about you many times: 'Someday, Jean will be back, and we will build a trellis in the yard. . . .' "

The next morning is overcast. Jean's daughters stand in the drive kicking the gravel as he says goodbye to his mother. "Mother, take care of yourself. With luck, I'll be back next year with Geralyn. She wants to meet you."

She places her head on his chest. "I am afraid I will be meeting her in another life. This is goodbye; tell her that I pray for her." Jean gazes over her head to the white house and the archway that leads into the basement. He holds her face in his hands.

In 1918 the news of the Allies' victory over the Germans and the Turks turned the country into a flame of celebrations. Everyone forgot the horror: the devastation, the starvation, the dead. Money and clothes arrived from abroad. Uncle Shebl's luck in America was changing, and he would visit Lebanon soon. However, the recovery was short-lived, for the Spanish flu struck the village.

Boutros and Elmaz were taken quite ill. Boutros had been sitting on a rock watching the few sheep. The sky was gray; the sun had not cut through in days. When dinnertime came, Boutros hadn't returned. Rachid found him slumped over his gun in the rain and carried him to the house.

Elmaz lay for days, her breath whistling through the house. The children took turns sitting by her bedside. The color in her face had faded to ash and her hands fell limply against the sheets. At night Jean knelt on his bed pronouncing loud prayers for her. His grandmother nursed her the next day. When his grandfather, the town doctor, looked in on his daughter, the children waited outside her room and watched as he rested his ear against her chest, placed water on her lips, and pressed her stomach. He said nothing as he walked through the hall.

Boutros recovered within a week, but Elmaz lay on, speechless, in her bed, the gloominess of early spring hanging over the house. At the beginning of the third week, sunlight pierced the clouds. After their grandfather left, the boys stretched their tense bodies on the patio. "I'm going to open the window so Mother can have some fresh air," Victoria said and unlatched the double windows and let them swing to the sides of the house. The sun poured in, bleaching the dark bedpost and throwing a beam across Elmaz's face.

One of the roosters began to prance across the patio. He was the biggest, almost two feet high and very black and shiny. He marched across the patio spreading his feathers like a peacock's tail; then he flew up to Elmaz's windowsill and crowed.

Her mother looked over at the rooster. He crowed again and stretched his neck. Grunting, she threw a pillow at him; he ruffled his feathers and crowed again. She rose to chase him. "Don't, Mother, he's my favorite," Elmaz said.

His grandmother turned. "What?"

Elmaz's eyes were open; she raised her hand. "Don't hurt him, Mother."

The children heard the scream, "My daughter, she's alive!" Rushing in, they kissed their mother. She slowly lifted herself onto her elbows and sipped the water their grandmother held to her lips. Her children leaned their heads on her chest.

In the sun the rooster's feathers glowed blue; he crowed again and flew down from the window. "Do you think it was a miracle?" Lichah stood beside Jean. Soon after it began to rain.

♦

CHAPTER THREE

The

Locusts

♦

Rachid

1916

(**P**e r h a p s l i k e a bat, he can hear the darkness, even when he doesn't listen.) These last two weeks in hiding, Rachid has not been able to sleep. He sits up and puts on the coat he used as a blanket. Daylight could be dangerous, but he doesn't want to move yet. Leaning against the cliff, he hears the rumblings of the earth before the sun rises: rocks on the hills shift into their places for morning; the leaves turn their silver backs toward the ground. In the town below, buckets held in the hands of women squeak

∴ *43* ∴

back and forth, a small boy squeezes the teat of a goat and sprays her milk into a can, a mother calls to a girl to go to the well. Rachid does not want to listen anymore, but he cannot escape these noises. He trembles as he had the day a year ago when his wife, Elmaz, called him to the house. He had been hurrying to pull the undersized squash, the tiny peppers spoiled with brown cavities—anything left in the soil.

Elmaz's voice followed him, came nearer, and he knew he had to reply, to return, and to listen. He had to stand among the men of Abdelli and say, "This is the straw that killed the camel." They told him what he already knew: the locusts had come back. "This on top of everything"—starvation, Turks, sickness, and European war moving toward them. His neighbors stood close and waited, and all Rachid could say was "This is the straw that killed the camel." Some closed their eyes; perhaps they thought the noise would disappear, but blindness does not banish the sounds. Locusts rushed toward them, and the buzzing was a storm in their ears.

He had tried to think, to come up with a plan. (Do you have a plan, Sheik?) Day and night the locusts devoured the very earth on which he stood, drowning out the crack of the branch he stepped on, the splash of the water in his tub. The locusts ate their way from the sea, and across the village, and into his home. Thinking of the soft skin of his children, he shuddered. When he saw his sons Lichah and Jean come running from the field wiping locusts from their faces, he ran and brushed them with long sweeping strokes. They pulled the cover off the wooden tub and climbed into the water tugging off their wet clothes.

As sheik, Rachid enforced the orders when they came from the district government, the mutessarifate in Batroun. The governor, the kaymakam, had ordered all the men to follow Rachid from Mount Lebanon to Roshanna by the sea. Every able body was to collect three *okka* of locusts' eggs—eight pounds strapped to the back of Nehman, and of Ibrahim, to the back of Nassif Ackly, Rachid's neighbor, to Salim, the messenger, to all of them. They stood in a line before him, placed the baskets at his feet; Rachid wrote the receipts, and threw the eggs into the sea, warning, *Save your wheat.* (They should hide everything.) The Turks will lose their food first and come to us, he thought, looking at a tree stripped to its blond skin, dotted with the black lacy locust bodies. Their loss is our starvation, he couldn't say. (This is the straw that kills the camel.)

The locusts hatched and crawled out of the sea and covered the land like a flood. Rachid! The new order from Batroun was very clear. No one could travel for food, and no one could stop and pick the pears from the trees. They must build fences of wood and heap bushes of cedar branch inside them. They listened as the locusts roared up the hillside and into the trap. Rachid set fire to an old chair and some dried vines. The men held torches to the crackling mountain, and inside those fences the locusts sizzled. More came— to the fields of Antoun Fares, and to the hills of Baraket. The flames jumped and the locusts' bodies burned like butter.

Rachid hadn't wanted to be sheik. The sheik was the town leader, and he had judicial powers. The mayor led the town council and presided at official town ceremonies. When the Turks and the French designed the new constitution in 1912, before the war, they provided for elections for the sheik and the mayor. Shebl, Rachid's brother, and Boutros Bike, Elmaz's uncle, were rivals for the office of sheik. Shebl campaigned vigorously among their neighbors, promising them land and crop arrangements, lending them money. Shebl won and Boutros Bike became the mayor. And then Shebl left for America.

The village, particularly the family, had not prospered. One brother had to go to America to make money; another stayed in Lebanon to care for the village. Shebl left his wife, Mayme, and his two-year child, Zina. Rachid stayed for Elmaz, for his five children, for the new baby soon to be born. Matters got worse: the Turks levied taxes on the village, rationed crops, and suspended elections. The kaymakam whispered to Rachid, "Take your brother's place." Three continents trembled with war, Jamal Pasha, Al Saffah, as he was called, sat in Aley, a city in the south of Lebanon. "The Bloodshedder" ordered his soldiers to villages, Christian and Moslem alike, to gather food, supplies, money—anyway they could. Every day sheiks were hanged: uncooperative in pressuring their citizens to relinquish their copper pots, treasonous in their associations with known blasphemers against Al Saffah. One hundred thousand Lebanese were dead, from famine, from murder, from the hands of Al Saffah. Rachid wanted to say "not now," but the kaymakam did not listen. He held Rachid's shoulders like a friend. The kaymakam kissed both his cheeks and substituted brother for brother. Rachid became sheik.

Rachid does not close his eyes; the night is his blindness. He is cold against the mountain and not sure where he is. A road runs over the cliff to his village and somewhere turns to Batroun. Below him to the west lies the Mediterranean Sea. Rachid raises his eyes and sees only a dark mountain. *Bitenjan,* he remembers, eggplant, helps vision in the dark. When had he last eaten it? He hadn't thought of it before. (Why should he?) Late in the morning, six months before, Rachid walked into the kitchen as Elmaz pulled the tray of eggplant from the oven. She stripped away the skin, which tore like delicate paper. Her face was dewy from the steam. She patted her cheeks with a towel and scooped the long stringy pulp with a spoon and dropped it into a bowl.

"Elmaz."

She turned, spoon poised in midair. Strings of hair fell around her thick face.

"I thought you were in the office," she said.

"I had to leave. The women are driving me crazy with their wailing."

"I know." She laid the spoon on the counter and dipped two cups of water. "Zihr el Ban visited me."

"What did she say?"

"She wanted to know what you could do for the gamblers." Elmaz answered.

Rachid's broad shoulders fell forward. He sat at the table and pushed his thumbs together. "I did what I was told." His wife's back shook as she beat the eggplant into paste. The sound of the spoon against the bowl thumped in his head. "Zihr turned her own husband in, you know."

Elmaz turned in profile. "She had to."

He knew that. Shutting his eyes, Rachid kept his hands on the table. He looked stronger than anyone in the village; when he spoke he moved his arms and stared at the listener. His brown suit had been pressed and cleaned the day before, but around the bottom of each leg was a ring of soil. He kept his hair short in the summer, a habit he had picked up eight years before when he was a rubber trader in Brazil. His cheekbones had thinned since the beginning of the war and now were angled as severely as his nose and chin. A small mustache was neatly trimmed over this thin mouth. If he grew his hair, he would look like the Indians of the Amazon.

(What do idle men do?) Many stooped at the edge of the fields afraid to touch the tarnished soil. The blackened wheat fell into the burned earth. No green or purple grapes, no tobacco, figs, pears, or squash. The men stood in darkness. The growing season was over, and the cellars, baskets, and larders were empty.

The gambling may have started as a friendly game. Rachid, as sheik, had to report to the local mutessarifate concerning taxes, IDs, and land exchanges. Villagers presented cases before him, accusing each other of property theft, negligence. He did not know the gamblers gathered. They sold their clothing and food for money to wager, then traded away planting seed and land.

On the kaymakam's orders, Rachid directed the police to round up the men and to close the houses. Thirty-six gamblers in all. As Rachid turned from watching the gamblers march with the police toward Batroun, the faces of the women hung before him, their hands reaching out, and then they cried. They rushed toward him. "Sheik, save our families."

Rachid rose from the table and stood beside Elmaz. Her hand held a lemon above the bowl, and drops fell into the smooth green dip. "Kaymakam Zuine is a good man and a friend. I am going to talk to him."

On the road above him, a wagon crushes small stones. Rachid grabs his satchel and turns toward the trees. The gambling incident was resolved easily. The kaymakam and Rachid devised an oath for the men to sign, and they were released into Rachid's custody.

But there is no oath Rachid can sign now for his case; no sheik to plead for him and his family. This was an accusation of treason, and he had been warned. "They asked that you be placed in irons and taken to Aley," the note had said. The pasha saw that everyone aided the Turks' war effort; with one sheik more or less, it didn't matter.

The morning Rachid received the warning of his arrest from the kaymakam's counsel, Touma el Chidac, he stood outside his door reading the letter and trembling. Elmaz saw his face redden and then pale. "What is that?" she cried. Rachid handed it to her. Boutros Bike and Deeb Maklouf's petition had been delivered to the court in Aley. They had accused Rachid of stealing the funds for the Red Crescent, monies designated for the war effort; they described how Rachid had blasphemed the Turks. He had proclaimed, "To hell with the Turks," they reported.

Elmaz grabbed Rachid's shirt. "What are we doing to do? Chidac says you will be put in irons, you will be hanged. My God!" Rachid knew he must flee, and he could not tell his family where he was going. "If they come here, you know nothing," Rachid commanded. Elmaz tried to calm the children. Rachid watched their confused and sad faces, then gathered his bag and left quickly.

Now he looks north toward Mar Hanna Maron, the Maronite Catholic seminary where the priests are hiding. He hopes to see the patriarch and get advice, perhaps sanctuary. He knows that one of the holy men, Father Boulous Ackle, swims from Cheeqa, a northern Lebanese port, to the island of Rhodes, where he meets an English boat that passes him messages from France. If French intervention is likely, Rachid will stay in hiding until freedom comes.

The French will not come, as they did in 1860 when the Christian districts of Greater Lebanon and Syria were burned. They will not pull into the harbor as they did when, sixteen years later, Bashir II was kidnapped and taken to the sultan; they will not come. (A house without a father). The patriarch must have some power. Perhaps he will provide the missing connection, the resolution. Rachid is helpless. He cannot find an answer. He cannot return home and look into the faces of the people there any more than he can stare at an eclipse.

Rachid stays in the trees and watches the road until it clears. Pebbles roll under his feet and he runs across to the other side and ducks into the brush. At the turn he crosses again. More people than usual are walking from their houses to the fields, from the Mount to Batroun. They have baskets on their heads and backs. The pasha's troops need more grain, Rachid guesses. He brushes his jacket and pulls his hat to his eyebrows. Will he look like a refugee to these villagers? A boy his son Jean's age sucks a turnip. Since the rationing of wheat and milk the children's stomachs are hollow.

Before approaching the next village, Rachid rests among the shrubs where he can see a strip of the road and sea. He wonders now if he was fair to the refugee Bustany. As restrictions increased, Rachid's major preoccupation as sheik became his own survival. Bustany showed up in the village two months after the distribution of the identification cards. A boy came to Rachid's office and blurted out the message of the stranger's presence.

"A new man in the village? Where is he staying? Who is keeping him?" he asked.

"Beit Khoury, Sheik."

Rachid dropped his pen. He should have been told immediately, especially if the man was a refugee. "Who sent the news?"

"The mayor. He is there now and thinks you should come."

Rachid locked his office and followed the boy. The walk was not
lengthy. Rachid traveled quickly, his long legs striding over the
dirt path around the edge of the churchyard and down the hill to
Beit Khoury. The boy was left far behind. At the gate, the mayor,
Boutros Bike, stood with three men. Behind them, near the ground-
floor entrance, Yousif Ibrahim and Jerges Shaheen watched the
stranger. Rachid joined the mayor, and they turned away from the
others. "Do you think he has escaped from army duty?" Rachid
asked.

"It is possible," Boutros Bike said. "He has no identification."

Rachid paused. Boutros Bike glanced over his shoulder to the
other men without speaking. The sheik asked, "How long has he
been here?"

"A week maybe."

Rachid stroked his eyebrows and walked toward the house. The
stranger bent his head as if he knew that this was the sheik. He
was thin, old, and dressed in western clothes like a Christian.
"Who are you?" Rachid asked.

"I am Elias Bustany." He turned to Boutros Bike. "Don't you
recognize me, Bike?"

Boutros Bike said nothing, and he did not look at the man.

"How old are you?" Rachid continued.

"Fifty-six years old."

"Are you married?"

"Yes." Bustany raised his hands to the Sheik. "Please, Sheik,
let me stay in your village; I can make wooden shoes that would

last for ten years." The stranger pleaded, "Bike, tell him; you said you would help me." Bustany's voice shook. Boutros Bike walked over to the group of men who had now gathered near the fence.

"I know him," Jerges Shaheen volunteered. "He's from Junieh." Shaheen approached Rachid and Bustany.

"You know, Shaheen, we can all lose our lives if we harbor a refugee," Rachid said. Shaheen glanced at the others. Bustany covered his mouth with his hands.

"Do you have anyone else to vouch for you?" Rachid asked the stranger.

Bustany pointed to the group of men. At first it seemed he couldn't speak, then he said, "Yes, Sheik, yes. Yousif Ibrahim, Nehman, Yousef el Doghl, Boulos Antoon, and the mayor."

Bustany's witnesses did not acknowledge him. They knew the presence of the man was a danger. If every citizen was not regis-tered, he did not properly pay his tax or contribute his fair share to the Red Crescent. This was treason. Rachid could not help a traitor. Every person in every village had to be certified and iden-tified. Why did the mayor let the man stay?

Although they were related by marriage, Boutros Bike had tried to undo Rachid again and again. Now he ground his foot into the dirt.

Three women came up the road with their scarves pulled down to shade their eyes. They stopped and stared. Rachid followed their gaze to the man standing before him. (Rachid hoped his silence was perceived as anger.) The villagers would not be ultimately responsible for Bustany; the sheik would be found negligent. Mershed, the soldier stationed in the village, might have already seen him, have already reported him. Rachid knew he could not ask, show his fear.

Silently he walked to Boutros Bike's office nearby. The men
followed. No one asked him a question; they kept their voices low
as they speculated to each other. At the door Rachid raised his
hand to stop them and went inside. On the mayor's desk sat a
Bible, a lamp, and a pen—nothing more. Rachid opened the Bible
and pressed down a page. A simple shoemaker could cost him his
life. (What a war.) Rachid closed the book.

"Boutros Bike," he called out the window, "have you some
paper?" Boutros Bike leaned over from where he stood with the
men. He wore a black suit and a white shirt as if he were going to
speak before an assembly. Boutros Bike smiled. "Yes, Sheik, I
can help you." He nodded to the men and went into the house.
Boutros Bike wanted the sheik to be hanged, but so did many—
Rachid was sure of that.

The rivalry between their families was historic, and now it was
complicated by the war. They had fought over property, funds,
even seats in the church. Rachid, as sheik, was vulnerable, and
Boutros Bike knew it. He wanted Rachid's power, and he would
get it if he could discredit Rachid with the Turks.

Pulling a piece of paper from a drawer, Boutros Bike slid it
toward Rachid. The sheik wrote a testimony for each witness to
sign to vouch for Bustany's identity. He called the men in. "Do
you know this man and verify his identification and all that he says
as true?" They hesitated a moment and exchanged glances with
one another. Shaheen pulled the paper toward him and signed it.
The others followed. Perhaps they did not know what the paper
meant, or perhaps they felt confident it would make no difference,
but Rachid would do his best to share the responsibility.

Rachid took the document and returned to his house. In his
office, he collected deeds and property transfers to put in the pouch

for Batroun that afternoon. The mayor's behavior puzzled him but did not surprise him. In the past year, the mayor had drawn a petition against Rachid, but it was not accepted in the assembly. Some of the names on it had been forged.

He hoped he could find the messenger and send everything off before dinner. A pounding on the door interrupted his work. Voices called to him. Through the window, Rachid saw on the porch the wives of some of the men who had signed on Bustany's behalf. Pounding. The refugee was with them. He opened the door. Ibrahim's wife led the group. "Sheik, take this man, give us the papers our husbands signed." She put out her hand and cupped it like a beggar's.

"I cannot. They are government property now. Ask your husbands why they signed them."

Nehman's wife wept quietly. "But Mershed reported Bustany as a refugee this morning."

Staring at her, Rachid shouted, "Why don't you take him to Batroun and turn him over yourselves?"

She followed him back to his desk. "We'd be admitting our guilt," she cried.

Before he could sit back down, Nehman and Ibrahim ran in. "Please, for God's sake, save us from the trouble we are in," Ibrahim asked. The others, except for the mayor, came in behind them, and Bustany stood frightened in the doorway. They must have run into Mershed after Rachid left them.

"Put him to work as you planned." Rachid pointed at Bustany, then sat and looked back at his work.

"Yes, yes," Bustany cried.

"But he might run away." Nehman bent over Rachid's desk.

Rising from his chair, Rachid placed his hands on the edge of the table and leaned into Nehman's face. "Then you will take his place," he whispered. "Now leave." They backed through the door, and Rachid closed it. He could hear them cursing Boutros Bike, and the house of Bustany.

"Do you know how I feel? Let Boutros Bike be the ground under Rachid Shebl's feet, let the sheik teach him a lesson," Yousef shouted. Rachid moved papers around on the desk and kept his eye on the door. His hands were shaking and he couldn't write. They had tried to trap him, but they were caught too.

Rachid heard Elmaz's voice: "If my husband doesn't obey the government's orders, he will be hanged." As she opened the door, the group pressed toward the entrance. Bustany was still with them.

"Nehman," Rachid called. "Take Bustany to Saad Allah's house until I make my decision."

Elmaz closed the door. "What will you do?"

"I'll write to Zuine, I'll explain the problem. What else can I do?"

He cracked open the shutter. Elmaz stood behind him looking over his shoulder. She closed her eyes for a moment. Two men held Bustany's arms and marched him down the road. Rachid returned to his desk and sat. He rubbed his forehead, stared at the table top, and dropped his arms to his sides. "Sheik Wilah was hanged two days ago. His family was killed, and the house was burned to the ground."

Elmaz crossed herself and cried, "Jesus, have mercy. Why would they do that? Why?"

"When they came to collect the accounts, he wasn't in his office. I think his wife was giving birth. They called out his name. He told them to wait, and he sent his brother down to explain. They grabbed him from his wife's bedside."

Elmaz fell into a chair and started to weep. "I don't understand what is happening." She raised her arm toward the window. "Do you hear? It's the bells again. Ringing for the dead so much, we don't even notice anymore. Hanna Doum's body lay in the road for days before someone took him in. I don't understand."

After Rachid finished his dinner, he sent his son, Boutros, to fetch Bustany so he could feed him as well. The man entered and stood frozen in the doorway. Rachid ordered him to stay on a mattress in the hallway. He warned, "You sleep here. Don't try to run; if you do, I will shoot you."

Bustany looked at the sheik and dropped his eyes as if sentence had already been passed on him. His hair was cut short and unevenly on top, and he had the beginnings of a beard. Rachid gave Elmaz a gun and repeated what he had said to Bustany. She looked at the man as he folded his jacket and placed it under his head. She said nothing.

Rachid wrapped himself in a heavy robe and walked out to the *roojme*. The letter to Zuine had to be composed carefully. The sky hung heavily with stars, a good harvest, lighting up the hillside. A small white line appeared across the horizon.

Abdelli knew that of all the regions in the mutessarifate, they were the luckiest because of the appointment of Zuine as their kaymakam—a religious man, humane and fair. An entourage of the twenty leading men of the Abdelli had traveled the dusty path to Batroun to welcome the new governor to his office. Idle soldiers wandered through the streets of Batroun. Vendors' voices filled the air. The men passed fabric wrapped around sticks sitting like large rolling pins on tables in the souq, sheepskins hanging from hooks, and hats piled in high stacks. Young boys accompanied shoppers carrying their goods as they purchased them. Soldiers, rifles resting against their legs, sat outside stores and cafés with cups of Turkish coffee.

The kaymakam was headquartered at the house of Indrawos, a local landowner. In the front hall, other groups waited for an audience. The kaymakam invited Rachid to sit at the table to drink wine. In his black suit Zuine leaned his bright face toward the sheik and told him he trusted him to be honest. As Rachid listened and Boutros Bike watched, a man from Thoum, a friend of Indrawos, entered dressed in an elegant galabiyas. The gown's green satin fell near the floor, and it was edged in gold. He wore a fez of velvet embedded with jewels on his head. The folds of his robes floated as he walked toward the kaymakam. This man owned much territory and offered his services to Zuine. The kaymakam rose abruptly and waved at the landowner, shouting, "Get from my sight." He turned to Indrawos and said, "How dare you bring a man to see me in his nightclothes." Indrawos tried to explain, but the kaymakam turned back to the table. Rachid's trousers were neatly pressed and fell to the top of his shoes, made for his large feet. Most of the Maronites had adopted western clothes years before. Boutros Bike, who sat nearby, mopped his forehead with his white handkerchief.

Zuine announced he had faith in his replacement of sheik, and he was certain Rachid would run an honest office. Rachid would be responsible to the government for everything.

He thought of this that night—how he didn't want to disappoint the kaymakam or put himself in danger. If he broke the law, what would the kaymakam do? He, too, was responsible to the Turks. *Where was Shebl?*

The next morning was quiet. The men who had signed the papers stayed away from the man who had brought them bad luck. Rachid sent a letter to the kaymakam giving him every detail of the case. Slipping it into his pouch, Salim, the messenger, started toward Batroun. Rachid expected an answer before night. Raps came from Bustany's shoemaker's hammer all day. Rachid rested his arms across property papers and listened. And watched. Three hours at the most each way. After lunch he went to the *bydre* to start the threshing of the wheat. Lichah had already hitched the oxen and spread the grain. The animals walked around and around. Rachid sat against a tree and listened to the grinding of the wooden platform against the wheat. Lichah held the oxen still while Victoria gathered the wheat into baskets. The fields emptied of the workers as the sun stood brightly in the afternoon. Most people stayed in their cool houses and canned vegetables or baked bread.

When Rachid returned to the office, he closed the shutters and wiped his neck and face with a handkerchief. Bustany's tapping ceased, and a scraping noise echoed from the basement. Rachid was jealous of Bustany's work. He could build shoe after shoe. Rachid poured some coffee into a small cup and examined a page of a ledger. (What had he planned to check? He couldn't remember.) The voices of his children floated from the dining room as the evening cooled. Rachid walked onto the porch and stared at the road. The shadow of the big oak at the side of the harra obscured the chalky path. Back at his desk, Rachid ran his finger down a column of figures. Taxes would be due soon. He untied his tie and leaned back. Someone rapped lightly on the door. Rachid pushed his chair back and ran across the room.

Salim stood panting as he let the door swing open. He held out a letter. The seal of the kaymakam was embossed on the flap.

Rachid grabbed it from Salim, wrinkling it in his fist. "Fetch Elmaz and tell her to bring the stranger."

He lifted the pressed wax, unfolded the page, and read, "Rachid, you have judged this case fairly, and I leave the final decision to you. You may bring the man to Batroun for investigation, or you may release him. God be with you. Kaymakam Jerges Bike Zuine."

Rachid lowered himself slowly into the chair. When Elmaz entered with Bustany, she reached for the letter. Rachid cleared his throat. "Bustany, the kaymakam has authorized your release." He knew he should have said something more, a moral note, a warning, but he could not go on.

Bustany fell at Rachid's feet and cried. "Thank you, Sheik." Within minutes, he was gone.

Rachid is not a poor shoemaker. (Although he feels much poorer.) On the road in the morning, he looks at his hands: empty, tired, but not broken with the tiny scars of splinters. They have sifted through the dirt of fields, laid stones on the terrace, and slashed the meat of a steer with a long knife.

By late afternoon, the sun has not penetrated the overcast sky. Like a large tombstone, the seminary looms on a hill with its single spire and a bare cross fading into the grayness. The students have gone home to their parents. Two of Rachid's children have quit their lessons with the priest. Jean excelled in languages even at his young age, but he and the other boys have had to stop. Each one, except the baby, has a job in the house, since some of the hired help have disappeared.

Rachid crosses himself before entering Mar Hanna. His hand stops between the head and heart, and he leans back to survey the tall doors. Inside, lights from the offices and classrooms fan across the dark line of corridor. Voices from down the hall rise together, then fall into silence. One voice presses his point finally, loudly. In the shadows, images of Christ and the Holy Family pass by Rachid's shoulders as he creeps to the stairs. His feet barely touch the floor, and he keeps his eyes on the stairway and the jagged light on the steps.

"Rachid!" He stops on one foot and turns toward an open door. Father Ackle approaches and puts his hands out to the sheik. Behind the priest, beneath a picture of Christ, on a small sofa, Boutros Bike talks with Bishop Sakre.

"Rachid, what are you doing here? Come in and join us," the bishop says.

Rachid drops his satchel, arranges his jacket, and removes his hat. "I have come to bid you goodbye."

Both priests begin to question him. "Where are you going?" Boutros Bike crosses his arms against his chest, gazing at the blank wall across from him. Rachid begins his tale of the petitions against him from Boutros Bike and other villagers. As he speaks, Boutros Bike does not shift, even under the surprised stares of the priests. Suddenly, the three men lift their faces to the door and rise. The patriarch stands and looks solemnly at Rachid. (How much of the story has he heard?) Rachid takes a short breath and kneels to kiss the patriarch's ring. The holy man raises his hands to the men in the room in a sign of peace. His figure fills the entryway. Putting his arm around Rachid's shoulder, he guides him into the hall. The two walk together. Rachid keeps his head bent slightly, and the patriarch stares ahead to the doors. His hands are clenched gently, and they hang against his robe. (A fallen prayer.)

They stop beside a painting of the Virgin looking into the face of the baby Christ. The child smiles, his face bright from the ring of light above his head. Flecks of gold are sprinkled in his skin. The patriarch steps in front of the picture. "Rachid, you must settle your differences with your wife's uncle. We hear from many of the problems in your village."

Rachid nods, glancing toward the room where Boutros Bike speaks to the priests. Boutros Bike's words spill from him rapidly. (The birds in the bushes chatter.) Rachid lowers his eyes to the hem of the patriarch's robes, clenches his teeth, and tries not to listen.

The patriarch's words sound as soft as the slow murmur of absolution in the confessional. Who is the sinner here, Rachid wonders. "As for your trouble, I can do nothing for you. We are hiding here ourselves." He puts out his hand, and Rachid genuflects and kisses his ring again. "Rachid, let Bishop Sakre negotiate your case with Boutros Bike. You will regret your differences later."

A boy in a long black cassock appears. Holding the patriarch by the elbow, the boy leads him away.

Rachid stands outside the room while Boutros Bike's voice travels through the door. He is the first to tell his story. *Be quiet.* The voices are getting louder. Rachid leans against the wall. The seminary will not bring him peace; he cannot hide here. But he has to make the priests understand about the mayor.

Once the voices cease, Rachid enters. Boutros Bike takes a seat against the wall. The bishop looks directly into Rachid's face. "Rachid, I would never expect this of you: to be at odds with your uncle and to try to oust him from the Baladeit, the town council."

"What my uncle has told you is far from the truth. He is the one who is trying to destroy me and kill my family. He went to Hanna Basbous with a petition full of lies against me to persecute me in the assembly. He accused me of forging my brother's name, of selling illegal identifications to fugitives from the army, and other criminal acts. He has twenty-three signatures on it." Rachid's voice cracks, and as he talks more, he talks faster.

"Twenty-three people signed it?"

"Yes." He shakes his head. "No, I mean, I asked some of the people whose names were on it, and they told me they never saw the petition."

"Did you protest it?"

"Yes, I wrote a letter to Saad Allah Bike, the assembly representative, and told him everything in the petition is a lie and that Boutros Bike as mayor is harmful."

Boutros Bike half rises.

The bishop wrinkles his forehead and places his hands in front of him. "What happened to the petition?"

"Basbous rejected it and wouldn't present it to the assembly."

The bishop walks toward the window. He looks at the yellow shutters without speaking. When he turns, his eyes are closed and he is holding his forehead. "Then what is your grievance with Boutros Bike, and why are you leaving?"

Rachid can hardly speak. His heart pounds in his arms and legs. "It doesn't matter now. If I am hanged, just let my children know who is responsible."

Boutros Bike approaches the bishop with his hands out. "This is not my problem."

"What is not?" The bishop looks at Boutros Bike, drops his arms, and then turns to Rachid. "What is not? Tell me."

Rachid tells him of the second petition drawn by his uncle accusing him of withholding Red Crescent funds.

The Turks demand money from all the villages to support the

army. The sheik has to deposit it in the Red Crescent account, and then pass it on to Aley. The order for the arrest came soon after the filing of the petition. "In irons, it said." Rachid nearly whimpers.

The bishop whips his head toward Boutros Bike. "Aren't you ashamed of what you are doing to your niece's family? You have put them in the hands of the Bloodshedder. What do you think God's patience can endure?" Boutros Bike retreats toward the chair. Rachid feels his heart beating in his head, his neck, his back. Shame before the village and the church. (Pounding, always pounding.)

Boutros Bike's face is red. "Bishop, Rachid is a very clever man. He can turn things around in his favor and convince everyone that he is right. Ask Abou Iskandar. He is here, is he not? He will tell you the truth."

As the bishop summons Abou Iskandar, Rachid stares at his uncle, whose eyes blink and look away. What is Abou doing here?

"I want you to tell me what is going on between the mayor and the sheik of Abdelli," the bishop instructs Abou.

Abou glances toward Rachid and Boutros Bike and addresses the bishop. "Your excellency, the mayor rides the sheik's neck, the sheik slaps his hand, then the sheik rides the mayor's neck and the mayor slaps his hand. And they both abuse us. Boutros Bike made a petition signed by twenty-three persons and sent it to the assembly with Hanna Basbous accusing Rachid, and Rachid wrote to Saad Allah Bike to fire Boutros Bike, the mayor, and to abolish the Baladeit. Then Boutros Bike consulted with other persons from the village and denounced Rachid to Jamal Pasha, and now he is going to be hanged. His family cries day and night. You can see what they are doing, my lord. We are concerned about food, and they work hard to destroy each other." Rachid closes his eyes and covers his face. The beating, the rhythm whirls.

Bishop Sakre and Abou Iskandar leave to join the council of priests in a nearby room. The holy men have settled many disputes in the villages before, with little interference from the government. Rachid tries to picture the pasha's courtroom, if one exists at all. Would it be anything like the bishop's office? Each wall meets another—perfect. One corner holds a small empty bookcase; a reflection from the candle shines in the glass. He cannot look at his uncle. Rachid walks into the hall and catches pieces of Abou's story. Over and over. His steps through the corridor are deliberate and careful, like those of the horses on the road. *Abou, aren't your figs drying on the trees? Don't you have any hay to bundle? Abou? I do, Abou. My sons guard our fields from robbers and intruders. All the people need food because of this war. I can't feed them all, not even the ones closest to me. All the arguments and the fighting. And now no one has food. And you, Abou, have time to come to condemn me? Maybe I am a crazy man, hearing voices around me, grabbing what I can to feed my six children? Am I wrong?* Rachid will say none of this to the bishop, or the bishop will transfer the care of Rachid's family to someone else.

As the bishop enters the room, Rachid sits down next to Boutros Bike on the couch. The bishop places his hands squarely on the desk. "Boutros Bike, retract the petition against Rachid and put the issue of the Red Crescent funds aside," the bishop demands.

Boutros Bike shrugs. "I have nothing to do with it."

The bishop takes a breath and slams his fist onto the desk, "It is a private petition. What are you going to do with it?"

"It is out of my control."

The bishop rises and goes toward Boutros Bike. Rachid interrupts, "Your eminence, my time is short, you have tried to help, and I have caused you enough headaches. I am not expecting to survive this. Why don't we write a letter to Saad Allah Bike stating that we came here, and we agreed to leave our grievances aside until after the war."

The bishop surrenders his hands to the sky and summons Father Ackle to write the letter. Rachid signs it and hands it to his uncle, who looks away.

"Sign it."

Boutros Bike waves him away.

"Sign it."

The older man drops his head. The bishop rises with his shoe in his hand. "I will curse you if I must spend one more minute with you." The bishop charges toward him. Boutros Bike's eyes widen as he backs out the door and runs into the hall. The bishop's shouts travel down the corridor and out into the courtyard.

Rachid bends down to get his satchel and the papers. The bishop's voice echoes from the hall. Father Ackle approaches. "Rachid, the charges against you are grave; I wish we could grant you sanctuary, but we cannot. Sometimes I walk onto the terrace and can see the fire of the soldiers camped below in the fields."

"I know you would help if you could. But I honestly don't know what to do—not just for me but for my family."

Father Ackle plunges his hands into his robes. "The last news I got at Rhodes is that the Germans are crossing the continent. No one can save the Christian world now." They walk through the hall; the priest looks straight ahead, focusing on something far away.

Rachid pictures him in his journey in the water, treading and looking at the horizon, a promise. His mouth is drawn and his eyes are circled with darkness. "Rachid, you know how much I love your family, but if you survive this, this is what you must do: pick the best of your children and save him, see that he gets what food and care are available, and let the others go." He puts his arm on Rachid's shoulder. "Otherwise, everyone will starve; they are rationing the wheat, the milk. You must save one or you will lose them all."

Rachid furrows his brow as if he doesn't understand the language the priest is using. The beating in his body stops, and he drops his arms limply to the side. He stares at Father Ackle, and the priest continues to talk. What is he saying? Rachid cannot hear. (Blind and deaf.) The wall behind him recedes and softens. The priest leans toward Rachid and whispers into his ear, "God help us." He steps away, and like a bird rising from a cliff, lifts off up the stairs.

Bishop Sakre approaches, stands, and rattles the letter at Rachid. He asks a question, but his voice falls like a slab of stone. A bat shrieks outside. Rachid turns and he can hear nothing, at last. The tall doors of the church are pointed at the top like tiny churches, and Rachid moves toward them. He steadies his bag on his shoulder, and as he runs down the hall, each picture flickers. Outside of the seminary, he stops. Perhaps he will die. His family will too. Rachid must go home. He must get to Abdelli.

Rachid rushes to a tree, leans against it, and bends over gasping for breath. Voices come from the road—loud whispers. The night is a shield if you are a bird and can hover in the darkness and pick your direction. Rachid pulls himself around the trunk and peers at the intruders not ten feet away. They are Jabali, mountain people, and speak dialect. The Jabali travel at night if they are hiding, or if they carry black-market goods. Rachid crawls to a grove of cedar. He sits and his face fills with heat. He drops his face into his thighs and breathes out slowly. Some decision has to be made.

Rachid has sent a message to his neighbor, Nassif, asking him to make one more plea to the office of the kaymakam. If he cannot get a district trial, he wants to go to Aley himself. And he would be sure to go or else the Turks would come after his family. The priest could be right. What will become of Abi-Nader? (Will Rachid be a murderer of children?) His eyes burn. He leans back onto the rough grass and rocks.

Below him, in the valley, the travelers have stopped. Their fire lights their faces. Rachid closes his eyes and listens—a quiet fire for cooking, good dry cedar, oil frying; water rushing over small stones. Soothing. When he opens his eyes, he sees a hand put something into the flames that flares up quickly, then dies. A paper, an identification card, a birth certificate, a deed, a letter, a photograph. He closes his eyes again: flame after flame rises, then shrinks. Blue around orange, white, red.

◆

The

Five

Families

◆

R a c h i d

1917

Two days later, Rachid slips in and out of Abdelli as quietly as he can. He has seen his wife and Nassif Ackly. Now he knows what he must do. He runs his hands up and down the sleeves of his jacket and looks down into the valley. (Is he lost?) The road switches back, but he cannot see it. White fog rolls through the invisible villages. Momentarily it breaks around a red tile roof or the cross of an old church. It was so thick when he left that morning that each object—rock, tree, animal—appeared suddenly before

him, often startling him. Rachid had to stop. He did not want to
meet the soldiers too soon. The letter Nassif had received said
arrangements had been made and gave clear instructions of when
Rachid should reach Batroun. *Arrangements.* A district trial, perhaps, but he had to go and meet the soldiers. Nassif sent a message
that Rachid was on his way, ready to give himself up.

In his house the night before, Rachid lay beside his wife and
listened to her sleeping breath stop and start as her chest rose and
fell under the blanket. She said she had waited for his return each
night, sitting up in bed with the sheets pulled up to her waist,
listening to the creaks and vibrations of the house. "Most nights
the baby made sure I wasn't lonely. I would reach to close her
shutters and find myself looking out into the dark."

On the road Rachid thinks of his father. When Rachid was a boy,
his father told stories with his pipe. First he tapped it against a
stone and lit it, then he waved it around as he spoke; when he
became quiet, he placed it in his mouth and let the fire die down.
The brothers sat around the fire while the younger children slept.
Their father nodded his head slowly. "Abi-Nader, Abi-Deeb, Koojock, Saleh, Elian—we had all been one, the five families of
Abdelli—until the invaders came: the Turks, the Matwilah, the
Shihabs."

The Abi-Deebs—at what moment had it changed? When Deeb
Maklouf and Boutros Bike's last and most successful petition against
Rachid reached the court of the pasha, Chidac wrote to Rachid
and warned him that the kaymakam could not help. At what moment
had the families turned against one another? He opens the letter
Nassif gave him and reads it again. The ink starts to fade in the

fog, and the words streak down the page. Touma el Chidac signed
this one too. He is the counsel of the kaymakam and a friend. Now
a local trial is possible. Rachid collected all the evidence he could
and started on his way.

There have been other petitions, usually generated by Deeb
Maklouf. They accused Rachid of acting as sheik illegally, and of
forging his brother's name. Signatures had been obtained to testify
he had manipulated property settlements for his benefit and over-
taxed the villagers. Each of these charges were turned away by the
kaymakam in Batroun. But this time Deeb and Boutros Bike delivered the charges to the court of the pasha, and the accusations of
keeping the money collected for the Red Crescent, and of cursing
the Turks publicly named Rachid as a traitor. He crumples the
letter in his fist. He knows if the petition is successful, he is dead.

The sea is smothered in white. The sky too is a smoothed sheet
with a barely noticeable spot of yellow. Before Rachid reaches
Batroun, the sun should burn through. He does not hurry and he
stays at the edge of the road. In the fog the ground softens and
feels like the mossy paths he journeyed along the Amazon. Once
when his boat broke in a strong current, he had to walk ten miles
along the bank. The day was hot and some of his merchandise had
floated away from him; the rest he hung to dry until he could return
with another craft. He was surprised to see his brother, Shebl,
approaching from the opposite direction. When Shebl saw Rachid,
he began to weep and hold his arms. "Oh, brother, I thought you
were dead."

Rachid pulled away from Shebl and looked at this face. "What
are you talking about?" he asked.

Shebl panted heavily. "Maroka Navis put a curse on you, and when I saw the ruins of your boat, I thought she had killed you."

"Why do you believe in witches?" Maroka's husband was president of the Masons and had tried to get Shebl to join. When Rachid wouldn't let him, she had manufactured spells against him and recited chants in Shebl's presence that promised to destroy his brother.

"I couldn't sleep or eat, I had to come looking for you." His eyes brimmed with tears. Rachid put his arm around his brother. Although Shebl was older, he fell victim to many hoaxes. Some saw him as weak, since he and Mayme had not conceived children in the fifteen years of their marriage.

"Come," Rachid assured him, "we'll find another boat and pick up the merchandise. Relax—God will protect us." They stepped over a fallen tree and headed toward a village.

"Rachid, another thing."

"Yes?"

"We received a letter; your wife had a boy and named him Boutros after her brother."

Rachid smiled. He had wanted to name him Floriano.

In Brazil, even though the government changed, Rachid conducted his business without interruption. Money to a harbor master went a long way. Now in his own country Rachid hides from his enemies; in his own village they try to destroy him. Maybe this is Maroka's spell.

Rachid enters Batroun from the northwest, where many of the merchants have their large homes. By Glabany's house four soldiers stand, their bayonets fixed. They wait for Rachid, as the letter said they would. He hesitates and looks at them momentarily and then advances.

"Are you Sheik Rachid?" A soldier with a large mustache steps forward to meet him.

"I am." Two soldiers position themselves in front of him and two behind. Rachid walks with them holding his satchel tightly with his elbow. He thinks: I am not afraid. I am Rachid, from the house of Nader Antoun.

Batroun has changed since the beginning of the war. The few merchants open only for three hours, serving mostly soldiers. In the souq, a vendor pulls his table in and fastens the cloth roof. It is late afternoon. Men in uniform surround a fire and eat a roasted lamb; others sit on the steps of the churches and schools. Groups of children, skinny and poorly dressed, dip water from the fountain in the square. They cross to the *sarraya*, the government compound. On the other side of the plaza, lines of people crowd the yards. An old Druze woman, her head wrapped in a black scarf, talks rapidly to the guard at the gate of the court; he shakes his head back and forth. Raising his hand, the sergeant waves to get the attention of the sentry at the door. He blows a whistle, and sixteen more soldiers join the party. As they climb the stair, Rachid lifts his head. Deeb Maklouf and at least twenty others from Abdelli watch Rachid's entrance into the court.

Inside the chambers, the prosecutor shouts as they approach, "Where have you been?"

Rachid does not move and stares at the man, whose jowls shake as he orders the soldiers out the door. Rachid stutters, "I walked from my village . . ."

"Sit down and sign this." The prosecutor pushes a paper toward Rachid. He picks it up and starts to read. The prosecutor puts a pen under Rachid's nose. "Sign it now—we are running late," he growls.

Rachid removes his bag and sits down in the chair in front of the desk. The prosecutor stares at him while he dips the pen and writes his name with a trembling hand. The paper is grabbed by a clerk and they walk into the courtroom.

Many people are standing and listening to the interrogator read the list of witnesses. Soldiers are scattered throughout the busy room. Each name is called, and the witness comes through a half-gate. Since he is not given a chair, Rachid leans against a door on the far wall. He is stunned by the size of the crowd. He cannot concentrate on the event in the front of the room. The names and people fuse together. Someone whom he has greeted each day in the fig groves joins the testifiers; another whose children went to school with his children steps forward. (His father's voice: _Abi-Nader, Abi-Deeb, Koojock, Saleh, Elian. We had all been one. . . ."_)

Deeb Maklouf sits first, takes a breath, and speaks. "I accuse Rachid of everything read in that petition." He describes blasphemy against the Turks, pilfering treasury money; he adds accusations Rachid has not heard before. He talks quickly and moves his arms toward the sheik and then against his chest. _But Deeb Maklouf, you have seen my daughter's hair. How it falls and shines. My son Jean's legs, long; he will be the tallest, surely. Have you met Maron, born three years ago at the beginning of the war, slow to speak?_ The prosecutor asks Deeb to sign the charges. His hand forms the curves of his name. Rachid's body is hot and he pulls his shirt away from his skin.

Deeb Maklouf glances toward him, and Rachid straightens his shoulders. He wants to faint and teeters a bit. (I am Rachid, from the house of . . .) Rachid mops his head with his handkerchief.

Deeb's uncle is the next to state charges. Rachid's head pounds louder, and he begins to pace in the doorway. Each word seems shrill; he wants to put his hands up to his ears but is afraid to draw attention to himself. He hears the list of charges again. Rachid cannot wait for death when it comes this soon. He stops and looks at the door. No soldiers stand by him, and everyone is watching the witness. He places his back to the door and turns the handle and slips into the adjoining room. It is a large office filled with books and three desks, he sees no other doors. At a desk in the middle is an officer of the mutessarifate, Said Afandy el Bitar, who looks up from his work. "What can I do for you?"

Rachid doesn't know what to say. (He could be crying.) "Your honor"—he approaches the desk—"I am a dead man. I signed a paper I did not read. He wouldn't let me read it."

"Who didn't?" Said Afandy rises.

"The prosecutor." Rachid turns his head toward the courtroom. "Nagibe el Kouri?"

Rachid nods and puts out his hands. "I must be able to tell my side or my whole family will die."

Said Afandy goes to the door of the court and calls Nagibe el Kouri. The voices stop. Nagibe pounds his gavel and looks across to Afandy and Rachid's face behind him. Afandy motions to Nagibe and then closes the door, leaving Rachid alone. Rachid stands in one spot and does not move until a few minutes later when Afandy opens the door again and says, "Come."

They cross the courtyard to the house of the kaymakam. Stars flash overhead, fading into the night. Nagibe stays behind Rachid while Said Afandy goes into the kaymakam's office. Rachid can hear Nagibe's strong breathing and his anger as he curses a soldier by the entrance.

Rachid remembers the last time he stood in this hall, surrounded by some of the same men who have come to testify against him. They congratulated him on the good impression the men of Abdelli had made on the kaymakam. They gave Rachid the credit— Boutros Bike was among them. When Zuine enters, Rachid steps forward and bows.

"Hello, Rachid." The kaymakam's voice is soft and slow.

"Hello for the last time, your excellency."

The kaymakam pats Rachid's back. "Don't worry, Rachid. Tell me what happened."

As Rachid repeats his complaint, the kaymakam looks at Nagibe and wrinkles his brow. His face hides in a gray mask. "Nagibe, destroy the statement and start again. Take Rachid's testimony." The kaymakam says nothing more.

Nagibe grunts and leaves without waiting for the prisoner. Rachid follows him to the courtroom, and when he enters, he sees Nagibe is in the front announcing the change in the trial. He blows air like a wounded animal and shouts at the witnesses and the clerks. Rachid finds a chair in the front row and waits for Nagibe to question him. "No, the Baladeit did not have eighty pounds in its treasury at all, nor was there money available for the Red Crescent." He displays ledger sheets, and letters of witness. (How many times in the night has he rehearsed this?) Rachid signs the new testimony. Others are called again.

("Abi-Deeb, Koojock . . .") As they speak the same charges they had before, Rachid walks to the back of the room and slips by the guard. In front of the courthouse, people sit and talk quietly as if they share a fire—some hope for news concerning members of their families who have disappeared or who were arrested. Rachid understands now. *Arrangements.* He descends the stairs. Soldiers stand near the entrance, and below him the faces of the frightened hang in the darkness. Some follow Rachid with their eyes as he returns to the kaymakam's house.

The kaymakam sits at the head of the table where they had first talked four years before. He drinks from a tiny blue cup.

"Rachid, how did you do?"

"I was able to tell everything, thank you, your excellency."

"You are welcome, when it is possible." He places his cup upside down on the little saucer. The grounds pour onto the plate and the future runs into a puddle. A servant takes the cup away. The kaymakam's face looks tired, and his voice sounds strained. "Now go to your family."

Zuine walks slowly from the room and up the stairs. Some things have changed in the last year. Each person's loneliness and fear wear different clothes. On the Amazon, Shebl became nervous when the current rose or an obstacle stood in their path. He was amazed when Rachid managed the boat through a tight channel. One night, less lucky, they were jammed and could not see how to get free. Rachid gave up when it became dark, and he slept with the rocking of the boat—a soft melody in his head. Shebl walked the boards all night. In the morning, Rachid released the boat from its cradle. After that Shebl returned to Moraka, the witch, and told her that no one could hurt his brother. Rachid was lucky or blessed.

Go to your family, the kaymakam told him. His case will not go to Aley, he knows that now. Out in the streets, uncertainty looms in the *sarraya.* Each heart beats unevenly. He passes through the city so quickly the lights streak a gold line on each side—suns rising and setting. On the outskirts, he looks ahead to the mountain road and stops and turns to the sea. The torches bounce stars onto the water. Masts impale the darkness. The kaymakam's face looked tired to Rachid. Something has happened in the government—it will change soon, he can feel that. Rachid will quit the office of the sheik immediately. He turns his back on the city and starts up the hill. When he arrives home, he will awaken his children and kiss everyone.

◆

The

Old

Days

◆

R a c h i d

1918

W h e n d i d t h e war actually start? Rachid wonders. Now in 1918 *before the war* is referred to as *the old days* in their talk. He reminisces about the time as if it took place in another century. Rachid remembers how the men sat in a circle after dinner on the velvet-covered dining-room chairs, their dark wood arms curled in spirals like a snail's shell. As his father spoke Rachid settled against the high back, sipped his coffee from a demitasse cup, and puffed on the water pipe. His mother circled the room and doled out pastries onto the small lace-covered silver plates on the end tables. As her arm crossed in front of his eyes, Rachid noticed the small beads dotting her gauzy lavender sleeves. Her skirt rustled as she walked from him to his father, whose large mustache was sprinkled with crumbs. She unfolded his napkin and held it in front of him. He continued to talk as he brushed his mouth.

Elmaz and the other wives cleared the table and retreated to the kitchen. Except for Aunt Madeline, who stood near the doorway until the men overturned their cups onto the tiny plates, sending the coffee grounds down the sides of the china. She placed her thumb against the bottom of a cup and swirled the grounds around and around. After turning it upright, Madeline peered inside. Everyone waited quietly until she uttered the words "In your future, I see . . ." Only then did the men suspend their discussions of the land, impending war, or news from abroad. Because they were Catholics they did not believe in reading fortunes, but they listened from curiosity and for amusement, they said. But they did listen. Madeline was particularly good at reading the grounds because she always included some truth about the character. She had once said to Rachid, "You will get important information from someone you don't know, but because you are bull-headed, you will not listen and you will regret it." He laughed and so did the others.

Now Rachid thinks of the old days and rocks back in his chair looking at his emptied coffee cup. Perhaps they need his old aunt's advice. Since the beginning of war, few dinners have been held. No one reads their fortunes, and often they have no coffee to drink. His father's chair is piled with old blankets placed there for visitors who had to leave sick houses. All the silver has been sold, but they still have the blue-and-white demitasse and the copper urns that keep the coffee from turning bitter.

Rachid rotates the grounds of coffee in the bottom of his cup and looks into the future. A line cracks through the middle of the silty design and separates the smear along the edge from the shadow on the bottom. (What does it say?) Rachid examines his cup. (Do you see an end to the war?)

He never sees a stranger with information, or wealth, or a long illness; he always sees a map in his fortunes. The grounds cover one side of the cup and curl along the bottom. This country is long and thin with a small point jutting on an ocean curving like a fish jumping from the water. Its mouth is opened and its back is humped. Rachid outlines the shape in the air with his finger. That long stretch of angular beach is not his own country, not Italy, Portugal, or France, but it looks familiar to him. Rachid has followed many maps. He pulls open a desk drawer and lifts a pile of deeds, sifts through land certificates, and searches through the letters. He closes it carefully. Where are they now?

Rachid leans on one elbow and copies the image on the back of an envelope. He peers into the cup and imitates each line. As he forms the curved line, Rachid can picture an old map he had at the beginning of the century. He pierces the paper at a corner where the coasts of Brazil, Peru, and Bolivia touch the River Acre, a spot where he once lived, where he followed a hand-drawn map like this one.

Rachid, Shebl, and Yousef established a rubber trade there. Two brothers traveled while the other managed a general store selling necessities to the laborers along the Amazon, Acre, and Purus. Wherever Rachid went he met other Libnani. Many of his countrymen also had businesses there and in the other nations of North and South America. Lebanon always surrendered her men to the stories of wealth abroad. Like their ancients, the Phoenicians, they took to the sea, and Rachid, Shebl, and Yousef followed this tradition and the water into a corner of Brazil that Rachid called its earlobe. When they returned to Lebanon, they brought a museum of wealth in furniture and adornments.

Rachid fills out the map and writes in the names of his towns in Peru: Iñapari and Purus; in Brazil: Río Branco, Brasiléia; in Bolivia: Cobija, Santa Rosa, Conquista. Three countries and three brothers: Rachid, Shebl, Yousef. All young, very young. (They were not afraid of each other then.)

No longer the sheik, Rachid has time to tend to his business and spends much of it in his office in Abdelli on the first floor of the house. In the early afternoon the sun shines and casts a pattern from the wrought-iron gate onto the marble floor. His desk is across from the door, and he can see a tangle of oak and pomegranate leaves through the window nearby. He rises and looks down to the road that borders the fields and orchards leading to the church. His son Jean walks two goats up the path and shouts to someone below the house. (All the fish they threw back into the Río Acre, the Amazon, the Purus—if they only had them now.)

Rachid holds the cup by its delicate handle, big enough only for a child's finger to poke through. Some of the grounds making up the dark ocean have shifted, cutting Peru's border. He wishes he knew the future. (How would this day end?) Rachid waits for something—for a baby to be born, for a rainstorm, for a child to call to him, for the war to end, for the *ringing for sorrow* to cease. The bells signal another neighbor has passed away. The bells ring alone. The keening and clapping ended along with the Sunday-night dinners. Too many deaths from war, hunger, disease, and absence.

The bells ring alone, splintering inside his head. He considers his cup again and searches in the grounds for monetary gain.

The villagers stay inside their houses more and more, hiding their animals in the basements instead of letting them graze in the fields. Rachid's sons take turns sitting with the livestock and guarding the figs, and if they have any extra food, someone stays in the pantry all night too. (The war has returned.) In order to get food, Rachid must travel again.

When Rachid is on the road, even with his son Boutros, he feels a loneliness that rings as hollow and deep as the caverns of Gheta. He can't describe what he misses or longs for. A story about Brazil or a religious parable fills the air between him and his son. Sometimes he thinks of music—a long high flute—and of dancing. The kind of dance where men stomp on the ground and whirl to exhaustion. The kind of dance where they hold each other's shoulders and beat their boots along the floor. The kind of dance that causes a friend to break from the line and twirl in the middle of the circle, waving a scarf. He doesn't hear music anymore. Some days Elmaz hums the babies to sleep. Rachid stops at the door and listens. An Aramaic hymn. Her light tones are like birds that cry at night: eerie, desperate. (Is war the absence of music?)

The last time Boutros and Rachid traveled, it was spring, and spring nights in the mountains are nearly as cool as the winter's day. They climbed the rocky path above the sea to Akar. They were returning from buying two steers. Rachid was pleased with the bargain because they had traveled so far, and because his wife's gold bracelets were worth so much.

The main road would have been warmer, but armed bandits were a constant threat there, so father and son wrapped themselves in sheepskins and turned their faces away from the wind. A donkey walked beside them, swaying as her hooves rolled over the stones. Rachid looked at his son's face. He tried to imagine the boy working on the Amazon River. Boutros was diligent and could sell, certainly, but would he watch the water there in the same manner he stared into the empty fields here? Rachid had come upon Boutros standing with a spear of grass in his mouth, staring at the wheat bending in the wind. He waited before approaching him; he watched the flicker of his eyes. Perhaps a thread of wheat flashed in them or a fig might be caught in his throat, but he never left the boy undisturbed.

As they walked, Rachid gave Boutros the instructions that they must follow on all the trips. If we are attacked, he said, do not stay and fight. Boutros nodded and kept his steps even. Boutros spent his life next to his father, learning to shoot and read, listening to him as he made deals with other merchants, helping him pull the oxen into the lower cellar. The oldest son closely repeated the actions of his father. He should be ready, just in case. But they were really nothing alike, Rachid thought. Boutros's voice was soft, muted. Yet coming from the town one day, Rachid heard Boutros's voice booming at the other children, giving orders to clean up the pile of rocks on the path and take the olives into the cellar.

At the age of fourteen, Boutros was as tall as Rachid. As they walked along the road, they might be mistaken for brothers. One of the animals wobbled on his back legs. They stopped and listened to his breathing. Heaving. Rachid shook his head. As they continued their journey slowly, Rachid's free hand waved in conversation. He told Boutros stories he never told the other children.

One of the animals stumbled through the stones, and the scraping of the hooves silenced them. Something must make the steer stop its noise. Rachid did not look at the steer, but at the road. He calculated the time from Akar to Tahoun el Sheik, from Haba to Abdelli. The rope in his hands pulled back. The steer shook and leaned to one side. *You will not die here, beast.* He yanked the animal's neck and the steer bellowed through his nose. (A ship's whistle.) The steer slid through the brush: *the keel scraping the bottom of the Acre, a terrible sound; they imagined each plank ripped away. Passage through the shallows brought them to the rail. This close they could not breathe; they did not speak until the river widened.* The healthy steer bobbed his head; the donkey and Boutros stood at the top of the hill waiting.

When Rachid and the steer reached the top, Rachid's face, arms, and back were soaked with sweat. "I think we'd better stop at Tahoun el Sheik for the night. I will find a place for them to sleep." They hurried down the other side. The sick animal tripped. Rachid pulled him up and thought his face looked bewildered.

The shed Rachid found could not hold both the animals. Boutros led the healthy one all the way inside. Together they shoved the sick animal in behind, but he did not fit, and his back was left exposed to the night air. If the creature could make it through the night, Rachid would have him slaughtered in the morning. The animal teetered a little and leaned against the wall. The boy unloaded the donkey and tied her to a tree near where Rachid began to clear a spot for their night's camping.

The shed had once been used as an outpost for a shepherd. The owner had lost all his animals at the beginning of the war. He stood in his doorway in his shirt sleeves and refused money from Rachid. After Rachid persuaded him to take a few lire, his eyes filled with tears and he shut the door.

Boutros built a small fire, and Rachid set a small bowl on the ground. He dampened a rag in oil and placed it inside the bowl and lit it. Rachid did not allow himself much pity when he was with his children. He did not speak of the past in the village, especially since Boutros was old enough to remember the times of large dinners in their new house—the long table filled with thirty people sitting around; the candles slowly melting beside the hands passing food up and down. He didn't even talk about the music with him, the music he missed so much. He told the long-ago stories of a life and place that didn't exist for Boutros. Why do men decide to leave the countries they love so much only to long for them once they are gone?

The tiny fire danced in the bowl. "Boutros, have I ever told you about Manuel Phillips?"

"When was that?"

"Long ago." 1899, maybe. It was Christmas, and Christmas on the Amazon slowed the traffic down. They traded more, visited a great deal, and held parties in every port of call. The price of rubber stabilized for about two weeks, and everyone felt generous. "Long, long ago."

"I don't think you ever told me. Was it on the Acre or the Amazon?" By now Boutros must have known Rachid's stories as if they were his own. He rested against the shed, and the uneven breathing of the sick animal faded into the night. The flames flickered on the brown face of Rachid, exposing only one side of his face and neck.

"We were on a long voyage in 1899 and my friend Adolf was the captain. Adolf walked the deck with a cane and watched the water. He was always dressed in white, and he rarely hoisted a rope or swept a deck. On Christmas Eve we were docked at a central point. Nearly twenty ships had decorated their masts and sails with flags for the holiday, and they each sponsored a party for the others' crews and passengers. They sang, they prayed, and spoke to each other in the broken languages they picked up on their journeys."

Rachid tried to converse in Portuguese; he had listened carefully to the captains and asked to read their Bibles. He engaged his customers in trivial how-do-you-do conversation so he could polish his Spanish and Portuguese. He counted the inventory three times, each time in a different language. At night he whispered in his sleep, *Dios, madre, mi país.*

"My friend Bashir Sharwool came from another ship to celebrate. At midnight a cannon was fired and fireworks were exploded. We stood on deck and raised our glasses to the red and blue flowers bursting in the sky—new stars, full of color. The band played Brazilian music and everyone drank and ate. Bashir gave a speech for the holiday, praising Brazilian hospitality." Rachid smiled. "I remember his voice stumbling through the Portuguese words, and then he lapsed completely into Arabic. I translated for him and everyone cheered. I don't know if they heard a word."

How much did he drink that night? (Long ago.) When Rachid awoke, he looked out his porthole. They were on the water probably going to Anti-Marie. The heaviness in his head persuaded him to go back to sleep. By afternoon he was able to pull his pants on and climb to the deck.

"By the time I was able to go up we were nearing Anti-Marie. Adolf was out of his cabin and watching the shore come nearer. I stood beside him steadying myself by holding the rail. His eyes were intently staring at the harbor. I turned and saw men running around and shouting to us. Adolf ordered a party to go over to see what the commotion was."

"Was it a war?" Boutros asked.

"Not this time," Rachid replied. The instability of the governments there was a constant problem for the merchants. They would return from a trip up the river and find that the government had changed and their currency was invalid. So they tried to trade only goods, but then they were forced to take trips into Manaus or São Paulo to get funds. "Not this time, no," Rachid repeated. "Pirates."

"Pirates?" Boutros raised his head.

"When the entourage returned, they reported that the ship, the *Libra*, had been looted. Manuel Phillips, the rebel, shot a cannon into the side of it, then went through and took everything. Captain Adolf told me that Manuel Phillips wanted to fight the Bolivians and make himself the governor of Alto Acre."

The Río Acre ran from Brazil into Bolivia and on to Peru. The area was rich in rubber, but the trade was not tied up in big plantations like the areas farther east. Natives and farmers owned most of it. From the Acre, the traders could go to the Purus that flowed into the Amazon. From there, the trip to Manaus, the central business city, was not long. Manuel Phillips had his eye on this trade and probably would charge tolls.

"Adolf whispered to his first mate, who nodded to his captain's words. He ran down the deck and gave orders to the crew, not in his usual blustery way, but quietly and clearly.

"Adolf watched the shore while his men pulled down the flags and sails. Our ship crept into the harbor as if it were a ghost ship— no signaling, no shouting. The captain went below. Unfortunately

Manuel's men waited, so we stopped just short of going into the harbor."

They stayed there for two days, frozen, not loading, not unloading. Rachid was to change ships in Anti-Marie and join the *Soprano*, captained by another friend, Justino. The *Soprano* weighed more and was larger than the other ships on the river. Adolf believed Manuel wanted it for a battleship, because he never bothered to board Adolf's ship or any other. He just waited.

"When the *Soprano* arrived, Justino docked in the far end. The shore had been silent and Justino was not warned of what waited for him. As he prepared to unload, four men boarded the *Soprano* and delivered an ultimatum: Surrender the ship and the cargo or it will be taken by force in twenty-four hours.

"Justino called a meeting of the captains of all the ships in the harbor. When Adolf returned, he told us that they had decided to cover the ships with sandbags. Together, they had three thousand men with arms, and they felt that they could defend all their ships."

Rachid wanted to fight too. Adolf and Justino had been very good to him, often allowing him to sell his merchandise among the passengers. He talked to his friends, and they went to Adolf to volunteer. The captain pulled him aside and confided, "Rachid, I would prefer it if you stayed to be my bodyguard." In 1899, Rachid was only twenty years old, but his height and rigid stance aged him. His face was sharp, and his steady eyes penetrated everything he could see. The passengers felt safe around him and often wandered into his room when the tension thickened.

"Half the day passed slowly. We waited for Manuel's move. Crewmen and passengers leaned against the walls in the hall talking idly. Rumors spread about Manuel's approach, but each time

it was a false alarm. Everyone was nervous, and I was tired. One
of the passengers said he was afraid. 'I've heard of these battles on
the water, but I hoped I would never experience one.'

" 'Don't be afraid,' I told him.

"The man shrugged. 'Who is going to protect me? You?'

"A couple of the crewmen laughed. I straightened up and fixed
my eyes on him. 'I am not afraid because I believe that God will
protect me.'

"One officer grunted and stood before me. 'What makes you so
invulnerable?' He looked me up and down.

" 'I have a piece of the Cross.'

" 'That makes you safe from bullets? Ha.' He turned and looked
at the men behind him. They laughed too.

"I neared him. 'Yes.' I stared him straight in the eye.

" 'Oh.' He pulled out his rifle. 'Let's see how good that piece of
the Cross works on this.' "

Rachid looked up. His son was no longer leaning against the
wall. He pulled his body forward as if he were hard of hearing.
Rachid moved in until his whole face was lit by the tiny fire. He
whispered, "The room became quiet and I felt I was a dead man.
My face was warm and I couldn't say a word. I stared into the
barrel of the rifle and straightened up." *Madre, Dios, mi país.*

They stood like that for a while feeling each other's hot breathing. Rachid's body became very warm. No one spoke. He stared
and the officer aimed. The captain approached and walked into the
center of the group. Everyone became quiet as he pulled the rifle
from the man's arm. "This is not the time to compare philoso-
phies." He threw the gun on the floor. "Tomorrow you can prove
yourself when Manuel Phillips attacks."

The officer snorted and went away. The others left slowly. Rachid fell against the wall, sweating and breathing heavily. (This is not my war.)

"About ten o'clock everyone came ready for combat. The ships were stacked with sandbags and salt bags. They fired the engines on all nineteen ships and four launches. Manuel Phillips saw what was going on and reiterated his threat. He boarded a launch and came down with thirty-two men to the side of our ship. I was below guarding the captain. This is all I heard: Manuel called for Adolf to come out and talk to him. The first mate told him the captain was sick and couldn't come out. Manuel tied his launch to the side of the ship. I heard the feet of the crew positioning themselves on the deck. He looked over the line of men and rifles standing in front of him. After a moment, Manuel returned to his launch. He walked up and down his boat. Our men did not move from their readied positions. When I climbed back to the deck, Manuel Phillips had already turned around and sailed down the river."

Rachid raised his hand and Boutros moved nearer. This was how his story could be told years from now, Rachid thought. Every day we lived another story and forgot about the hours that passed quietly or in prayer or accompanied by the ticking of an old clock in the hall.

In the middle of the story, the animal wobbled; he heaved air and swallowed, his eyes rolling back and forward again. Rachid dropped his arms and rose, and Boutros drew himself up and waited for his father's order. Rachid pulled at the animal, but he collapsed.

Rachid looked at his son. "Are you going to stand there and do nothing?"

Boutros began to push the steer. The animal could not walk at all. Rachid tugged the collar while Boutros shoved the back. "Come on, hurry," Rachid groaned.

"Where are we going?" Boutros pressed his head and shoulders into the beast.

"To the river."

The animal lurched forward, and Boutros tripped and fell onto the hill.

"Get up," Rachid shouted. "What are you doing?"

Boutros rose quickly and wiped his head with his sleeve. He saw the moon's reflection swimming on the river. The final fifty feet of ground sloped sharply, and the steer rolled and bounced to the river's edge. Rachid, Boutros, and the steer puffed like the *batalon*'s smokestack. The river was silent. Rachid wanted to fall back and stare at the sky. He imagined a small boat taking him down the river—no engines, no smoke, no wheels, just the current in command.

The steer grunted and then dropped his head onto the grass. Boutros stopped beside it and stared at his one open eye. Rachid stood and pulled a knife from his belt.

"Are you going to kill him?" Boutros watched.

Rachid did not look at him. He knelt at the head of the steer. "We'd better do it now, and we can sell the meat in Bjarfadel or someplace nearby. They must need meat too. We still have the other one. We might be able to get a worthy price for it." Boutros dug a small hole in the ground near the river's edge and filled it with leaves and twigs.

The steer seemed to balloon in front of them. Rachid stabbed it and slit the neck until the chin dropped forward and blood ran into the river, soaking the mud. A fetid smell rose and Boutros moved his head back. Rachid squeezed his nose, then rolled the animal over. The sickness had taken over. Rachid wondered if the meat would be edible. Much of what they had eaten since the beginning of the war has been questionable. They would have to boil it a long time; no raw kibbee from this animal. As Rachid struggled with the steer, Boutros stood and faced the water. "Did you ever see Manuel Phillips again?"

Rachid had to wiggle the blade to get it through the flesh. He paused a moment. "What did you say?"

"Manuel Phillips," Boutros repeated.

"Oh, no, I never saw him again, but that wasn't the end of his handiwork. Apparently he took over another ship, the *Primo.* He and his men ate and drank everything until they fell ill. They boarded another ship, the *Spencer,* and Manuel ordered the engineer to start the engine. The man refused, and Manuel beat him. The captain saw what the pirate was doing and gathered his men together. They cornered Manuel at the rail. We heard he looked at the crowd over and over, then called to his men, 'My friends, take care of yourselves,' and then he jumped into the river and disappeared."

"Were you frightened?" Boutros blocked the moon's shine and cast his shadow over the steer's body.

"Boutros, move out of my light."

Boutros squatted and watched Rachid spread the hind legs of the animal. "Hold this."

Boutros took the leg into his hand and pushed it toward the ground.

"Frightened? It was a tense time for all of us. That wasn't the end of Manuel or people like him. His reputation sailed by in the form of mutilated passengers and crew members floating down the river. Their bodies were torn apart as if savages of the worst kind had attacked them. I had never seen that kind of destruction before."

Rachid stopped and sat back. The smell was overpowering him—worse than curdled milk, or a decaying squirrel, or a skinned rabbit. Would sickness spoil a human body? Without all the perfumes, would we be one more rotting animal in the ground? He placed his tired hand into the water. Boutros kept his gaze on his father. A brown puddle formed around Rachid's hand. Burnt milk, bodies, squirrels. His son's face was cocked away from the butchered animal. His son had seen bodies hanging in the square in Batroun, and the swollen children begging in the *sarraya*. Why did he turn away now? Rachid rose to his knees and wiped his blade on a cloth. The animal was one more of Manuel's shredded bodies. He felt sorry and tired. "Boutros, go up to the shed and guard the steer until I return."

Rachid watched his son climb up the hill and disappear into the darkness. No matter what he had seen in his own life, perhaps his son had seen enough. Had heard enough. The ones who died now from the sickness or hunger were not buried promptly or even claimed. The bells rang every day. Rachid had not thought of this before, not about Boutros, or Lichah, or any of the children, not about Elmaz, or Mayme, or Sahda, or their children. What they heard, what they saw; what they thought. But he had no choice. He did what he could do and he failed at all of it, so it seemed. The tenure as sheik, the renewal of the crops, and now this meat purchase. And where were his brothers all this time? They left their wives and children for him to care for, but where were they and where was the promised money? Surely, his son understood. He did what he didn't want to do. Everyone did.

Rachid knelt beside the remains of the animal. He had no choice but to sell it. He could not ask much because of the condition of the meat. But it was meat all the same, and people would be happy to see it. He wanted to rub his aching shoulder, but his hands were soiled, and he preferred to keep his clothes as presentable as he could.

How would he carry it to them? He figured out a plan as he walked to the shed. The only way to reach the people in Bjarfadel would be to go to the priest. Boutros had moved inside and was sleeping next to the animal. His son looked smaller lying next to the steer. The animal raised his head as Rachid entered and knelt to tap his son's shoulder. "I'm going to see if Simon Mounat will lend us his cart so we can move the meat to the Salha Heights. I shouldn't be long." He crouched beside him. "Listen, if anyone tries to take the steer, give it up. Do not fight." Rachid pulled a blanket from his satchel and swung it on his shoulders like a cape. He glanced at his son as he withdrew. The boy opened his eyes when his father spoke to him but closed them again. Rachid found himself wishing the boy were not with him. Too many things to think about. Too many things to fix. Whom could he trust these days?

When he returned to the riverside, he placed one part of the carcass over his blanketed shoulder and dragged it to the shed. After six trips up and down the hill, he piled all the meat against the wall. The sky lightened to gray. At the water Rachid cleaned himself for his trip into Bjarfadel. He combed back his hair and ran his hand through his five-day beard. The blanket was completely soiled. Rachid threw it into the shrubbery. He washed his face and hands, and the water darkened in the spot he touched and beyond.

When Rachid came back from Simon Mounat's to pick up the meat, Boutros was pacing around the shed. Simon Mounat walked beside Rachid in silence, and behind them two boys pulled a wooden cart. Boutros stopped at the sound of the cart. The healthy steer was tied to a tree, where it nibbled at some grass in the church-yard, their belongings were in their satchels and strapped onto the jackass, and the small oil dish was gone and the fire was out. Boutros almost lurched toward his father. Rachid waved his hand, pointing from the meat to the cart. Boutros dropped his bag and began to carry the meat toward them. He held it at a distance and kept his eyes turned away.

The two Mounat boys watched until their father turned.

"What are you going to do with the other one, Rachid?" Simon walked over to the healthy steer.

"I will probably take it home and give it to the village."

"It has been a long time since any of us had meat."

"It is the same with us."

The boys looked very healthy. His and Mounat's family avoided starvation, that was easy to see. Perhaps this village was doing better than his own, but he did not see any fields in production.

"What time did you tell Father Nehmetallah the sale would start?" Rachid asked.

"Ten o'clock."

Father Nehmetallah was the bishop of the region. He would have notified the villagers of Rachid's arrival after the morning mass. Naturally Rachid would give him and Simon their pieces in advance. As they walked to the heights, Simon and Rachid discussed the war in low tones. Boutros followed the cart, holding the ropes of the jackass and the steer. He stopped occasionally because one animal or the other wanted to push its nose into the rocks or grass and chew whatever it could find.

"Rachid, you should have told me you were here yesterday. You and your son would be welcome in my home."

"We didn't know we would be stopping so soon, Simon. Thank you." They climbed the final hill, where they saw other people walking toward the plaza. Villagers began to gather around the cart. These are my customers, Rachid observed. The women were scarved with large dark haloes and the men's necks shone red. Some children wriggled through the legs of the adults; they seemed to be with no one in particular. He was wrong. These people looked as gaunt, tired, and as hungry as the people of Abdelli. Color had faded from their cheeks; their clothes hung loosely on their frames.

Rachid felt uneasy. Father Nehmetallah hadn't yet arrived. He and Simon stood in the square by the well. The boys turned the wagon around behind them, then Simon inspected the meat and whispered to Rachid. He instructed Boutros to take two pieces out and place them under the wagon. Simon nodded to Rachid, then turned and stepped through the crowd to talk to friends. How many have died here? Rachid wondered. Not more than thirty or forty people had come to the sale. Yet this once was a fairly large village.

When Father Nehmetallah walked through the plaza, he spoke to no one until he reached the well. "As you can see, Rachid, I told as many people as I could."

"Thank you, Father, I appreciate that."

"But I must warn you; they have no money for meat or anything else. They came because they are desperate."

Rachid ground the toe of his boot into the dirt. He glanced at the now silent villagers. (Which ones were we?)

"You do understand, Father, I paid for this meat. I have a family to feed, too."

Father Nehmetallah contemplated the crowd. They stared steadily at the two men. "What do you propose?"

Boutros stood by the steer, holding the rope in his hand. Rachid regarded him, then waved for him to come over.

"Father," Rachid said, "tell them to bring whatever they have to trade, and they can have a piece of the meat."

"That's a good thing, Rachid." Father Nehmetallah patted his back. He walked toward Simon and the other villagers. "Rachid will take whatever you have to trade for the meat. Go to your homes and pick something which is an honest trade."

The villagers left quickly. Rachid and Boutros unloaded the ass and piled their coats and clothes and tied them in a bundle.

"Boutros, you take what they bring and put it in the bags. I'll choose the pieces of meat to give them."

"How many people can one steer feed?" Boutros asked.

"Not enough."

The sheik's wife was the first to approach Rachid. She carried an armful of figs wrapped in a small blanket. Boutros emptied the figs into the bottom of the first bag, and Rachid and the woman wrapped a slab of meat in the blanket. Figs and olives were what most of the villagers had to offer. Rachid said very little to his customers. Figs and olives were what he had enough of in his own orchards. He hoped for a little wheat, even grapes (but who would have grapes?); something new to offer his wife.

After all the people had left, Simon Mounat lingered. "You have done a good thing, Rachid; it's a shame you have no money from it." Rachid squinted his eyes and looked toward the church. In the middle of the day, after the ground dried from a dewy night, the sun turned white, and faded everything to a paleness. In the spring, he might forget the sun was there. The breeze in the mountains kept him cool. Grass that had not been there the week before surrounded his ankles. He liked to feel it against his legs. Bjarfadel is rocky, though, and spring produced only the white buds on the trees around the church. What little grass they have was strangled by roots and rocks.

"Simon," Rachid asked, "could you send your boy to Kroom and tell the butcher we are coming with fresh meat? We will be there by dinner."

"You won't be taking it home after all?"

"It seems useless."

"More olives, Rachid?"

Rachid smiled. "No, no more olives or figs. Only money this time. I hope."

The healthy steer lay on his back, and Rachid and Boutros watched as the butcher and his wife, Badre, quickly slaughtered and divided the animal. The butcher needed to cut through the gut two times before he reached the middle of the carcass. They filled basket after basket with deep-red flesh. Badre placed the fat and hide in a wooden box to the side.

The sale took three days. Neighboring villagers came with raisins, pots, pans, and cloth, and some had money that recently had reached them from relatives in the States. Each came with a story of not having had meat in a year, maybe more. Rachid learned to watch the hands and not the faces as his customers traded with him. They were not the mangled victims of Manuel Phillips, but their eyes were circled in black and the children's bodies were swollen from hunger.

Boutros packed the bags to the brim and hid the money inside a pouch in his shirt. A small child came to him and touched his sleeve. Rachid was giving the boy's mother some meat. When the child and mother left, a black print of the child's hand was left on Boutros's clothes. (How would their story be told?)

Rachid surveyed their loads before they left Kroom for Abdelli. The jackass carried two large baskets, two bags, and a roll of blankets and coats. Rachid had a small satchel strapped across his chest and carried another pack on his back. Boutros held the top of the jackass's wobbling packages as they walked down the road. Their paths were obscure animal trails toward the sea; then they switched back into the mountains. Rachid carefully picked the deserted routes, because their cargo would draw too much attention. They could not be quick lights, shooting stars, trees rustling without wind, running, boots in hands, faces covered with scarves. Too many days. Too much to carry. They needed to be home. The boy should have been with his mother.

At sunset their shadows created large beastly shapes on the ground. Ahead of them, coming from the west, other shadows fell over the rocks. Voices droned. Rachid pulled his son behind a rock. He put his finger up to his mouth. The jackass followed them off the road. "Stay here; do not come out where you can be seen, no matter what happens."

Rachid tied the beast to a tree and paraded into the open as if he were alone. The group he had heard seemed to be standing and talking. Rachid saw three men and two women. A young man approached Rachid, who stopped. The stranger was thin and dressed in dirty brown clothes and carried a large tied bag. Obviously he was not a soldier, but he could have been a bandit or a deserter.

Rachid waited without moving. "What do you have there, young man?" he bellowed.

The stranger braked in his tracks and tightened his grip on the bag. "A few pounds of wheat, my lord." His companions came near to where the two men stood.

Rachid did not step back. "Would you sell some of it? How many *rotl* do you have?" Perhaps money would have sent the strangers on their way.

"Twenty *rotl*, my lord."

"Where did you get it?"

"I can't tell you," he answered quickly.

Rachid stared at him. "How much do you want?"

The man put out a hand. "Just a few pounds, my lord. My wife is expecting our first child."

Rachid peered at him and pulled two coins from his breast pocket. "I'll take it, but I am going to weigh this when I get home, and if it is short, I will ruin your contraband business forever." Buying black-market goods was dangerous. The neighbors would smell the bread and wonder where the wheat came from. He clutched the bag. The flour jars had been empty for very long. Besides, where would he get it otherwise? The Turkish government took it all. Rachid waited for the group to leave. He waved at Boutros to come. His son and the animal rushed toward him.

"We can go now."

"Who were they?" Boutros asked.

"Just some people selling wheat."

Boutros took the bag from his father and slung it over his back. The two walked quietly for a few minutes at a quicker pace than usual. Rachid said, "We will have to stop to have the wheat ground tomorrow."

"Where?"

"Haba."

Boutros nodded.

Before they turned to descend into Cheeqa, a voice called, "Sir, sir, I want to talk to you."

Rachid stopped when he heard the young man who sold him the wheat. "Boutros, go ahead of me. If you see a fight develop, go on anyway, and I will meet you in Haba at Shehid's house." Rachid sighed and turned toward the voice. Boutros pulled the loaded jackass behind him and fled down the road.

"Sir!" The young man ran up to Rachid. "I need to tell you something." He took a long breath. Rachid put his hand inside his jacket and held the handle of his knife. "Sir, I must tell you. We bought forty *rotl* of wheat, my brother and I, and we divided them to carry. My brother thinks the shares are uneven. If you wait for my brother, you can look at his and pick the one you think is fair." He pointed to the others coming up from behind.

Rachid set his load down and offered his hand. "You are honest, and I don't need to check his share. I will stay with the pack I chose." Rachid pivoted and retreated, still gripping the knife.

"But my lord—"

"Don't worry. Goodbye." Rachid followed his son down the road.

"God be with you, sir," the young man shouted.

Rachid and Boutros neared their village. Their days had been long and their packages grew heavy. Rachid reviewed the decisions he had made on their journey. What could he do with all the goods he had received? He and Elmaz would plan how they would use them, what they would give to their parents, and where they would hide the rest. No place was safe. The relatives walked in and out of their pantries and cellars without asking. They would find everything, and before Rachid knew, the food would be gone and he would be on the road again. His clothes were sprinkled with the grains of the ground flour.

As Rachid ate lunch at Haba, he had overheard a conversation between Boutros and a mill worker.

"You are a Nader, aren't you, son?"

"Yes, from the line of Shebl Antoun."

The man offered Boutros water. *"Nader.* It is the word *rare.* Why would someone be named such a thing?"

"My ancestor was in the service of the king when his own brother led a revolt against the throne. Shebl volunteered to lead the king's men to suppress his brother's soldiers. He did and killed him. The king named him *rare,* Nader, because it is a rare man who kills his brother."

The man wiped his mouth, "Yes, there is one story like that in every family, in every village."

Boutros looked down at the ground. Rachid walked over to him and put his arm around his son's shoulder. "We are leaving." Boutros trembled under his father's touch. Rachid squeezed his shoulder. Wars were part of everyone's history, Boutros. Was that what made you tremble? Or was it the story itself? Was any brother *rare,* different from another brother?

When their last child was born, he lay on Elmaz's stomach while she stroked his head. Boutros watched. Maron, his new brother, sucked his thumb and his grandmother pulled it out. He put it back in again. As she reached to him, Elmaz said, "Mother, let him have it, he's hungry."

Her mother stared at Elmaz. "They are all hungry and there you are with another baby. Don't feed this one, Elmaz, only to let it starve later. Let it die now. With God's mercy let it die."

Elmaz's eyes widened. The children screamed at their grandmother, pounded on her, and pulled her hair. "Devil," they shouted. Elmaz screeched at them to stop. None of the children forgot the brother who was almost sacrificed.

Rachid's own brother, Yousef, died in America in 1916. When Rachid's mother heard the news, she threw herself down the steps of the house. Her screams and moans filled the village. Later she remarked, "A mother never loses her dead children." Boutros would not allow the death of a brother. Rachid understood this as Boutros quickened toward Abdelli. Not even for a king.

It was night when they climbed the hill leading into the western quarter of the village. The good road was below them. Instead of taking the path around the rough rocky hillside, they slid down, pulling the protesting ass behind them. At the bottom side of the road a dog was smelling something large. It shook its head back and forth violently. Rachid moved toward the dog.

"It's a body, Father." Boutros stood staring.

How could he have distinguished it from there? Rachid knelt beside it and unstrapped his satchel. A woman with a thin gray face sprawled in the dirt. She was young, perhaps in her twenties.

"Is she dead?"

Rachid put his ear to the woman's chest. He lifted her eyelid.

Her gray eye rolled. Rachid nodded. He lit a match and examined her face.

"It's Faris Shababy's daughter."

"How did she die?" Boutros stayed on the path.

"I don't know." Rachid rose and took off his coat.

"Boutros, go home; I will get Father Michael." He covered the body and walked toward the priest's house. He heard the jackass's hooves echo through the street away from him.

The rectory of Mar Elias was dark. The shutters were closed and it looked abandoned. Rachid pounded on the door. Behind him stars crowded around Mar Elias's wooden cross. Rachid rapped one more time. Inside a light went on, then the door opened slowly. The priest clenched the handle. His face was white, and his eyes nearly shut. His robe drooped from his thin body. Rachid scrutinized him; something had happened. "Father, I found a body."

"Who?" Father Michael breathed out.

"The daughter of Faris Shababy."

Father Michael trembled and nearly fell. He rested his body against the edge of the door.

"What is wrong, Father? What is happening?" Rachid grabbed his upper arm.

"I am sick. I can do nothing. We are all sick." He held on to the door, which closed before Rachid could respond. A breeze spun some dead leaves around and around the road. He glanced back at the rectory. *We are all sick.* Rachid rushed to his home.

It was not long, perhaps a few weeks, before they had a name for the plague. The Spanish flu. Even nameless, it killed entire families. When Rachid and Boutros had left for ten days, some neighbors were sick with a fever. Now they were gone. Children fell in the fields and died within days. The churches were empty. The healthy did not stay with the sick and helped only from a distance. "Send the maid to our aunt's house with food. We cannot infect our own children." For days the priests buried the dead. The workers walked the back roads to the fields to avoid the cemetery. (The enemy was inside.) Most of all they waited—for medicine, for a cure, and for money from America.

This was happening all over the world, Rachid knew. Some other man in another place sent his sons to the fields to plant tobacco they hoped to sell and went himself to carry another body from a empty family parlor to the church. Other women like Elmaz shook lentils under water, picked the stones from them, and made soup for the third time this week. Six children must eat and fight the sickness. Another friend died. God's will.

Rachid hung his head more from fatigue than sorrow as he returned from the burial of two of the children of Hannah Michaels. Hannah sat outside her house and stared at her open hands. Her husband had died months before. Rachid watched the widow. Her black clothes were made for a stouter woman. "Madame, you tell me if I can do anything for you and your two boys."

She raised her head and cried, "Oh, Sheik, Deeb is trying to buy my husband's notes for ten percent of their worth. I have no choice but to sell them. What do I have left?" She lifted her upturned hands. His neighbors unconsciously held out their palms like the beggars on the streets of Tripoli. He wanted to grab Hannah's wrists and shake her. (We are not beggars here.) She dropped her head into her lap and wept loudly. Rachid placed an arm on her shoulder and his other hand on the porch post.

Although her house was not large, it was one of the most beautiful ones of the village. Small diamonds of blue stone were inlaid into the pillars and around the windows. The roof was layered with red shingles that resembled overturned sea shells. The wood on the door was split, the base was crumbling, and a window on the north side was missing altogether.

"Hannah, listen," Rachid said. "I will buy the notes from you at a fair price if you release the rights."

"Oh, Sheik." She grabbed his sleeve. Her swollen red eyes filled with more tears.

"Come to my house and we'll fix it."

Rachid didn't know what good the notes would do him. Hannah swallowed her sobs and thanked him. She rose and stroked the front of her skirt.

Rachid noticed that the grounds around the house were unkempt. Weeds grew where there should have been rows of tobacco shoots and wheat spears. "What will you do now, Hannah?" When she was younger, Hannah had been considered the best singer in the village. She stood at the altar's side while Elmaz and Rachid married, filling the church with her voice. A tremor from the earth. Hannah did not move as she sang. It was both beautiful and terrible.

"I am going to Batroun to live with my father and take care of him. I will leave the boys to tend the land." She had two living sons: Tanous, twelve years of age, and Boulos, fourteen. "I can give them some money from the notes."

Rachid continued walking, and she released her grip and stood. "I cannot stay here." She put her face into a handkerchief. Abdelli was the tomb of her family.

Everywhere else on earth, fathers and mothers were praying for the health of their children. Perhaps everywhere else on earth, they spoke of nothing else. Elmaz kept her children away from anyone who was infected. But she waited, as if their turn would come. Walking through the village she asked from the path after the health of those in the house.

Who took care of the children of the dead, of the refugees? Not me, said Rachid. I have six children to feed. A mother and father to care for. Who then? His brother's wives sent their children to his door for food, and he turned them away. (I can do nothing.)

Two weeks after Hannah left, her sons had not been seen in the village.

"I have not seen them," Elmaz told him.

"What did they do with the money I gave their mother then?" Rachid left the kitchen and walked to the house with the blue diamonds in the columns. The door was slightly open.

Rachid peeked his head into the gray living room. "Hello," he shouted. He beat on the door with his fist. "Hello!"

"Mahraba," a voice inside mumbled. Rachid pushed the door, and it swung, spraying light on the empty living room. All the furniture, handmade by Hannah's husband, was gone. Boulos was sitting in dust on the floor, and his brother, Tanous, leaned against him asleep. The shutters were closed and the air was foul. A towel soaked up vomit, and a glass sat in a puddle of water. Tanous's clothes were caked with sweat and food; Boulos, red-faced and dripping, coughed.

Rachid quickly ran outside and took a breath of air. He untied the kerchief from around his neck and placed it over his nose. When he returned to the living room, he opened the shutters and slowly approached the boys.

"Boulos, how are you?"

"Sheik," he whispered and tried to push himself up from the

floor. Rachid motioned for him to stay. "Sheik, I am as you see me." He sucked in a short breath. "My brother is dying."

Rachid knelt beside the boy. "Tanous, Tanous."

Tanous's rough breathing spurted from his mouth. Both boys were emaciated, their faces were pale, and their clothes were stiff and dirty. Rachid went into the kitchen. It too was empty except for a bucket of water on the table. He filled two cups and took them to the boys. Tanous would not awaken. Rachid shook his shoulder, but the young man lay barely breathing on the floor. Rachid dampened his handkerchief and placed it on Tanous's dried lips. Boulos opened his mouth for the cup. His throat gulped loudly. Boulos's eyes closed, and he started to fall to the side. Rachid held him by the shoulder. Had their mother left them knowing they were sick? Rachid had to take them home. He pulled up Tanous and put him on his back. He was surprised at the boy's lightness. Boulos leaned on him as they walked through the village.

The brothers were put in the big kitchen while Rachid burned their clothes and dressed them in his sons' old things. As Elmaz forced yogurt into Tanous's mouth, she tried to talk to him. "You will be fine; pray a rosary and eat everything." Boulos sat by the fire, his face dewy with fever. Rachid gave him cool towels for his head. The boys slept for days in the basement below. Elmaz did not allow the children near them. "We can't leave them here. Not while I am pregnant," she warned Rachid.

Rachid agreed. He told Tanous and Boulos that they would stay with Mayme, his brother's wife. She had only two children. They could not require much food. The boys moved to Mayme's house. After they left, Elmaz had the floors scrubbed, their utensils buried, and all signs of the boys removed.

Rachid did not see the boys again for a week until he found them outside of Mayme's basement picking up kindling. Tanous talked animatedly to his brother. When he noticed Rachid, he stood near Boulos and pulled his brother's sleeve. They bowed to him. "Good day, Sheik."

Rachid wiped his chin with one hand. "You look better, boys. God has been good to you."

"Thank you, Sheik." Tanous hugged the wood against the old shirt Rachid had given him.

"I am sorry to tell you boys that your mother has died." They shifted their eyes to the ground. Mayme opened her door. Rachid said nothing more and walked away.

♦

A

S h o r t

J o u r n e y

♦

R a c h i d

1918

T h e   s t e e r' s   m e a t and the supplies Rachid had received helped his family eat throughout the early spring. He gave something to Mayme and Sahda for their families too. Nothing remained but what they could grow and what they stored of bulgur, lentils, and fava beans. But before Rachid could return to Tripoli, others died or were taken ill. He went to visit the widows with baskets of figs. He planted lettuce in the rough soil of a sick family; he emptied the slop bucket of the dying priest.

Elmaz had slowed down in her seventh month of pregnancy. Their eldest daughter, Victoria, prepared the dinners and kept the boys out of her way. By the beginning of May, the shortage of food and supplies had reached a crisis point. No one had sugar or flour. The voices of the children cut their ears. Rachid was tired of them and sent them to the fields for days. Boutros had become quieter and Lichah noisier. When Rachid could finally go for food, this story would end, he thought. He left on May 14 and returned in three days with coffee, wheat, and lamb. When he arrived, the house was quiet. The children were asleep, and Elmaz padded around the kitchen in Rachid's felt slippers. Her hair was falling from its pins. Rachid dropped his bag in the doorway and watched her back. Elmaz was wide, but not round—a small square woman with agate eyes and a veil of hair. "How are you feeling?" Rachid asked.

She turned to him. "Fine."

"How are the children?"

"Good, very good. They worked hard while you were gone."

"How are my parents?"

Elmaz put plates on the table; she watched her hands and avoided Rachid's face.

"Why don't you eat your food first. We will talk later." She maneuvered between the kitchen and the dining room carrying one plate at a time. He stood by his chair waiting for her to join him as she always did. She sat for a moment, then rose to get him yogurt, then to tend to the baby, then to clear the dishes. When she reached for his plate, he put his hand over hers. "What is the matter, Elmaz?"

She pulled her hand away and fell into the chair. She began to cry. "It's your parents."

Rachid arose. "What happened?"

"They are ill. They both have a high fever and are getting worse."

Rachid held her by the shoulders. "Who is taking care of them?"

"I try, but I can't go over there."

"Is anyone there? Has the doctor seen them?" He put on his coat. "Someone must be with them. Where is Mayme?"

Elmaz grabbed his sleeve. "Don't go over, Rachid."

He shook her off. "Are you crazy?"

She lowered her voice. "Mayme is there, yes. She and Nassif are stealing everything that belongs to your parents, even their clothes. I went to see them yesterday, and your mother screamed your name and cried, 'They are stealing everything, even our lives!' " She put her head on the table. "The house is a mess."

Rachid ran down the stairs. It was after midnight, and he walked through the garden to reach the back entrance of his parents' house. The soil was soft and his breath puffed out like smoke. He started to run. His heart seemed to have grown and taken over his entire body. When he reached the yard, he saw someone at the door. Another neighbor, Nadia, slowly closed the door; and as she turned, she saw Rachid standing there. He looked at her and recognized his father's quilt under her arm.

She stopped. "Rachid, you have returned!"

He leaned toward her. "How dare you take my father's comforter and leave him naked!" Rachid grabbed the blanket and unraveled his mother's wedding silver, which fell to the ground. "You witch," he yelled, and he pushed her. Nadia collapsed to the steps and supported herself with her hands behind her. Rachid towered over her. "Is he still alive?"

"Yes, Rachid." She dragged herself up. "I only took these things

because I was afraid that Taminy Michael would steal them." She
cried with her hands held out in front of her. (The upturned palm.)

Rachid went into the house and ran up the steps to the main
hall. A candle glowed in his father's bedroom, and Rachid entered.
His father lay on the bed with a thin sheet and a pillow of straw.
His special pillows and bedding made for his large size were gone.
Blood rose to Rachid's face, and he knelt by his father. "Father,
my lord." The old man breathed long and shallow. He did not open
his eyes to his son.

Rachid turned to his mother's room across the hall. He carried
the candle near his face, and his mother lay in darkness. "Rachid,"
she screamed when she saw him. She hollered words he could not
understand. Her voice was raspy and slurred. Waving her arms
about, she signaled toward the closet. He put the light beside her
bed. She tried to rise, and Rachid held her shoulders, pushing her
body against her mattress. She groaned. Her face was ghostly and
her lips were dried and cracked.

He stared at her. "Have you eaten? Have you seen the doctor?
Who is taking care of you?" She threw her head back and forth
and tears rolled from the corners of her eyes.

Rachid ran down to the kitchen and came back with warm yogurt.
He propped her head with one hand and placed the spoon in her
mouth with the other. She dribbled the food down onto her chin.

Rachid sat by her and stared at his father across the hall. What
had happened? His father's large body was heaving and drawing
in the air as if it would evaporate soon. His chest looked hollow.
Rachid paced between their beds. This plague was crazy, too much.
He should have dropped to his knees, prayed, or run to bring
someone. Instead he leaned against the wall crying into his elbow

surrounded in the dark hall by the unhealthy breath of his parents—puffing bellows, gas hissing into the lamp.

In the morning, his parents had not awakened, and they had not died. Mayme and Taminy would come to feed the silkworms soon. He would ask one to return to his house for some supplies. As he drank his coffee he wrote what he needed on the back of a letter he had sent to his parents years before. He found it on the floor where the desk once was. That too had disappeared.

The two women came and greeted him and went about their work. His mother opened her eyes and saw them standing in the hall and cried aloud. They looked at her without a word. Rachid pocketed the list he had been writing. When he rose to go to his mother's side, his cup crashed to the floor. He dabbed her with wet towels, and she mumbled incoherently.

Rachid stayed the entire day, talking aloud, telling them stories of Brazil. He tried to think of a happy story, but he began to cry and could not continue and dropped his head on his mother's stomach. His parents listened with their coldly gray faces. Out the window the church bells were quiet. An occasional wagon rolled by on its way to the fields, where some workers were grooming the trees and tending to the crops. Rachid boiled coffee three times, tilting the brass urn over another small cup, but not drinking. Elmaz brought blankets and dinner, and they talked at the door. He ate alone.

As he took the dishes to the sink, he heard his father grunting loudly. Rachid dropped the plate and rushed to the room. When he reached the door, his father was half risen, and his face was twitching.

"What do you want?" Rachid asked.

The old man looked at his son and leaned back. "God bless you, and God bless Shebl, and God bless Elias. Goodbye for now." His eyes closed for a moment, then opened again. His mouth formed more words.

Rachid sat closer. "What, Father?"

"God bless your children," he rasped. Rachid put his head into his hands and cried.

"Don't cry, Rachid," his father whispered.

Rachid paced the entire evening, watching his parents struggle with the fever. By midnight his father's chest was puffing rapidly; air was escaping him. No doctor came. (What do I do?) Rachid knelt in the hall under a mother-of-pearl cross. Three days. It had been a short trip. He would never leave his parents again, he vowed. Rachid poured out his cold coffee and watched the rivers run through the used grounds. (You will be traveling soon.)

At her bedside, Rachid moistened his mother's face.

She said, "Where is my husband?"

He carried the bucket to his father, who was gulping air—a whale, a door falling, a boat scraping a shallow bottom. *Take mine, take my air, have all you want, father.* Blood flowed from his father's nose. Rachid cupped his hand and caught it, but it seeped through his fingers and onto the sheets. (My father's blood.) Rachid scrutinized the hand splashed with blood, then he plunged it into the bucket and ran down the stairs to get the priest. As he stepped through the door, he heard a scraping below him. He crept toward the shed and found Yousef Michael trying to steal the goats. The man saw Rachid and fled.

Rachid's children gathered on the porch as the priest gave their grandfather last rites. Rachid stood back and the prayers echoed around the walls. Smoke from the incense filled the room, and Rachid swooned a little. The priest turned to Rachid and said, "Now, Rachid, he has said goodbye."

Rachid and Father Simon knelt together. Rachid then went to the door and announced to the group: "Abo Shebl is gone."

The deacon left to begin the bells of sorrow. Rachid listened. Mayme and Taminy placed the candles around the bed and arranged his father's clothes. They washed his body inside the wall of light. And the bells began to ring.

Where are my brothers?

From the other room, Rachid's mother called him in a quiet desperate voice. She growled at the women in her husband's room. "Get out of there." She squinted at the candles. (Lightning, thunder.) Rachid went to her, and she held his arm; she moaned, "I think Abo Shebl is dead." She lay back crying. He wiped her face and she convulsed.

"Father Simon," Rachid summoned, "my mother is ready." When the priest entered, she closed her eyes. Her breath stopped and her hand fell from Rachid's sleeve. Rachid dropped to the floor and wept again. The priest touched his shoulders. Rachid rose, turned, and wiped his eyes. Mayme stood still holding a shawl inside her sweater. She pulled it out. "I wanted to take this." Rachid waved her away. It belonged to his sister Hanny.

New graves had warm soil on them, but the fields were frozen, white and still. Abdelli was having a frosty spring. The day his mother and father were buried together, Rachid saw their faces were the color of the sky, smoky white. He kissed their lips before they left. He wandered back slowly from the funeral to his parents' home, and he lingered in the hollow hall. The relatives and neighbors had looted every dish and pan. The women accused each other and fled. Rachid regarded the wall where the mother-of-pearl cross had hung; its shadow marked the spot like a ghost. The closet doors were open and the drawers were pulled out.

His parents had no home anymore. For two days the church would ring the bells for their death; Rachid would clap and kneel for the dead until the ringing ended.

Rachid has been sleeping, although he doesn't remember closing his eyes. He picks up the cup that has fallen onto its side—Peru spilled into the saucer. The fish is gone. Rachid unlatches one shutter and pulls it open. Night frightened Rachid as a boy; now it covers fear. Sometimes he will say to Elmaz, "Remember when we walked in the village at night and found Ibrahim or Fares outside their houses in chairs telling stories?" They become quiet as they picture the old life. But eventually the images fade. Everything is so immediate. He knows he cannot bring back the past. Perhaps his mistake was looking to the future. Perhaps nothing can be done. Ever.

The next day, Rachid stands in the field listening to his rake move through the soil. He feels as if he has not talked to anyone in days. The rake scrapes across stone. His children are nowhere to be seen, and the neighbors have already gone in for the evening.

Rachid drops the rake and climbs up to his house. As he enters, Victoria comes to him. "Father, I have a new brother."

In the parlor his sons wait outside the bedroom. Mayme and Taminy are with Elmaz. Her face is puffy. She receives the baby from Mayme and pulls its blanket around his face.

Rachid's parents missed the new baby by only a few days. They are in a tomb and their house stands like a sepulcher. Mayme is wearing Hanny's shawl. It dangles off her arm as she offers Elmaz some water. Rachid sits on the side of the bed. Elmaz lifts the baby toward him. "It's another boy."

"Not another one," Rachid says, "a new one."

How will the story be told? The pictures will show them standing with the five boys lined up behind the two girls.

"What will we name him?"

"Do I get to choose?"

"Yes." Elmaz smiles and coos toward the child's wrinkled face.

Rachid takes hold of the baby's tiny hand. It is smaller than Rachid's thumb. He kisses the baby's palm. He glances to Boutros and then back to the infant. "Nader," he announces.

Elmaz presses Nader to her face. Mayme and Taminy leave, allowing the other children to enter. Elmaz sits with the baby, whispering to him in small bird tones. Rachid sits in a chair and watches the baby's eyes blink tiredly. It's hard to be born, he supposes.

◆

Life

of a

Stranger

◆

J e a n

1935

J e a n   c o n s t a n t l y   c o u n t s   what is missing in Abdelli—what is not the same since he left nine years ago. He searches for the ones who are living and the ones who are dead. Grandparents, great-aunts and -uncles. Gone. He looks for old things—wildflowers growing around the steps of the church; the *roojme*, and its neat walk and elegant trellis—but he does not find them. His father is closing the business in Brazil, but where are the others? Work, children, school, wives. Jean has lost count, he forgets litanies; his dreams are in Portuguese, in Arabic, in Spanish. He misses his father.

His brother Joseph comes out and watches Jean's brooding face. "What are you thinking?"

Joseph, only fifteen, was born after the war and he does not understand Jean's reverence for the land. Unlike his older brothers, Joseph did not guard the fields or watch Rachid tip a torch into the vines to sizzle the locusts. Jean has talked to Joseph often about those times since he returned. He is beginning to sound like one of the old folks. "Before you were born, Joseph, we couldn't go to school in new clothes, we didn't have wagonloads of food delivered to the village each week, or automobiles transporting us from Abdelli to Batroun in two hours." Joseph did not place one rock upon another to press the earth back into steps along the mountainside. The younger brothers are accustomed to sleeping until nine o'clock or later. When they do awaken, they argue about who will let the cow out; Elmaz usually silences their fighting by doing it herself.

Jean is tired of only walking around the village. Although he writes and reads and helps Elmaz, he feels aimless. He sees his brothers' lazy life-style and he is sad. All the money the family has been receiving from the States is dwindling because of the depression, so Jean has made a decision: to bring the land back. This will be the year of their new harvest, Jean enthusiastically tells his brothers. With a little hard work they can have fruits, nuts, vegetables before the fall. Nader joins Jean as he tours the land to see what needs to be done. The task is enormous: the stone walls have fallen down and the field is being used as a path from one place to another, so the soil is worn dry. Bushes and thorns cover many once-rich gardens, and the orchards are overgrown. The brothers walk all day planning where they will cut and where they will plant.

In the evening Jean sits at the table and wonders where the money will come from for the materials. He considers the family assets. What they do have is a gnarled, woody jungle. What could be saved from it? Jean decides the only way to raise cash is to make charcoal: they have the trees and they could build an outdoor oven somewhere on the land. At the turn of the century, charcoal was one of the main profit-making products of the village. It is settled, then. He tells his brothers that the next morning, they must arise at dawn.

They begin the first phase—building the wall around the vineyard which begins in Mar Simon and reaches more than a half mile. The brothers work side by side, passing stones from one darkened hand to the next and placing them on the ground. They do not stop except to stretch or to sit under a tree with lemonade or iced coffee. They drive a two-mule plow through the dirt and rake the land until the soil pours through their fingers. They cut the tangles from the trees, prune the branches, and stake the vines. When they reach the *alkornee*, a corner where the thorns are very thick, they can't move. Jean takes an ax and a sickle and cuts through the bristle. For many days he chops away until he can walk through, and then he crushes the shorter bushes by trampling over them. His brothers take the thorns to cover the top of their wall to protect the land from intruders. The brothers work hard. The blisters on their hands turn rough and leathery, their arms bleed, from the pricks and scars of the brambles, and their faces tan a deep Saudi brown.

When fall comes, Jean's brothers must return to school, and still the village has no grapes or olives. He becomes more desperate about making the charcoal and asks an expert, Hanna Matta, to start the charcoal fires. He sets up the site and leaves Jean and his brothers to watch the furnace. It has to be kept ventilated to stay aflame and yet it can't burn too fast, or the charcoal will disintegrate to ashes.

The first week of this endeavor, they have a terrible rainstorm with high winds. The charcoal pits fill with water. Each morning they stand drenched while they dig ditches around the charcoal stack. The rain is cold and the strong wind is as unbearable as the storm is unrelenting, and every time they return to check on the charcoal, the rain has filled their ditches and they have to dig again.

After five days the rain stops. Jean, Joseph, and Nader clean the wood away and find the fire is still burning. They open up a hole to give it air and then send for Hanna Matta to look over the situation.

The expert stands scratching his head. "When you sent for me, I was not going to come because I was certain everything would have washed away. This is amazing." He takes the shovel and throws some dirt in the corner where smoke is rising. "When you see it smoking like that," he points, "cover it with dirt. That's a sign that the embers are burning to ashes." He picks up his shovel and turns to the three brothers. "You, gentlemen, don't need me anymore."

The next year on the Feast of Our Lady in August of 1935, before the boys return to school, they harvest their first fruits. Jean walks along the rows of trees and under their roofs of wide leaves. He inspects the bark of the trees in the orchards, plucks a dead leaf from the berry vines, and examines the bugs on the lettuce. He has accomplished his goal, and he is glad.

Before the cold weather comes, Jean visits Lichah in Tripoli, where he works on the Persian pipeline. The brothers decide to take a tour, to visit some friends, to see their Uncle Elias, who is in the seminary, and to walk through the famous Cedars of Lebanon. With satchels and bedrolls on their backs, they trek through the high mountains above the tree line where there is nothing but the sandy rocks. On the particularly hot days, they descend to the groves and the small forests of cedars and pines. In the middle of one afternoon, they lie on the ground to cool off. While Jean is resting, he sees a big rock on a cliff above them. "I'm going up there," he announces.

Lichah opens his eyes and looks up. "Why?"

"The sights must be wonderful from there."

The two men climb with their hands and knees until they reach the top. Crossing his arms, Jean stares at the view. He cannot believe how the mountains look purple against the white sky. They look dreamy, like a mirage, as if they would float away at any moment. Lichah grabs Jean by the arm. "Wake up, you. You're turning into the rock yourself."

"What?"

"I have been talking to you for several minutes."

"I didn't hear you."

Lichah points below them. "Do you see that tent down there? Look at all the goats around it."

"So," Jean says, "I have seen goats before."

"Where there are goats, there is water," Lichah tells him. "Or goat milk for us to drink anyway."

They descend toward the tent, and before they reach it, a group of children greet them. The women are sitting by a natural spring, making butter.

"What place is this?" Jean asks.

One of the women says, "Have you not heard of Hine Neeha? Haven't you ever heard the song about the spring?"

"I have heard the song, but I didn't know the place was real," Jean answers.

The family gives them bowls of milk to drink. The brothers asks what town they would find next, and they are sent on their way to Hannoush. They travel through a cedar forest until they arrive at a hotel and restaurant on the edge of Haded. They stop and eat a large meal of shish kebab and stuffed eggplant. They sleep there, then go on the road again.

Often on the tour with Lichah, Jean thinks of Brazil and how he slept under the mango trees and listened to the flute on the water. He remembers his loneliness there, and he had expected it to disappear once he returned home. But it is worse. Everyone has something to do with his life. Boutros and Zina are preparing to return to the United States, Maron is in the seminary, Joseph is attending school, Nader is working as a carpenter, his sister Selma keeps the Beirut apartment for the family, and even his youngest brother, George, is taking lessons with the priests. Jean can only think of revitalizing the land. But then what? He is not a farmer, and farmers are not needed that much anymore. He stays quiet for days wondering where his life will go.

Out in the field he sees his American cousin Camille. He has seen her often since she and her parents, Aunt Mayme and Uncle Shebl, came from the United States. This is the cousin he is expected to marry. Is picking crops what she is accustomed to? She works easily and quickly. Her sister, Zina, married Boutros. Jean is sure Camille is not his type. She acts shy, but tries to be sophisticated. Besides, he doesn't know if he wants to marry at all. Still he keeps company with her, because they talk like old friends and because he wants to be near her father, Shebl. His uncle is not like Rachid, at all. The doctors say Shebl's stomach bleeds inside constantly. He is gentle, not only because he is dying, Jean thinks. All the stories of Shebl's philandering and bad business deals are legendary, but Jean finds him wise and generous.

Shebl grips the rail as he walks down the stairs. His skin is light, and his eyes are gray like Camille's. As he reaches the landing, his legs wobble beneath him. In Brazil, Jean had met people who knew him—they did not mention the unpaid debts or the parties that lasted days. *Your uncle is a good man. Generous.* Generous to a fault, Rachid mentioned more than once. Shebl believes anything people tell him, Rachid says. The country of pennies. Jean likes to imagine him in the United States with Abraham Lincoln and a tall hat on his head. The country of dollars. Is he rich now, Father?

Shebl asks Jean to accompany him to Cheeqa, where he will meet an old friend. His hands open wide like a priest's as he talks, and his white shock of hair blows high. "Do you know, " he starts each sentence, "that there was a time, maybe it's possible still, when your father could hit any bird in flight?"

"Do you know . . ." His face crinkles as he tells a story and wipes away the tears. In Cheeqa he puts his hands out to the merchants and nods as they talk about the businesses and how much the country has changed. He stoops to tease a little girl. She tucks her chin into her shoulder as he gives her a kiss on the cheek. "I had two little girls," he reports. Jean doesn't tell him how much he likes Camille. He stands aside and watches his uncle buy fruit.

They drink coffee by the sea, and Shebl does not speak. The sun through the café windows leaves squares of shadow on the sand, two dark eyes. Jean lights a cigarette and looks at the sky. The horizon is dusted slightly pink, layered with a white and a flat solid-blue line.

"Uncle, what time do you think it is?"

Shebl rises, buttons his jacket, and looks out. "We should return now."

Jean flicks his cigarette out onto the sand, and Shebl wrinkles his brow. He loves all things natural and clean. On the drive he pointed to a newspaper on the road and complained, "Who lives here, anyway?"

"Aren't you going to visit your friend?" Jean asks.

"He's dead." Shebl puts his straw hat with a striped band on his head. At the door of the café, he shakes the owner's hand. Jean follows him, feeling a little out of reach of his voice. They walk toward the place where the *service* will pick them up and take them back to Abdelli. Across the bay one boat with its high sail breaks the line from the sand to the rose horizon.

They stop at a corner where an old man sits with his feet tucked underneath him. His head is tied in a gray cloth, and his shirt is soiled. He looks up when the two men greet him. "*Mahraba fikoom,* and God's blessings, sir."

Jean steps to the opposite corner, but Shebl does not follow. He bends toward the man and holds his hat in his hand. "The season is cooling, sir."

"Yes." The old man pulls his mustache from side to side. "Winter will come upon us soon."

"What do you think, sir, how should I prune my vines this year?"

Placing his packages on the ground, Jean listens to the old man give his uncle instructions. Shebl asks him many questions about gardening and planting, and the old man talks and talks. He pulls a gray handkerchief from his pocket and wipes his face. They don't leave the old man until the *service* arrives. Shebl shouts to him, "*Ha tirek*—may all your wishes come."

The old man's eyes sparkle, and he raises both arms and proclaims, "*Allah wa fik*—God go with you."

They settle into the backseat of the car. The sea becomes a white strip along the road, and they climb away from it.

"Uncle." Jean turns to Shebl. He is resting his back against the high seat. "Why did you ask the man questions you knew the answers to?"

Shebl breathes in. "Did you notice how defeated and old he looked when we came and how excited he was when we greeted him?"

Jean nods.

"The old man is useful to me. His happiness is a kind of knowledge, or maybe it's a promise. It must be hard to wait along the road for your happiness."

Jean stays quiet after his lesson. Shebl talks about faith as the taxi slows behind a donkey cart; he chatters at the birds and waves at the workers in the field. He asks the driver about the car. His face on the window floats against the white mountains as they near home.

For six days Camille works in the orchard. With the bushel balancing against her hip, her hands pull the grapes and fill a three-bushel *kassusa* which she carries on her back. First grapes, then figs, quinces, and olives. The American cousin makes wine, arak; she dries grapes, cooks figs, and stirs quince jelly. Her freckled face drips with steam, and she smells sugary.

At the end of the week, she and her mother travel to see some relatives. When Camille returns two days later, it is clear she hasn't slept. She barely says hello to Jean and she enters the house and drops her bags on the terrace. She is no sooner in the house than someone knocks on the door. Her friend Toufic and his brother greet her cheerfully. Camille returns their greetings, then excuses herself to change and refresh herself. The men wait and wait for her to return. Jean sits with them without saying a word. Finally Toufic says, "She could be hurt."

Jean knocks on her door, but she doesn't answer. Going outside, he climbs up the wall, then enters the room through the French doors. When he steps down, he sees Camille fast asleep on the bed half dressed. Her hands are stretched wide and she has her face turned to one side. Jean stands and stares at her, at her white neck, shoulders, and breasts. Her skin is as white as tulip petals, he thinks.

The visitors knock on the door again. "Is she okay?"

Jean clears his voice to answer. "Yes," he croaks. He places a blanket over Camille and goes out to the guests. "I am sorry, but she is exhausted; you'll have to come some other time."

When the men do return, Shebl, Mayme, and the neighbors are having a large dinner. Everyone knows that Toufic is going to ask for Camille's hand in marriage. Throughout the meal, the old folks talks about the past, and Toufic drops a line or two in Camille's direction. She looks at him with puzzlement. After the lamps are lit, Jean leaves.

The next day, his uncle tells Jean that the visitors didn't like to see him leave. "They were not in my house, they were not my guests; I wasn't obliged to stay," Jean answers.

He repeats himself when he meets Toufic on the road in Batroun. Jean is carrying many packages and doesn't want to stop, but Toufic stands in his way and says, "You left that night because you didn't want me to marry your cousin."

"If I didn't want you to marry my cousin, Toufic, I would have stayed, not left. I wasn't there to be your host. If you want me to be your host, come to my house."

"But," Toufic says, "I've been told I should forget her, since she has you in mind."

Jean drops his parcels to the ground. "Everybody thinks he knows everything, but Camille and I never discussed it."

"Well, don't feel obliged to either." Toufic smiles.

Jean knows he will propose to his cousin now.

After the harvest, they go to Beirut for a holiday. Bashir and his fiancée, Muntaha, and Jean and Camille walk along the sea. "Look." Camille points at a drugstore near Zytoony. "Ice cream sundaes, all flavors." Camille begins to cross the road. "Come, let me treat you to an American-style dessert."

The winter in Beirut brings tourists, sunbathers, and shoppers. In the hotel district, signs advertise in English, French, German, and Arabic. The city is white and warm, and the buildings rise like stairs from the seaside.

"Can you eat Sunday on Monday?" Bashir laughs. The group

follow Camille into the store and sit together at a small table by the window. Camille talks about Pennsylvania and its large green hills and the truck she drove for her father's store. Jean tries to picture her at the wheel bouncing through the groves of trees and fields of blackberries she describes. Without brothers, Camille was raised like the boy. She's tough and strong, even though her crossed feet barely reach the floor.

After they eat they continue down Embassy Row. A small sea breeze cools them. Jean points to Pigeon Rock, standing in the sea like a primitive Arc de Triomphe. The water crashes around its base. Jean tells of the lovers who in despair leaped to their death from its flat top. Birds circle the rock and they fly through the keyhole. "Have you ever known anyone who jumped?" Camille asks. No one has.

They turn toward the boulevard. The streets are crowded, and Jean holds his shoulders tightly as they pass among the people. Cars travel closely to one another, practically sharing bumpers. Jean remembers the trains in Brazil that looked like snakes on the ridge above the river. Camille walks ahead, chatting confidently and smiling without hesitation. The road is wide and is split by a small strolling park. Camille pauses and looks toward the middle of the road. Some women in the park begin to scream. "Look!" Camille calls.

Two women are surrounded by at least a half-dozen French/Senegalese soldiers. The women yell, "Get away," first in Arabic then in French. Jean and Bashir step into the street and head toward the women. Although Bashir is holding up his arm, the cars zoom along by them and blast their horns. Across the park another car screeches to a stop and four Kata'ib nationalist soldiers pounce on the Frenchmen. Jean and Bashir keep their distance while the

Kata'ib knock five of the soldiers out and chase the others away. When they look around, they discover the girls have fled.

Muntaha and Camille walk silently arm in arm ahead of Bashir and Jean. They pass the St. George Hotel and Pigeon Grove without speaking or stopping. The afternoon traffic thickens—drivers honk their horns unrelentingly. The group leave the boulevard and stay by the sea. "Do you want some iced tea?" Jean asks.

"Yes, sure. Let's have some tea," Bashir agrees. They lean on a vendor's stand, sipping silently. Bashir shakes sugar into his glass.

"Bashir, look how much you are putting!" Camille says.

A small white mountain of sugar sifts slowly into the yellow water. Muntaha giggles. Bashir waves his hand. "Shh, shh, don't you hear it?" His brow wrinkles. "It's coming from the direction of the Basta Mosque." Yells ring and gunfire cracks through the air. The sunbathers run to the rail to listen. Everyone on the street stands still. "Let's go see what is happening," Bashir suggests.

Jean did not want to get in the middle of a struggle between the Kata'ib and the French or Muslims. "Bashir, I don't feel like taking my shoes off. Let's go home."

Camille sets her glass on the table and rubs the back of her neck. "I am tired anyway."

Everyone is frightened, Jean thinks. He quietly leads them to the *bourj,* the midtown district. Bashir looks back every few seconds. Many of the shopkeepers begin to close up before dinner. "Something is happening," Jean says. People are running up from behind, screaming. Jean and Bashir spin around trying to avoid them. Muntaha and Camille lean against a building. Jean catches a man. "What is the trouble?"

He pants and speaks quickly, pulling himself from Jean's hold.

"The Muslims, they are storming the *sarraya* and killing the Christians."

"How did it start?" Bashir asks.

"Some Christians invaded the Basta Mosque." The man runs off into the souq. The four do not move. Killing Christians. Jean tightens a fist. Standing beside him, Camille puts her hand on his shoulder.

"We have to go now. It isn't safe."

It has gone too far. As they walk to their quarter, people are driving or running. They see many men holding weapons and going toward the mosque. An old man charges into the street from his house holding a large radish and hollering, "I am going to kill every one of them." A tall woman follows him. "Stop, remember you are a refugee."

Traffic has seemed to stop. The sounds of gunfire fill the air. The men place their hands around the women and hurry to the apartment.

As Camille sets each plate down for dinner, the china rings as it touches the table. The room is quiet except for Bashir's friend reporting the damage that occurred during the riot. While he speaks, Jean paces the area of a small rug that lies in front of the sofa. He stops when he notices his jacket that he had flung over the back of a chair. A button is missing. Raising it, he strokes the empty spot. A blind eye. He thinks, I will never replace this button. This is my country, not Peru, where the government changes overnight, where people disappear on their way to the market. They cannot kill Christians here.

The burning, looting, and shooting last through the night. After dinner the men blow smoke into the air of the salon and the women sit at the table. *Lebanon must belong to the Lebanese,* they all say.

In the morning, before they start for the village, they return to the seaside. The city is quiet. The stores they passed the day before are unrecognizable. Glass is broken, doors and windows are missing, and many of the shelves are empty. Walking through the rubble are French/Senegalese soldiers. They stand on each corner. Bayonets shine from the rooftops. Bashir mumbles, "Oh my God." The lemonade stand where they drank the day before is flattened, and the counter is tipped on its side. "No one is here," Bashir says.

"Maybe it's not over." Camille says.

"It's over for now," Jean answers, "but let's get out of here just the same." They walk to the boulevard and hail a *service* and head out of the city.

The road winds around and around. Some areas are not ready for automobiles. As in the shallow parts of the Rivers Acre and Purus, the driver must slow down on the turns. He honks his horn to warn oncomers behind the mountain. The valley and sea appear and disappear during their climb. Camille leans to the front seat. "Jean, you are so quiet; what are you thinking?"

Jean shakes his head. "Nothing important." Again Jean feels very lonely. Lonely for what, though? He has his family and his home. Everything will work itself out. He will eventually get a good job and start his family and build his house. But what is it, after all?

The year of the harvest—1935, Jean wrote at the top of a sheet of paper. He is trying to compose a letter to Boutros in Pennsylvania,

U.S.A. The bushels of fruits, the barrels of wine, and the sweet fig paste to spread on the flat bread fill the houses of the village, but Jean doesn't have a penny to his name. Twenty-five years old and he feels as though he is wandering. After the crops are in, he visits his brother Joseph, who goes to school in Beirut. Joseph's friends drop by, and they speak in French. Jean chats awhile but often leaves and walks by the sea. The boats flutter their sails far from the harbor, and Pigeon Rock stands like a secret passage. He sits on the benches, smokes a cigarette, and watches the tourists walk out of the St. George Hotel. Some come to the rail and stand while another takes a photograph. They run off to the shops.

His shortcut home takes him through an alley with a garage at the end. A large white sign hangs over the entrance—BICYCLES. Inside rows of shiny bicycles wait to be rented or bought. Jean lifts one by its handlebars and spins the wheel. It clicks and blurs a star. A young woman playing with a baby on the counter calls, "Would you like to rent it?"

He drops it and walks over. "How much?" Within minutes Jean is leading a blue bicycle to the Corniche.

When he reaches a fairly clear spot, he hops on and begins to weave through the crowd. His knees nearly hit the handlebars as he pedals. Sliding back onto the thin seat, he tries to get comfortable. When the cars stop on the boulevard, he crosses and heads down a small hill. The bicycle speeds up. Jean pedals backward, then grabs the handbrakes and squeezes and squeezes, but the bicycle crashes into a house. A young lady sitting on the steps in a yellow dress runs down and pulls Jean up. Laughing, she puts the bicycle upright. Jean looks at her and his face reddens. He gets back onto the bicycle and rides away from her.

At the garage, he wheels the bicycle toward the owner, a man who stands in a dark blue apron and stacks baskets on the counter. He takes the bike from Jean. "How was your ride, young man?"

"It was good. How much for the time?"

The man does not answer. "Where are you from? What do you do for a living?" He asks.

Jean shakes his hand and tells him about Abdelli and Brazil. The man nods as Jean talks. He finds himself reporting to the man his frustration, and the man seems to listen.

"I have a son, younger than you. He'll be going to college in France this year." The man wipes the frame and places the bicycle back in the line. "I am looking for someone to run the shop for me."

Jean surveys the room. The bicycles stand with one wheel cocked toward the door. Tires hang on the walls, and baskets and bells are piled on a counter. "I'm afraid I don't know much about bicycles."

The owner puts his hand on Jean's shoulder. "Listen, my niece could teach you in ten days. After that you can hire some boys to help you when it is busy." He holds up his finger in a "wait" and greets another customer, who wants to rent bicycles for himself and his son. The owner shows him a selection, and while the father chooses, his son rings a bell on the handlebars. After they leave, the owner joins Jean.

Jean puts out his open hand. "When do I start?"

The man smiles. "Come tomorrow."

The year of the harvest. On the first day of his new job, Jean learns how to run the books, what rates to charge, and where everything is. On the second day, he rolls up his sleeves and changes three tires. He takes a shiny blue bicycle to the house to ride to and from

work. On the third day, as he passes through the residential section, the girl in the yellow dress waves at him as he cruises down
the hill. Jean raises his arm to her and turns into the alley. She is
there every day: on the third, when Jean meets the owner's niece
and they organize the parts; on the fourth, when he runs the shop
alone for more than half a day; on the fifth, when Jean feels the
chilly basement of his mother's house is far away. On Saturday the
owner returns to find Jean oiling the gears on an English bicycle.

"My niece tells me you like the business and you do well." He
stands near to Jean. "Listen, I am glad, but you got a message over
at the house. Your uncle is dying."

Jean watches a gold drop of oil run down the silver rim. He
places the can on the counter, wipes his hands, and hangs the
apron on a nail by the baskets.

Jean leaves for Abdelli immediately. He doesn't stop to change
his clothes or pick up anything from the house. As the taxi spins
into his village, the bells are ringing already. Jean checks his watch;
no masses are being held at this hour. His uncle has died. In the
harra Camille is putting white sheets on the large bed. Mayme sits
in a high-backed chair, and she is wrapped in a black shawl. She
seems to be looking at her shoes, but tears are streaming down her
face. Selma hands her a cup of tea. Mayme holds it very still, then
stares into it. Is a picture inside, does she see something? Her
eyes move back and forth as if she were watching a moving picture.
Three women from the village pray in the salon.

As Camille's fiancé, Jean must help Mayme with the arrangements. He is the only man in their lives. He stands in the hall.
Once the body is ready, death lapses into a strange inactivity.
After you wash and perfume the corpse, lay it out and place the
candles around, you can only turn to yourself, to look at your hands.

Perhaps Mayme is afraid to speak because her voice might echo in the empty chamber. Mayme's cup rings as it hits the floor.

When Jean arrives at his parents' home, his mother rushes to kiss him. She runs her hand along his cheek. "I am sorry, Jean." She leads him to the table. Everyone knows that his life will change, that these women will depend on him now. *What should I do? I am fine, Mother.* Elmaz and Jean sit at the kitchen table, and she holds one of his hands in hers as he writes a list: announcements, masses, coffins. Devotions too, she says. Yes, he writes that too.

Jean arrives at the harra with his list. Mayme has gone to sleep, and Camille is on the terrace. Jean enters the parlor and looks at his uncle's body. It is beginning to turn blue. Why didn't anyone care for him? Where is the mortician? He looks around the empty house, then charges through the French doors onto the porch. Camille sits near the railing looking out into the valley. Jean stands and watches.

Camille curls her legs under her. Her face is bright and freckled, and her head is wrapped in dark braids. She fumbles a rosary around her fingers. Jean sits with his back very straight, peering over the edge of the balcony into the valley. He cannot imagine what it is like to have your father die, and to have no one to share the memory with. "Camille, do you remember the village when you were young?"

"A little, during the war. Mother has kept my memory vivid. She got very homesick, especially when Zina came here."

Jean leans toward her. "My father and your father competed a great deal at the games during the feast of St. Elias. Do you know *fashba?*"

"The jumping?"

"Yes, your father was particularly good at that, but my father was a shooter—he still is. He could shoot a bird in flight with a rifle."

Camille twists the rosary around her hand. Earlier in the summer Jean went to visit the priest and wanted to tell her about the visit, but kept it to himself. He looks at her carefully. Her face is sweet, but her style seems old-fashioned to him. When he asked the priest if he should marry his cousin, the priest asked Jean if he loved her. Jean wasn't certain. "I like her; she is a good friend." The priest nodded. That was good. He then asked if she was a religious girl. Jean was certain. Camille and Mayme attend church every day; they carry rosaries in their hands while other women wear gold bracelets. Yes, the priest thought they should marry.

A breeze rises and blows stray hairs into Camille's eyes. She does not brush them away. Jean knows she is thinking of her father, but he doesn't know what to say. If he could sing, give her a song to drop her sadness into like that flute on the river, she might shut her eyes and stop her busy hands.

"How is Aunt Mayme?"

"A little lost." Camille pushes her hair back. "My father knew he was dying; that's why he came back. He accepted it, but mother can't. She's afraid. He had a serious operation at home. I overheard him once describe his death to my mother—the lights in the hospital, the time of day, everything. He knew as if he had planned it himself." Camille fiddles with the beads, then pulls the cross out and holds it between two fingers. "When the priest came to give him communion, he offered to hear his confession. My father said that he was in a state of grace. He knew."

Jean shrugs. "Maybe we all know." Jean looks at the sky. He remembers what his mother told him: every person on earth has a star. Orion, the Big Dipper, the Bear. He wonders what star will go black.

Is it because of death or because Jean must travel to make the arrangements that it rains again? For days lightning and thunder flash and rumble through the mountains. The roads washes out in places, and the cars slide around the small hills. In Junieh he orders the announcements. In Beirut he chooses the coffin. Camille and Mayme wait for him. The year of the harvest: 1935, *Shebl George Nader dies. 1935, Jean Rachid Abi-Nader sits in a car that spins mud at the windows.* Jean gets out and in his wet suit helps to push the vehicle up the hill. Pushing toward what? He sees Camille in her long plain dress placing food before him and offering him a drink. His hand pauses before he takes it. Recognizing her face and her quiet hazel eyes, he finally takes the cup from her hand. Where will Mayme be? Rachid said women should not live without a man to take care of them. Everyone agrees that Jean should move into Shebl's house and after the mourning period marry Camille. He shrugs. Perhaps he should have done it long ago.

After the funeral Jean takes his last trip to the city. He stares at the sea and waits for it to rise. He and the owner of the bicycle shop walk together as Jean explains the change in his life. The man shakes his hand. "Jean, if you ever need anything, let me know." The girl in the yellow dress waves at them. Jean stands alone and watches the small boats rock back and forth. No lovers cling to the top of Pigeon Rock now. Below it a ship passes, going west.

Jean takes the next car to Batroun and settles back in the seat alone. The driver's head is wrapped in a red-and-white cloth. They speak a little, then Jean closes his eyes. He hears a whistling, or is it the flute from Brazil? Perhaps it is Rachid's voice talking to him as he did when he placed the cool towels on Jean's feverish head.

"Jean, you are home," the driver says.

Jean lifts his head and looks out the window of the automobile at Shebl's harra. The rain falls steadily and water fills the ruts in the gravel road. Jean opens the door and steps across a small puddle. He pulls his bag onto his shoulder and begins to climb the stairs.

PART TWO

◆

Mothers

and

Daughters

◆

M a y m e

1918

Mayme tucks her dress beneath her thin legs and sits down. The other passengers on the ship around her scrape tin spoons across metal plates. She slowly rubs the left side of her face and closes her eyes. Now she can think. People have stopped moving around; she has stopped moving around. Although she needs food, she does not want to eat. She prefers to sit, to let her back curve in a posture she would correct on her daughters—to drop her head slightly, to not look at anything very hard; to place her hands together, not in prayer. The deck rocks beneath her long flat feet. Her daughters, Zina and Camille, sit quietly on the bed above hers. Soon the lower deck will be dark. Boats stir a sickness inside Mayme, and the view from the rail petrifies her with its infinity. The passengers cannot watch her down here; the girls will not see. *Lie down girls, sleep. Sleep for days. Hold your shiny rosaries of olive seeds and close your eyes.*

Mayme cherishes solitude and quiet. She did not have it in Abdelli, not even in the old days before the war. When they moved into the big house, she imagined she would sit on the veranda sipping tea and watching the water, but she did not. If she could have escaped through an open window for a little while, just a little while, and disappeared while Shebl's friends drank black coffee and smoked Turkish pipes; if she could have shrunk and crept along the roads like a mole, she would have loved her home. In the early years of their marriage, she liked company, and set food for everyone at a moment's notice. After all, she was the sheik's wife, and from her hands came plates of stuffed grape leaves, stacks of homemade bread. She placed a diamond of baklava on each plate. They called her Sheika and thanked her. She bowed, smiled, and backed into the kitchen, never speaking or mingling with them as they sat on their chairs watching her come and go.

Now without light or examination, she pauses, stops, stares as she could not in the busy "palaces" in Abdelli, in the basements and ruins she was sent to live in, or in the shanty in Batroun, where she could not look beyond the flicker of the fire. Now Mayme is taking her daughters away, and that's all that matters. No one will notice if she rests for just a little while, or if she remembers, allows herself to think back and remember the faces, hands, and voices of the dead. And when the deck has gone quiet, Mayme will think

of her nieces, the children of Shebl's brother Yousef. His wife—
she forgot her name, although they spoke often—had run away,
leaving the two daughters on their own. They were not only the
same ages as Mayme's own daughters, they had the same names,
except in that family, Camille was the elder and Zina the younger.

No one could have known the girls would die. Not the women
who had named them the same, nor the fathers who lived in America; not the mother who had left them, nor the mother who stayed,
and maybe not even their uncle, Rachid, the new sheik. Could
anything have been done? When they try to explain, people will
say: The girls were born into a hard time—it was World War I, the
Turks occupied Lebanon, and those who weren't dying of starvation were ill from the Spanish flu. Everyone counted these events
in his history.

Mayme knew to keep her daughters close to her, to veil them in
her skirts, to create chores for them so they would not stray and
find a body or touch food that was contaminated. Mayme made
them sing. *Love singing, girls. Listen to my scratchy voice as I beat
the bread. Repeat and sing.*

After the wife's disappearance, the nieces had no mother to
whisper to them, to take them away from the sickness, or to take
them to another world. *Who actually found them?* she asked Zihr
el Ban. Zihr was visiting Mayme in Batroun and brought the news
of her nieces' deaths. As the village teacher, she knew all the
children. Zihr explained, "After the girls' mother left, they refused
to leave the house. The older, Camille, found food, washed herself
and her sister, and went to church each day. Suddenly they disappeared. Some thought their mother had come for them, but she
had not. The flu took them quickly." Mayme tried to picture the
two girls in their house, alone, dying.

A few years after Shebl left Mayme, her two girls were not allowed to visit their cousins. Shebl had left many debts and no money. Rachid had to liquidate his brother's property to satisfy the creditors. He sold the furniture, sold off the crops, and eventually rented out the house. He allowed Mayme and her two daughters to live in the basement, but they could not return upstairs to the large rooms. Also they could not cross their land or enter their groves. Rachid needed the crops to feed his large family, so he guarded the land carefully, allowing no one to trespass. Yousef's house was on the other side, so it was impossible to visit the other Zina and Camille. After a while, Mayme did not think of them, filling her time only with thoughts of her own escape.

Two girls, Camille and Zina, had died in a room beneath their father's house. Did they then lie there slumped against the wall until an angel gathered them in his arms? Two other girls, Zina and Camille, lay together in the dark on their way to America. These thoughts were hidden in the darkness, or in the depths of Mayme's lungs, until she breathed out all the air, clean. Start over.

The basement of their harra had once been a small store. Crates, drawers, and bins on the dirt floor served as their furniture. Mayme sang loudly to puff away the clouds of dust that filled the air. Perhaps her girls did not see the brown particles shaking from the walls, rising from the floor, floating into her mouth. Mayme tasted the dust, saw it, and tried to rub it from her daughters' skin until they cried. Rushing through the room, she took little breaths as she worked, trying to beat the dust from coming in every crack.

She sang, prayed, waved her hands through the air, watching it fly. The girls' steadiness sometimes bothered her. She tried to move them: get water, sweep, dance, walk around . . .

Two years before, when Mayme's mother died, Mayme could barely see because of the dust. She splashed her eyes with water before she cleaned her mother's body. It had become soft, like a rolled carpet, and in her arms, her mother's body hung to the ground. She moved quickly—get the priest in and out, the doctor, the neighbors, or they would all choke.

While she was preparing food for the visitors, her youngest daughter, Camille, only two, came out of the pantry where she slept and stared at the wooden box sitting in the middle of the parlor. Her *sittie's* old mattress, dressed in a tight white sheet, was pushed against the wall. The blankets had been folded and placed at the foot. The day before, Sittie had laced strips of rags through Camille's hair, and Mayme could see it needed to be fixed. Camille looked through the door toward the bleached morning. Putting her tiny hands on her hips, she examined Sittie's bed again. It was smooth and unwrinkled. She turned toward her mother and her sister. Mayme chopped onions with slow careful slashes and watched her daughter. She hadn't thought of what to do with the little girl. Her mother had died in the night, and the funeral bells were not rung, so Camille had slept through the commotion. Zina poured chick-peas into a bowl. The large box in the middle of the floor had its lid propped open. Camille slipped her feet into her felt slippers. Mayme raised her eyes and saw her little girl approaching the coffin. "No, miss." Her voice became shrill and immediate. "Don't go near."

"Where's Sittie?"

"I'll comb your hair out later." Taking some bread and yogurt to where Camille had stopped, Mayme instructed, "Go and eat your breakfast outside, and when you're done, go down to see your cousins."

Camille held the bowl for a moment, and her mother waved her out twice. She walked away from the box and out the door; then she sat on a stone with her food. The first neighbor who came to pray greeted Camille. The little girl scooped her yogurt with pieces of bread and mumbled, *"Mahraba."* She did not look at the others who clutched rosaries and wore black scarves pulled down over their eyes. Throughout the prayer, Mayme lingered in the doorway—a shadow on the threshold.

Mayme prayed for her daughters and for herself. Her mother was gone, and her husband has been in America since before Camille's birth. This was the only life the girls knew—the life of this basement, this loneliness and foreboding. They have taken on the traits of gypsies. Camille often wandered through the village alone looking for animals of any kind: oxen pulling wagons, asses carrying loads, or a bird sitting on a stone wall. She said they waited for her too. That one partridge on the pomegranate tree blinked sideways into the sun and watched for Camille's golden hair. A work mule in its journey across the tobacco fields shook his head to see Camille march up to him and talk in a high voice. Sometimes she was chased away by a farmer, but some old women listened and smiled.

As she walked, Camille limped, because her left leg had been injured. She stayed on the road to avoid climbing down through the thickets. Her foot skimmed the pebbles, and she raised and dropped it again. It didn't hurt anymore, but she was slow to get going. The scar was nearly gone, and Mayme prayed there would be no permanent damage from her daughter's foolishness.

About six months before, despite her mother's warning, Camille had dawdled in an open doorway during a thunderstorm. "Don't wander out into that rain, little miss." Camille put one foot in, one foot out. In, out, in, out. Mayme steadied her eyes on her own fingers twirling threads around needles. She hoped the girl would tire soon and sit down. The scream that came from Camille was not part of the game. Mayme rose, shook the strings from her fingers, and ran to the door. Camille crumpled forward, and the back of her knee burned red. She had been struck by a hailstone the size of a tomato. Carrying the child to Sittie's bed, Mayme laid her on her stomach. The spot blazed from the heat, and the knee swelled. What could she do? Zina ran into the storm to get her great-uncle, and Mayme watched as Camille's leg turned blue.

Uncle Nassif looked at the little girl's leg, which had doubled in size. She had started to run a fever. He shrugged. "You had better take her to Batroun." Zina and Nassif helped wrap Camille on Mayme's back and tie her with a shawl. Pulling on a scarf and shoving her shoes in her satchel, Mayme started on the long journey with Camille sleepily bouncing up and down.

The treatment for blood poisoning was cleaning out the wound with a spindle and thread. The doctor watched as Mayme imitated his actions. Camille's face and dress were soaked with tears. She moaned, and Mayme's own eyes filled with water as she worked the needle and then replaced the bandage. For two months, each morning and each night, she let the blood while Camille's sobs choked in her chest. Mayme talked to the leg and told it Camille might be a dancer, if she would not cry.

When the mourners started a second rosary, Mayme gave instructions to Zina to serve the food, and she went to find Camille. Her daughter had stopped at the top of the hill, from where she could see her cousins. The bright morning sun cast short shadows on the dusty ground. Uncle Yousef's girls were returning from the well. Camille held her sister's hand and carried a jar with the other. Mayme's Camille descended and stopped the girls and asked with her head lifted, "Whose Camille are you?"

"Bint Yousef," the older one replied. The younger echoed, *"Bint Yousef, unna Zina."*

"Whose Camille are you?" Yousef's Camille asked.

"Bint Shebl," Camille automatically replied to their ceremonial greeting. She followed them, and her curls, still in rags, flopped against her shoulders.

On the way home, Camille asked Mayme where her cousins' mother was. Gone where? Mothers don't leave, except for a day when they to to the souq as Mayme does to get food.

Once a week Mayme held a bracelet or ring up to the light, polished it with an old cotton shirt, placed it in the belt at her waist, and headed north. Taking the roughest mountain roads, she walked quickly, speaking to no one. Many women she knew traveled to Tripoli too, but Mayme had to go alone. She did not want them to know about her jewelry; besides, she moved faster than most. From the road a traveler might sense a rabbit scampering through the field below. Her mother had taught her this route and how it wove in and out of the mountains, coming near the road only twice. She kept her hands on her waist, impressed with the shape of her treasure.

When she reached Tripoli, she went to a man she knew, a Syrian, interested in nice things. She did not stop to examine anything in the bazaar. The odor of fresh lamb sifted by her. Her eyes did not notice the bolt of brocade fabric open on a table or children's shoes lined on the street. No one's eyes met hers except when she raised her jewelry up to the man. *My bracelet.* She related the story of how it had been brought from Brazil or France and there wasn't another like it in all of Syria or Lebanon. She fingered the design and told him to feel it too. Mayme begged the merchant to take another look. He nodded his head as he did to all the village women and handed her small bags of flour, a skin of oil, a handful of salt, lentils, and rice.

Behind the church Mayme wrapped the food in her bag and placed it under her skirts, between her legs, and she left the city through the fields of a friend who owned a house there. She would be lucky if the Turkish soldiers didn't search her; she would be blessed if they didn't rape her. They stood at the archway of the city, throwing flour into the wind, spilling salt onto the ground, taking the last shawl, the pair of shoes, a locket from a neck, pulling the hair of the women down into long black waves. A village woman had been raped by soldiers. Some remembered her in their prayers.

Climbing down the cliff, Mayme let her body drop into the brush. She crawled on her stomach in the ditch, scraping her elbows on the stones. Dust filled her nostrils and sweat soaked her body. When she heard horses on the road above her, she lowered further until the dirt filtered into her dress and the rocks ripped her sleeves. Her face turned hot and red and the bags skimmed the ground. Their weight pulled on her stomach, her arms, and her breasts; her face scraped shrubs and her knees absorbed tiny rocks. Mayme prayed on her stomach and wiped away sweat and tears. She crawled along the road. She would feed her daughters. In spite.

On the day Mayme and Shebl moved into their new house in 1903, Mayme tilted her head in the parlor and twirled under the mural that her husband had commissioned a well-known artist to paint. The figure on horseback revolved, the Virgin Mother turned, the angels descended. It was beautiful, and visitors paused under it when they entered. And many came, to sit in a circle in the salon, drinking coffee and tea. This is when Mayme heard the voices around her—the persistent declarations—but she imagined they were only the wind fanning leaves, the door cracking open, or her voice singing as she worked at the stove. The women of the village talked among themselves. Grabbing their right calves, they shook them. "If Mayme could get pregnant, so could this leg." Mayme's legs were thin, long, and muscular; her body stayed lean. And the women commented again. Her husband might have many children, but no one was ever sure. *Poor Shebl,* they thought, *eighteen years with a barren wife, and he so handsome, and the oldest of the brothers. What else could he do?* Mayme did not care about his other women, though they came to her house.

As a couple they did not fit. Shebl's tall robust frame overshadowed Mayme's entire body. She would look up and see him gazing out to the fields. He was bright, with gray eyes and blond, nearly white hair. A lighthouse. Even when he sat, he dwarfed the furniture. But the face, when it bothered to look, to examine, to pause, melted into softness. Is this what made him a Don João? That face, with the thick line of a pink mouth, talking quietly to others as if every word were an intimacy? Mayme was not a tree. A twig perhaps, small, tight, and drawn into herself. None of her features protruded. Her dark eyes were recessed, her nose sloped. She pulled her hair back. She did not mind what they said because her house was so beautiful.

Now years later, just the sound of trotting horses made her cringe. Mayme stopped. She was afraid of becoming too exhausted, and she would not be able to run if it was necessary. She sat in a pile of weeds. She could make herself very small, by pulling up her thin legs and wrapping her arms around them. Below her a young couple leaned on one another. They did not seem to be hiding. The girl talked rapidly to her lover. Without speaking he raised his hand and outlined her nose with his finger. Shebl was not Mayme's lover.

When she was married at thirteen, Mayme did not know what to expect from a husband. Would he beat her? At twenty-one, she begged him to take her to Brazil with him; at twenty-eight, she hoped that he would sleep with her in their new bed. Perhaps Mayme did not pray enough, eat correctly, or work hard. She asked priests, gypsies, old wives. "Rub the olive oil, pray to Saint Anne, relax." In Brazil, she bought incense and fried bananas, and bathed in freshwater ponds.

Three years later, dressed in a hat from paris, a still childless Mayme returned to Abdelli. Her husband combed his hair back off his browned face and wore a white suit and white hat and carried a cane. Wicker baskets, chests of statues, vases, and jewels were carried up to the mount, and the couple received guests for weeks. Neighbors came to see Mayme's new dresses and statues, and to listen to them speak Portuguese. The men followed Rachid, Shebl, and Yousef to the table to survey the plans for the new houses. They admired the large rooms, the kitchens upstairs and down— the way a sheik should live. Mayme brought her sister-in-law Elmaz to sit with them. She gave her a new shawl, served her, and remarked on the beauty of her daughter's hair. Elmaz was pregnant with her third child.

When Mayme put away her hat, she did not know she would not wear it again. Fires were lit and the ground for their houses was cleared. The three brothers started to build on the outskirts of the village. Men carried stones from the quarry for the plaza behind Rachid's house, and Yousef imported tiles from France for his floors. The Italian marble for Shebl's stairs weighed down the ox cart on its way up the hill. He had traveled to Persia to buy rugs, and he returned with two hundred little bells to tinkle when the wind blew. He and his brothers supervised the work on the houses. Walking back and forth along the road with the carts, they ordered a larger window, perhaps a balcony in back as well. Every day a hundred workers waited for the meals that Mayme made. Running from the house where pots boiled in the kitchen to the fields, she raked, picked, and pulled. She steamed onion skins to make paint for the outside of the house. Taken from its French knot, her hair fell in a long braid on her back.

After the homes were completed, Shebl opened a business in the bottom floor: a bank, a general store, and on one side, the chapel, which the district bishop dedicated to Saint Elias. He constructed a public oven outdoors and hired a man to bake and sell, then he departed. He did not watch over his house, store, or land. While Mayme tended to the customers and his twelve-year-old brother, Elias, kept the books, Shebl traveled. Mayme baked bread, milled flour, picked figs, tobacco, and olives, and pounded coffee. Thin, barren, looking ten years older than her husband, Mayme stopped mid-action to watch: she thought she saw him standing with his cane at the end of the road. As she carried the laundry out to lay on rocks, she may have heard his boot thump overhead. When he did return home, he handed Mayme the merchandise to shelve, he ate her meals and slept in their bed. He did not wait for long—Mayme became pregnant.

After she felt the weight in her womb, a heartthrob on her own, the business slowed down. The Turks took away Lebanese autonomy, and money was scarce. No one could buy their goods. Shebl lent money, then borrowed more. He lent, spent, and promised. Taking the baker's place, Mayme propped her belly against the public oven, and she beat dough against the stone all morning. Her husband, now sheik of the village, and his brother Rachid worked together as they had in Brazil: dining with friends in Tripoli, Beirut, Batroun. Mayme's thin frame stooped under her new weight. Would she ever walk without pain? She rubbed her legs. Some did not believe she was pregnant—not even Elmaz, who had her fourth child before Mayme had her first. And the women offered quite casually to feel her stomach, to listen to the rhythms and gushes inside of her. Mayme did not draw back.

The day her labor pains started, her mother was in church praying. Victoria, Elmaz's oldest, heard Mayme scream, and she brought the midwife and several neighbors. In the cold of November, Mayme lay on the floor as her womb contracted. The baby wrestled inside of her. The women's faces hovered above her, and she breathed as hard as she could. She shivered and saw their faces swing. When she released the pain, they withdrew to look below. Inside the dampness of her clothes, in the fog of her own cold breath, she heard the midwife say, "It's a girl."

Mayme thanked God and screamed, "I have a daughter," lifting her arms to heaven, to her friends. But the women moved away from her. The midwife did not stay. Each neighbor retreated, backed out the door. *What a shame,* they said, not sorry, half expecting it. *Barren eighteen years and only a girl.* Her husband would leave her now, they guessed. Then the room was empty.

With the baby still tied to her, Mayme crawled to the bed and screamed for help. She leaned her body against the leg of the bed and buried her sweating face into the cool linen. She tried to reach the daughter between her legs and wept as she bent over. Her mother ran in and saw her daughter and her granddaughter drenched in blood and water. Kneeling, she lifted the child and cut the cord. She bathed them together—placing her hand on the face of her daughter and her daughter's daughter.

She laid the girl, Zina Marie, on her mother's chest. She was a small olive-skinned girl with a ruffle of brown hair. Mayme hugged her all the day and night, held her head, and felt the moon in the palm of her hand. Untying her own long brown hair, she let it rest on the fingers of the baby.

When Shebl returned a few days later, Mayme stood at the door. He had heard that a child had been born in his house and he hurried through the groves and orchards, up the stony paths to the bottom of the stairs. His wife waited in the doorway, and in her arms a child lay, tiny and dark. He examined her, lowering his flashing gray eyes until they became agate. His shoulders fell into a slight curve until Mayme thought she looked at him eye to eye. He put out his arms, and Mayme laid the infant in them. The baby barely reached his elbow. He kissed his wife and daughter over and over, then stretched beside them on the bed. That night he arranged a twenty-one-gun salute. The smoke misted up to the stars, and Shebl, too, thanked God. He prayed until the sun rose.

The road was quiet once more. Rising from the dust outside of Tripoli, Mayme wiped her face and ran home. Mayme didn't like the girls to be alone at night—Camille especially. She wandered away too often. Mayme might find her behind the church crawling in the bushes or walking on the edge of the mountain singing to herself. Something could happen. Last month Zina had been bitten by a scorpion. Anything could happen.

Pausing at the bottom of the stairs leading to the main rooms of the house, Mayme allowed her hand to graze the railing, but she turned and entered the basement, where she really lived. A small fire inside glowed orange on the faces. The two girls sat on the dusty floor, and beside them the Michaels boys rested. Tanous and Boulos had the Spanish flu. When their father died from it, and their mother had fled to Batroun, Mayme had taken them in, sick as they were. The four of them shared one room—small, square, and damp. Crates served as chairs and tables. The girls slept in fabric bins; Mayme used her mother's mattress.

Months before when the men carried out the sofa, the chairs, and the Persian rugs, the girls sat where their beds had been and cried. Mayme spun around trying to stop them, grabbing at their sleeves, pulling on her possessions, shouting. Above her head in the mural, the horse, white and sleek, posed without flinching; the light around the Blessed Virgin did not die. Mayme stopped a man with a chest. Opening each drawer, she ran her hands around the empty wood. Where were their clothes and the sheets? The mattresses and linens lay in a heap where the master bed had rested. When the men were gone, Mayme sank onto the pile. Zina began to fold what articles were left. Rising, Mayme ran to the priest's house. He listened and wrote a letter for Mayme: *My dear husband*

*. . . your brother said we must leave the house . . . your brother let
a man take the furniture . . . we must leave tomorrow . . . money is
needed.* Closing the door behind them, the mother and two daughters carried their clothes and two mattresses below.

Before she could untie her packages and shake the dirt from her
clothes, Mayme saw something scampering along the wall. She
raised her finger to her lips to signal the girls to stay still. Holding
a hot poker over her head, she crept to the corner. Camille screamed
and jumped as a rat ran toward her feet. Mayme swung her weapon
and smashed the rodent again and again, then dropped it. The
smell of burning fur penetrated the dusty air. Both girls began to
cry: Zina leaned against her mother, and Mayme wiped some dust
from Camille's face. She was covered with dirt. Mayme rocked
them, enraged. The brightness of her daughters' rosy cheeks had
become coated with brown. She imagined the Bedouins lived like
this, walking through the desert, turning their eyes away from the
sand blowing on them. They covered their faces and wore long
black robes. As she sat, the gravel she had picked up on her journey filled her underclothes and settled around her waistband, around
her ankles, between her toes. Yes, it enraged her that her own
body crumbled away into tiny bits of gravel. That her children spit
on their hands to wash them and created palms of mud. And now
tears on Camille's cheeks ran roads down her face. "Take my
handkerchief, little miss." Mayme removed her scarf, and dirt cas-
caded from her hair onto her lap.
    Mayme rose and pulled the groceries from inside her clothes.
Sometimes she wanted to speak of America where her husband
lived and how they all would have food and clothes. But the checks

did not come often. She spoke of none of it—not the future, nor the past.

Mayme handed Zina a small bag of flour. "Steal yourself to the house of Yousef and give this to your cousins. Stay with them awhile and let me know how they are." Zina pinned her hair up and wrapped her mother's shawl around her shoulders. As she walked in the shadows, only bugs chanted in the still night. She crept among the fig trees in her father's grove. In the valley, her cousin Boutros sat inside a tent. A small fire glowed. She did not speak to him; instead she climbed onto the road and hurried toward the last house.

Camille lay in her bed; the Michaels brothers also slept. Mayme covered her eyes and pressed her sweaty face. Since Shebl had left, Mayme spent only half each night sleeping. She thought of the strong cedar-and-velvet furniture they had placed atop the red ornate rugs in the master bedroom. Gone. Fortunately, she had tucked away her jewelry—a few bracelets and a brooch for her daughters. She put her hand inside her shirt and reached under her arms into her *hoobee*, a secret place they could not guess or get to. Inside the deep cave of her underarm hung the wrapped and tied pieces of jewelry. She never took them out except to show her daughters where they were. They too hid treasures: a piece of cake, some cheese, an apple in their *hoobat*, and when they thought no one spied them, they rustled through their blouses to reach the treats, warm and crumbly.

Before Mayme slept she prayed very quietly for her husband to come and recover her possessions. Shebl would send money, she told Rachid, but he did not believe her. She wept before Rachid and pounded her tight fists on his table. "Nothing is yours anymore, Mayme," he said quite clearly.

∴ *159* ∴

She wondered if she had heard a snicker from the kitchen. Elmaz had replaced her as the sheik's wife. She dressed her six children and paraded them to church—two girls and four boys, holding hands and walking in shiny shoes. Elmaz claimed she wore the first hat in the village. Mayme's eyes narrowed. *You are nothing, Elmaz; I may have nothing, but you are a peasant.* Rachid looked away from Mayme, talked to his son, tended his ox, drank his coffee. She cried, "At least let me have the goat for some milk for the girls, some yogurt for soup—something." He turned his back but left the goat with her.

Mayme could have blamed Elmaz—they argued between themselves about food, clothing, ownership, who could tat, and whether Mayme could continue managing the silkworms that she had bought. Elmaz won nearly every battle, because she had Rachid nearby. No one took anything from Elmaz, because she had attended a convent school and was one of the few women in the village who could read. People addressed her as Sheika; they admired her clothes, her children, and even if they plotted against the house of Nader during the war, they were intimidated by Elmaz's certain manner. She always stood on solid ground, boomed across rooms, pointed fingers at anyone who bothered her children. But Mayme did not blame her, because with all her children to look after, Elmaz too was often alone.

Mayme curled on a blanket on the floor and waited for Zina to return. Zina worked hard and was obedient. Every task Mayme performed, Zina did too. Unlike Camille, Zina, now six, had known her father and hoped for his return. Her brown eyes followed the needles closely, her hands separated the grape leaves carefully; her back rippled as she lifted the mattress to flip it over. She never spoke of her father. She prayed for him and cried only once.

One afternoon Mayme heard Zina whimpering at the door. Mayme lifted the handle and saw her daughter standing with a basket, as empty as when she left. Her mother had instructed her to pick some figs, just one basketful, since they were not ripened. They had only flour and beans for dinner. Zina had surveyed the grove and tried to see which of the fruit would be near ready. When she walked forward, her cousin Victoria stepped into her path. "Where are you going, Zina?"

"To my father's fields," she said, looking up and brushing the loose strands from her face.

Victoria moved closer. "You cannot have any figs." She pointed her finger at Zina. "You can have nothing of your fruit, until your father sends money." She breathed into Zina's face and wagged her finger. Zina drew a short breath and watched the finger, and then looked at Victoria.

Victoria's mouth folded into a line as Elmaz's did when she didn't like the people in the room. Zina glanced at her finger again, turned, and ran home to her mother.

Zina had wanted her cousins to like her so much. When they walked to church in front of her, she stared ahead as Victoria held Selma in her arms. Although only two years older than Zina, Victoria wore dresses cinched at the waist like a lady and stood erect always. Zina followed behind, talked to her sometimes, but now it was Victoria who made Zina's lips quiver and her fists draw tight. Mayme knew Zina would see more of what Rachid's family did to hers, but she could not tell Zina that her father was a bad businessman, that he had left them with debts. And all was taken away: no house, no furniture, no clothes, food, sheikdom, and no love. *I will never forget,* Mayme's oldest daughter muttered. You must not forget, her mother didn't say. How could she explain?

Aren't cousins supposed to love each other? Telling her war is wicked wasn't enough or accurate. *Because I live, crawled in, and ate dirt. Because I couldn't breathe for years and years. Because my monthly bleeding stopped when my husband went away. Do not forget.*

Her wiry body shook and her voice crackled. "What do you want from me, Rachid? Shebl has sent me nothing." Zina heard Rachid's voice again, rising against her mother. They stood in the parlor, but Zina could not understand the words anymore, because her ears flopped back like a rabbit's (so she thought), but she saw. Rachid slapped her mother's thin face and he slapped her again. She sank to the tiles, her bones cracking against the hardened clay. Mayme curled forward, black and weeping—the rugs piled for dusting, the blankets folded for the season, heaps of tossed-aside fabric. Her daughters surrounded her—Camille's small hand patting her shoulder and Zina looking up to see Rachid walking away clasping his hands behind his back.

Zina watched the wiggling fingers, the curve of the arms, the shoulders like shelves. His long feet spread outward as he clicked down the corridor and went through the door. Mayme dropped her head and wept, "Naum, Shebl, where is everyone?" She called to her dead brother, Naum, and her absent husband. She began to cough, and her body echoed with emptiness. Grunts forced themselves from her throat; she covered her mouth and stood. The power of her lungs threw her body around the room. Both daughters watched the convulsions. Mayme dropped her head again. She understood why Yousef's wife had run away. Zina and Camille approached her. "Naum!" their mother screamed.

Perhaps like the little cousins, the other Camille and Zina, these three females were alone. Truly alone. Perhaps what lay outside their door had nothing to do with them. This could be a stranger's village. What signs did she have that she belonged here? The village women had walked into her house as if they didn't know her and taken her clothes. "My husband said I could have this; Shebl owes him money." Then the furniture disappeared. Camille would not be able to remember how beautiful the house was. She would never read her father's books, or see her mother dressed in a gown with gold bracelets ringing her thin arms. Mayme had no family; everyone was dead or gone. She didn't even have her brother, although he visited her in the dream.

Over and over she and Naum entered a cave with pails and small shovels to bring the dust to whitewash the house. How many times did she have to go there? Ahead Naum's candle sprayed stars on the walls; long rays curled over her head. Their voices echoed in the tunnel. Naum's arms flashed in the light as he scraped the walls. When Mayme walked toward him, she began to feel dizzy and stopped. His voice swirled around her as the cave began to move. The ground growled and the ceiling flaked down onto her hair. She stood stiffly. "Naum!" Her voice faded behind the rumble of the cave, the collapse of the ceiling. She dropped her implements and fell to her knees and crawled backward to the opening. Mayme could not remove her eyes from the descending cave. Dust billowed into clouds, rocks rained onto a heap. She imagined the flattened body of her brother below, breathing inside the earth. Perhaps he could burrow like a mole and arise beside her. Wrapping her arms around her head, Mayme covered her ears, shut her eyes. "Naum," she shouted, louder and louder, into the storm until her voice rang flat. When she opened her eyes, Mayme saw a wall of rocks. Staring at the mountain of rubble, she screamed his name again.

Once she had explained to Yousef's wife why the men had to go away. "Think of the things you can give your girls with the money they bring back. Brazil was good for Shebl and Rachid. If it wasn't for their manager, who stole everything, they would be there now. America will be the same. A land of dollars, not of pennies, you know." Both women were suckling babies—Yousef's wife had her Zina, and Mayme held Camille. Later Zihr told Mayme, as she poured lentils into a pot to soak, that the mother had left. As Zihr spoke, Mayme watched the cloud of brown water settle onto the beans. "Where did she go?" No one knew. "So how do they know she won't be back?" Zihr responded, "She won't be."

Mayme stirred the beans. Yousef's wife did not come back—Zihr had been right. The Michaels boys left too. Their mother had died in Batroun; so they went to Tripoli to look for work. Mayme waited but knew she herself must leave soon. The "little miss" had tried the day before to get banana peels from a dog, but he had growled her away. Mayme found her daughter staring at the animal, who was tearing the rinds apart and making fierce noises. She wanted to go somewhere where food grew on boughs that bent down so her daughter could reach it and eat as much as she wanted. In Brazil in the jungles, fruit fell to the ground and rotted and an animal would come along, sniff it, and pass by. She wanted to be in a place where there was only singing, so instead of the bellowing of the empty stomach, the roar of anger, Zina might hear music. Angels.

Mayme decided to get the figs herself. Grabbing the basket from Zina's hand, she started for the fields. Mayme had always been pleased with her agility. She could climb anything, carry more than many men, although her bones were brittle. Approaching the groves from the west, she pulled herself up a tree on the edge of her land. Kneeling on a thick limb, she cradled the basket in her lap. As she stretched toward the outside fruit, Mayme slipped and fell to the rocky ground. As she hit the stones, she knew she had broken her back. Lying on the ground, she felt a rod bury itself inside on her. Mayme could not move and began to yell until a nephew found her and carried her home.

When the doctor arrived, Mayme lay on the basement floor stiff from pain. "We have to set the bones, Mayme. Can you sit up?" the doctor asked. She could not move her head to answer him. He dragged her body along the floor and raised her upright against a post. Pulling her shoulders back, he tied her to the pillar. Mayme screamed. He warned her, "Do not move for any reason or your back will be damaged forever. You must stay this way for a month." Mayme winced and tried to move, but the pain shot so hard and far she became dizzy. There was not much to do. Tied to the post, she watched as eight-year-old Zina cooked the meals, washed the clothes, and ran all the errands. Eventually Mayme could sew buttons and comb her daughters' hair. She wanted to twist her body away and walk, do the floor, tuck Camille into bed, but she could not even wiggle. She cut the vegetables for canning, crocheted a tablecloth, and leaned her head back to pray.

The month passed slowly. Her uncle brought food for them, a neighbor helped with the clothes and fed the silkworms, but Mayme was captive. She could talk, yell, wave her arms a little, and nod off to sleep. She prayed the rosary almost five times every day. And she tried to take deep breaths, but her breast pulled tightly. Since she could not go outside, the dust would bury her.

One late afternoon, Zina took a basket and went to buy some flour. As the night became cold and dark, Mayme pulled a little at her restraints but could not get up. She asked Camille to go to the neighbors to get an ember to light the fire. Turning from where she lay, Camille said, "I don't think so." *Camille*, Mayme shouted over and over. The little girl rose and walked around the house. "No, no, no."

Mayme pulled at her ropes in anger. Her voice bounced, squeaked, and growled. She poked her chin out, kicked her legs. Her clothes wrinkled into a ball beneath her. Camille moved as far away from her mother as she could. Mayme wrestled with the ropes again. She looked around her for something to throw. Picking up a knife by the blade, she flung it, handle first, at her daughter. The knife flipped in flight and stabbed Camille in her left leg, then dropped to the ground flashing its blade. The girl fell, and Mayme screamed. Her blood rose up and her voice echoed in their little room. She fought the ties but could only scream more loudly until her voice surrounded her, shook the dust from the air, stabbed the walls. Camille's godfather ran in. The girl's leg bled into a pool on the floor. He grabbed the broom handle and reached for a cobweb from the ceiling. He placed the web atop the wound. The bleeding stopped within a minute. Camille lay sleepily on the floor soon after, and Mayme wept quietly at her post. Later Zina made a strong fire, but Mayme shivered all night.

Perhaps her mind was gone. Mayme did not understand how she had crippled her daughter. From her position, she watched Camille's wound heal to a broad purple scar. The girl could barely rest her leg on the floor before she had to lift it again. For the next two months, the mother carried her youngest daughter everywhere, although Camille asked to be allowed to walk. When she became too heavy for Mayme's still tender back, she let the girl go. Camille limped without complaint.

For six months, Mayme received nothing from Shebl. Zina stood once again watching Rachid's fingers. This time she could not stay idle. She pulled and shouted while his fingers clenched behind his jacket, danced in his hands. In front of him in the archway of the house, a tax collector beat her mother. Mayme had screamed, as the man grabbed her by the shoulders, "Zina, get your uncle!" Zina ran toward her uncle's house, where Rachid stood, outside, like a spectator, squinting his eyes from the sun. Mayme was being kicked. Rachid's fingers danced. "Come, can't you see what is happening?" She grabbed his arm and he shook her off. She fell into the dust, then ran from his unmoving figure. Her mother writhed on the ground. When Zina helped her mother to her feet, she looked across the road. Their audience had departed.

When the Spanish flu invaded the village, Mayme nursed her husband's mother and father as they both lay dying on their beds. All of the men were gone. Rachid's trips to the north sometimes lasted weeks. Elmaz was pregnant and did not let her children come to the sick house. Neither did Mayme. She left her girls alone when she went to wash down her in-laws and feed them. And as she had every morning for the last year, she harvested the silkworms that lived on shelves in their pantry. The silkworms crackled like rain on a tin roof. She stopped for a moment while the chorus rustled. A loud moan came from above. Mayme climbed the stairs to the room of her in-laws. Their large bodies had withered quickly in this last week, their faces had turned to slate. As she entered the room, her husband's mother shrieked and tried to chase Mayme away.

When Mayme returned home that day, Camille stood outside their basement talking to a woman in modern western clothes. The stranger wore a felt hat tilted to one side and had a golden cross pinned to her lapel. Mayme rushed toward them as the woman handed a pear to her daughter. "Who are you?" Mayme grabbed the fruit.

This American lady was from the *Ship of Hope*; they had come to care for the stricken, she told Mayme. The Spanish flu was a worldwide epidemic.

"But we are not sick here—" She started to point to the house of her husband's parents.

The woman interrupted her. "Your daughter tells me your husband is in America."

Mayme nodded.

The stranger continued, "I need a woman to come to Batroun to work for me. Do you sew and crochet? Could you and your daughters go to Batroun?"

Mayme invited the woman into her basement home. Zina prepared anise tea and Camille sat on the floor. Mayme wanted to know about the job, but she asked many questions about America and Pennsylvania, where her husband lived. The lady of *Hope* had only traveled through the state once and remembered some steel mills and very green hills. The lady talked on about her mission and Mayme's opportunity. Mayme watched the woman's hands, pale and smooth, as they lay in her lap. Her eyebrows were very thin, but she wore no color on her white cheeks. Mayme could work by pieces. The nurses and doctors needed some sewing and darning; the sheets and towels needed patching. Could she do this? Could she find a place to live? They would give her some food and a little money. Mayme did not know how much would be enough. Anything would do. Could she come soon?

She would take the job even though she could imagine the warn-

ings: stay away from this woman, she is a Protestant. But Mayme
had known Protestants and missionaries in Brazil, and she was not
worried. Instead of thinking of this, she tried to recall the names
of people in Batroun who could house her and her daughters. Some
owed her husband money. What were their names?

Before she left, the stranger shook Mayme's hand. She would
see her at the clinic, and she told her the address. Somewhere to
go. When the woman was gone, Mayme surveyed their basement
room. Her daughters sat quietly. Dust settled everywhere. Impossible to clean. Yes, she would take the job, but she would not leave
until could do no more for Shebl's parents. They died a week after
the stranger's visit. They died together.

Mayme placed a basket of pots and pans on Zina's head. Clothes
and shoes had been rolled up in the mattresses; Mayme would
carry these, and Camille, who now was four, cradled only some
sheets and towels. Each girl was pinned with an important piece
of jewelry on her undershirt—Zina a ruby ring, Camille a brooch.
They were leaving without much notice. Mayme did not stop to see
Elmaz's new baby. The other villagers tended to the sick in their
homes. Mayme tried to imagine the village fading behind her, dis-
solving into a cloud, and finally into dust. Yet she was sure that
they would walk with everything they had and with all their strength
and find it there again when they stopped, when they rounded a
bend, when they shut their eyes, or left them opened.

None of the three wore a hat, although the day was hatefully hot.
The rocky road sizzled like embers beneath their bare feet. Mayme
sang to the girls as they walked. She recited the only Portuguese
word she remembered from Brazil: *sarava*. They repeated it obediently. They recited the rosary and they sang.

Other families traveled the road. Some had carts piled with furniture and children. They stopped and talked to the three females, shared water and stories. They met a group of five on their way to America. "We are going to live in Brooklyn, U.S.A.," a girl of eight announced. Mayme asked them if they would send a letter to her husband. "See us in Batroun." They snapped a whip and rolled away. "Do not forget!" Mayme shouted after them.

As the family left the hillside and reached the main road, they also left the rocky surface to walk on limestone. It seared their feet; they could hardly bare to allow each foot to touch. Mayme began to walk faster, but Camille could not keep up. She cried as her flesh burned on the road. She stood in the shade and would not move. Mayme stopped and looked at her in frustration. The girl was only four years old. Mayme tied the mattresses onto Zina's back and put Camille on her own shoulders. Beside them motorcars formed clouds as they passed. Walking with their heads down, they hurried along the road. Below them the sea rolled in and out, the white houses on the hillsides pearled the hills, but they bent with their loads and rushed toward Batroun.

◆

The

Lemon

Tree

◆

M a y m e

1919

The main road in Batroun was laid neatly with stones of different shapes. Wagons pulled aside for the automobiles. Bells on donkeys, oxen, and mules rang as travelers moved through the town. Batroun was a crossroad, and the downtown bore signs to every little village in the north on Mount Lebanon, and every town south to Beirut. Some corners had twenty signs stacked atop one another, pointing in all directions. The side roads to the residences remained narrow and dusty.

Mayme did not blink at the strangely crowded streets of the town, but both girls leaned toward their mother and watched her face as she surveyed the roads from the square. Behind a tree, she placed a blanket around the girls and put on the clean and pretty dresses she had made for them. They didn't raise a hand to help her. Lifting their arms obediently, turning to allow her to button them, they seemed to have gone limp. She combed their hair and tied it. With her handkerchief, she wiped the dust from their faces and from hers. Mayme instructed Zina to stay with the bundles by a church while she, holding Camille's hand, visited the houses of her husband's friends.

Mayme and Camille walked up and down the streets looking for a place to stay, and when turned down, they wound back through the busy streets. Beggars called out to them. People leaned against the churches and stores. A school had been transformed into an infirmary. Mayme brushed her dress off and straightened her daughter's ribbons and they approached the houses. Some did not remember her husband. Others could not help. By the time the night came, they had received only one offer. The woman of the house pointed into an alley where a roof, a portico, stood over a small section of cleared dirt. Two trees grew beside it like columns. They could live under there until they found a suitable home.

One night, only one night or two, Mayme thought. She returned with their belongings and a chattering Zina. She reported on all the new sights of the city—she described the long gowns of the Arabs; they all looked like priests to her, and about the old man who smelled funny and said something she could not understand. Zina became silent when they stopped at the new *house*.

Mayme arranged their mattresses under the roof and started a fire. The girls were tired and lay against the bundles. Without walls holding them, their shadows faded into the darkness. The fire cast little light into the night and meager heat onto them. They could not stay this way. Out there, beyond the fire, was Mayme's house, with rooms for everyone, with more than one fireplace, with a kitchen—a house of stone, not of air. Her job with the woman from the ship, Mrs. Bayly, did not begin until the following week. She told the girls they had to be careful with food. Sitting on their mattresses, they watched the bulgur wheat bubble in the pot. Each meal would be like this: a cup of rice, wheat, or beans. One meal a day.

The girls' stomach would swell into a hollow bloat. They would search the boxes of restaurants and large homes. They would stand outside stores looking at the oranges and figs piled before them. They would spend their days gathering discarded fruit. Mayme laid her hand against her stomach that night. A little tight ball pressed against her palm. She had always been thin, small, and Zina was like her. But Camille burst through Zina's hand-me-downs, and her cheeks glowed like two giant strawberries. People liked to touch her, put their hands on her golden hair, pull her cheeks between their thumb and forefinger. Mayme dressed her with lots of bows and lace. *Like a little doll*, they would say.

After their mother started to work for Mrs. Bayly, the girls became wanderers—they did inspect boxes and cartons for food, walk in the streets, but they were always dressed better than the others around them. They found a yard with lemon trees not too far from the house. They snuck through the fence; Zina pushed Camille up to pick the fruit. Each time they took only three lemons. They squeezed out the juice and ate the pulp. And saved one for their mother.

A month later Mayme found them a shanty to live in. It was near the edge of town crushed among other similar structures. These houses were not surrounded by grounds, nor did they have view of a sea or a valley. They sat so near each other that barely a footpath divided them. They bordered the road where dogs and children picked through garbage. In the morning vendors rolled carts past their doors only after they finished with the other neighborhoods. Not many families spoke to one another.

The first thing Mayme did was hang a rosary on the wall. Again the girls shared one room with their mother. Camille and Zina wrapped themselves in blankets as the wind pierced the loose boards. Every day Mayme curled their hair and dressed them in fresh clothes. After she went to work, the girls walked through the markets and around the fountain. They stopped at a nearby church, prayed, and stayed warm. One day they returned home and all their clothing had been stolen. Mayme did not like this neighborhood. The other residents dawdled in the streets all day and night. One had asked, "Are you a refugee?" Now Mayme wondered if her pride did her harm.

That night Mayme looked at the girls sitting on the bare mattresses. She sat quietly. Her daughters did not understand her silence; they thought they had done something wrong. Rising to make supper, the girls whispered to each other and glanced over to their mother. Many nights when she returned from the hospital ship, she had told stories about patients and nurses. Once she had taken them to see how it looked. They walked along the clean corridors with their mother and peeked into the swinging doors, but only glimpsed rows of filled beds. She sat in a small dark room beside two tubs filled with water. Two women cleaned the sheets, towels, and uniforms while Mayme sewed. Their heads beaded from the steam.

Camille stirred the small pot of rice while Zina cut a loaf of bread in half, then cut one half in thirds. As the dinner simmered, they placed the plates around the fire. Camille picked up the crock and walked toward her mother to serve her, but the pot broke in half and fell onto Camille's left foot. Before anyone could speak, the three dropped to the floor and tried to salvage the grain. They smashed hot handfuls of rice covered with dirt into their mouths. That night Mayme snuck into the lemon grove. When she returned with their fruit, she sang to the girls. She sang song after song, massaged Camille's foot until they slept.

"My dear husband . . . we are living in Batroun . . . Camille was hurt again . . . there is no food . . . when . . . I miss you . . . my daughters want to see their father . . . we are all well . . . My dear husband . . . the weather . . . our bones clatter . . . love . . . money . . . Mayme. A check for three dollars arrived at the end of the month.

Zihr came to visit later that year with news of Abdelli. On a rainy day, she found Mayme and the two girls huddled against the back wall of the shanty. It had rained all night and water poured in around their feet. Wrapping themselves in shawls, the two women and two girls walked to a church where they could stay warm. Mayme's daughters sat in a forward pew playing a game. Zihr told them of marriages and deaths in the village, particularly of the deaths of Yousef's Camille and Zina. "No one took care of them. Their mother never came back and their father never sent money. They died together, though." Upon hearing this the girls turned to the women. Camille stared at Zihr and Zina began to cry. Later they saw their mother remove her gold bracelets and hand them to Zihr.

Zina didn't want to cry; after all, Camille was the baby. But Zina missed her father a great deal. For a few days she would not eat, but would only cry. Camille pulled on her, tried to get her to sing. Mayme bought a small melon for them to eat. Zina prayed very hard and very loudly for her father. She repeated one particular prayer every night. "Take care of my father, my mother, my sister, and the whole world." At this point she opened and closed her arms. "Good night, Jesus, good night, Mary of mine, good night, my father, wherever you are."

The rain stopped the same week the *Ship of Hope* pulled out of Batroun. Mayme searched for other work, doing laundry, cleaning houses, anything, because she could not bear Zina's weeping any longer. She saw her daughter's lined face as she covered miles of streets and visited many homes. After work she didn't always stop at the American Consulate for her mail because her legs ached. The streets were choked with travelers, mostly shopping or passing through on their way out of the country. On Fridays she pushed through them to get to the government building. A pulse beat in her legs as she stood in line at the counter. The young man looked up. "Mrs. Shebl Abi-Nader," he announced tiredly. He handed her an envelope. She stood there. He pushed it under her hand and she opened it.

"What is this?" She pulled out three pieces of paper and a little book.

The man picked each object up. "You have a passport"—he held up the book—"a check, a letter from the government, and a letter from your husband."

Mayme fell to her knees, crying and kissing the ground of the consulate. The man ran around the desk to help her up. "How much, how much?" It was not enough money to get to America or even to Marseilles. She asked the clerk to read the letter and she wept as she heard, *"My dear wife, here are the money and the papers to bring you and my daughters to America. Please write when you are arriving. Your husband, Shebl."*

Before she returned to the house, Mayme reserved a car to take them to Beirut the next week. What would she tell the girls? She stopped. People streamed around her. Young beggars approached her and searched her pockets. Mayme shook them off and started down the street, splashing in puddles along the way. She paused at the door of the shack, then burst in. "Zina, Camille, we're going to have our pictures taken."

Mayme sent a message to the village they were leaving. They spent the rest of the week packing, curling hair, visiting the consulate every day to check, and crying.

Camille was very excited to ride in a touring car, a large Ford. She ran out as it pulled up to the church where they met it. Her reflection stared back at her from its shiny door. She sat in the backseat. From there she watched the Mediterranean and its rhythmic flow, she saw trees waving above her; she looked way down at the road below as it slipped under the wheel. The car went very fast. Camille's stomach bubbled, and she started to sweat although the air rushed around her face from both sides. She poked her mother once, then a second time. Mayme saw her daughter's pale cheeks. "Stop, please." Camille climbed down, walked over to the bushes, and vomited. She took her seat beside her mother and tried to close her eyes for the rest of the trip, but the same thing happened.

Mayme held her purse and opened it twice as they rode. The money, the tickets, the passport. She straightened her daughters' collars and fussed with their hair. Camille had two blue velvet bows that matched her skirt. Her cloth jacket was pinned with her mother's brooch. Zina's hair was pulled straight back. Her exposed pointed jaw mirrored her mother's. They had matching lace collars and cuffs. Mayme pulled her skirt down, then reached down to brush a spot from her shoe.

When they reached Beirut, Mayme spoke quickly to the girls. "Hundreds of people are going—someone will be left behind. Hurry through, do anything you can to get on that boat." Camille pulled her bad leg, and she hobbled as quickly as she could.

People with packages and luggage, children, and animals crowded around them. Mayme shouted to others from the village, but no one stopped. They pushed forward until Mayme could present her papers and her children to the purser, who stamped them and handed them back. She stood on the wooden planks and her daughters joined her. They went to the next man, who directed them to steerage in the near bottom of the ship. Descending the steps and turning to the left brought them to a large room with beds lined against the walls like shelves. They located the numbers of their beds and the girls sat by their mother and didn't move. Others crowded into the boat. Some flung their bags onto the shelf beds or dropped things and left to go to the railing.

The room had lights hanging from the center in a row. Metal basins were stacked in the corners. Mayme waved her hands through the air. No dust. She looked down at her clothes and saw they were clean. She put her hands in her lap for a moment and watched porters and passengers, waiters and children rush through the room. Camille slid down and wandered through the door. "Zina, go with her." Zina followed her sister. Mayme stood and opened their bags.

Mayme unfolded her hands and looked down at her nails. In Brazil she had had them painted a pale pink. They were long and pointed. She rolled her thumb against the overgrown cuticles and broke off a stray unclipped nail. One small bracelet dangled around her thin wrist. These were not the arms and hands of a sheik's wife. Gone are the days when the women sat in parlors silently examining each other's arms. Counting the gold bracelets. Checking their groomed hands.

She grabbed her purse and dug through it for scissors or a clipper. When she raised her head, two men stood in front of the bed holding her *sundoot*. "Mrs. Nader, is this your trunk?" She spoke very little French but nodded her head and placed her hands on its wooden slats. They lowered it and bowed to her. Mayme waited by it until they passed through the room.

The families in the bunks around Mayme had their heads deep into their belongings. Another mother with six children sat them two on a bed and lectured them about their behavior on the boat. An old man with a very large mustache wrote in a leather notebook. The bottoms of his pants frayed around his shoes. He looked up at Mayme and nodded. She bent her head quickly. Pulling the key from inside her dress, Mayme knelt beside the trunk and opened it. The *sundoot* had been her mother's, and at the last minute, she had sent a messenger to Abdelli to bring it down to her. Inside the lid, red flowered paper flapped away from the wood. She sighed and reached into the box.

Everyone guarded their possessions. When she traveled to and from Brazil before the war, they had stayed in cabins on the middle deck. The merchandise was stored in steerage, and their room had closets and drawers for their clothes. She had peeked over the railing at the people herded below—they wrapped themselves in dark clothing and sat together in large groups. Occasionally, the faint sound of a guitar and singing rose like smoke. It was impossible to enjoy it because of all the noise. She had strolled away into the lounge to play cards with other women from the village. She had forgotten how the steerage passengers looked, that they slept on shelves of beds last used by troops during one war or another, that their belongings would be forgotten in a rush—lost or stolen.

What these travelers owned was with them. Mayme touched a lace tablecloth neatly folded atop the stacks. She put her hand under it to see how the pattern swirled around it. Beneath the tablecloth was a pair of gloves. Had she worn gloves like this or had she just seen a picture of them? They had long flouncy cuffs. Raising herself up, she bent her head into the chest to lift out a porcelain bowl and pitcher. She placed them on the floor at the head of the bunks. No one had told her where to get water. Standing, she surveyed the room. No one seemed to have any, although she could not really tell. Beside these she set a jar for waste. Running her hand along the other folded items, she stopped at her blue-and-white flowered dress. Polka dots and flowers, bows and lace. She wouldn't resemble the other third-class passengers in the boat in these. All she needed was two good dresses—lively ones, elegant and clean. This is what she told the girls as they scratched a leg with one foot and then the other, waiting for her to finish with their hair and clothes. So much fuss, so much fuss. This was important, *we are not refugees.* Tucked beside the dresses sat her husband's jeweled hat. A round velvet box with red, white, and green gems set around in a pattern. Men had the most beautiful hats in Lebanon, and women had the best in France. When she visited Paris ten years before, a woman in a shop had placed a tiny hat with a large feather on her head, then brought a veil over her face. It was not in this *sundoot* and probably had been gone for years, but she plunged both arms into the contents and lifted each thing—all the way to the bottom.

Her father had a hat like her husband's, except the jewels were
arranged symmetrically around the crown. When she looked down
at him coming to the house, she thought it resembled the top of a
perfume bottle. "Do you remember your grandfather Elia, Zina?"

Her daughter turned sleepily over and propped her head up on
the pillow. "I remember his shoes."

"His shoes?" Mayme couldn't remember anything but boots, brown
with soil.

"The noise they made on the marble when he came to the house
on New Year's to bring the New Year's presents." Zina sat up. "I'd
be sleeping and I'd hear the taps outside and I'd open the windows,
both sides, and shout. 'Happy New Year, Jiddi Elia!'"

Mayme's father reached the height of the window. His legs were
long, and he had a small head. Zina looked into her open palm.
"Then he'd give me my gift. A halfpenny."

She had held that coin in her hand for a while, then tied it in
her handkerchief—the white one with the pink crocheted edge,
her best one. When they went to church, she tucked it into her
sleeve; she patted it during the New Year's Mass. Afterward the
vendors stood at their posts around the church, and Zina ran to
everyone until she found the one with the taffy. She scrunched her
shoulders while she secretly removed the handkerchief and released
the coin. When was the last time the girls had taffy? Mayme wondered. Camille now sat up and listened to her mother and sister
talk.

"Do you remember Jiddi Elia, Camille?"

She stared blankly at her mother and answered, "Jiddi Jerges."
Mayme's father-in-law was the only one she knew.

"She's too young, Mother, she doesn't know him," Zina said.
"She doesn't even know Dad."

Camille slumped down into the sheets; Mayme rose and knelt in front of her. "No, you're Daddy's present when we get to America. His blond daughter who was in my belly when he left. You're his beautiful girl."

"Will we see Uncle Elias?" Zina asked.

They all wanted to see Elias, her husband's youngest brother. He had played with Zina when she was a baby. His red hair and sapphire eyes captured everyone's attention. Elias worked with his brothers, but he also wrote. A poet, a playwright, historian—he didn't seem interested in finding a wife, only a new craft. He learned to sew, bake, and build sets for plays.

"Uncle Elias," Camille repeated.

"Yes, Elias too," Mayme responded.

Maybe she'd have another child in America—a boy. Her daughters raised their heads as the whistle blew the departure.

Here are the things we carry with us. Mayme placed the hat back into the trunk and closed it. Sheets, towels, bowls, a flowered dress, a bow, combs, pantaloons, hardy stockings, as many shoes as we can afford, a memory of songs, a heart full of prayers, the names of two young cousins now departed, a hand impressed with a halfpenny, hair when braided feeling like a branch, when loose covering like a bridal veil, two daughters, one dark and one fair, a few words of Portuguese, two bracelets, one ring, and one brooch; and her hands. Mayme stiffly raised each finger and checked the nails. She would work on these soon. The girls stood beside her at the rail and waved as they sailed out of Beirut.

"Do mine now." Camille spreads her chubby hand on her mother's knee.

Zina admires her new manicure. Her mother filed round ends at the top of each finger. Mayme takes Camille's hand into her own.

A little brown line grazes each nail. "Little miss, I do only clean hands." Camille jumps down and crouches at the basin. The water is murky and has soap floating in it.

"You and your sister go for more water. Fill the jars and the basin," Mayme instructs. They load their arms with the containers and march through the door. In the last week they have learned their parameters—the lower deck, steerage, and around, but not in the kitchen. More than once the porter has escorted Camille back to her mother. "I'm sorry, ma'am, she was upstairs." He is a Lebanese man, too, and already has accepted some money from Mayme to supply them with fruit or vegetables once in a while. She smiled, pretended to scold Camille, and watched her leave again.

Mayme raises her head and sees a woman from the village, Souad, watching her. "Hello, Souad, how is your boy today?"

Her friend walks toward her slowly clutching brown rosary beads. "He's worse, I think. He can't move." She grabs Mayme's hand. "He can't hold anything in his stomach, his fever is very high, and he cries to me. Can you let us use your slop jar?"

"Yes, Souad. I am sorry Yousef is so sick." Mayme bends her head to where the recently cleaned jar sits.

"Your girls seem better today."

Mayme hands the woman the bowl. "They are. I guess they inherited seasickness from me. I was hoping they'd be spared, but I just look at the ocean and ooh." She raises her flattened hand and rocks it back and forth.

Souad holds the vessel against her hip. "What about your husband?"

"No," Mayme laughs a little. "He can take anything—in Brazil he could eat any food at all, no matter how spicy. And he swam in ponds so cold they were fringed with snow."

"Mama!" A cry comes from Souad's bunk.

"I'd better go, Mayme."

"Yes, do. My girls will be back soon."

Mayme stretches her hand on her knee and brushes the emery board against her forefinger nail. She saw Shebl even in the darkness, taking his clothes off by the river late at night and plunging into the freezing water. Did he think she was asleep? Did she ever sleep when she was with him? Being responsive, attentive, tired, more than tired. Hearing her own voice crackling against him, accusations to him, to her, back and forth, a squeaky teeter-totter, swinging doors, unoiled wheels, Rachid, bursting into the room, complaining, "Why can't you be quiet when the store is open, Mayme?" Then, quietly, Rachid saying to a friend who drank their coffee and ate from their stock, "They are a barren couple; you must feel bad for them."

"See what your brother tells people, Shebl," Mayme pointed out.

Shebl turned like a closing door, left the room, the store. Gone to the witch's house, she supposed. This was what I came here for, she thought. This was why I traveled for a month on the Acre River in a launch, after watching the ship burn in Anti-Marie, a seven-day trip turned into a month, and the boatmen shouting *Jew* at me when I went to eat, or walk, or look out on the murky shore. I am a *Christian*. My stomach churned on that small boat, turning to liquid in my hands, on my clothes, over the side. Reaching the point where I'd kneel at the rail all day, and the river slapped us, and the heat melted my body and yellowed my clothes. I, alone, and instead of clenching fists, I held a rosary, always. She tells her girls, "Prayer instead of anger." How many rosaries did she recite in Brazil, when her husband had left for a few days' fishing, or in Paris, where they stopped, feeling happy and together, or in Abdelli, or Batroun, and on this boat?

Kneel up straight when you pray, point to heaven when you pray, save a decade for your father, and one for Uncle Elias. "And one for Mother," Camille announced.

Mayme lifts her left hand. The nails are perfectly pointed and white. The sound of Camille's foot thumping down the hall approaches the room, and Mayme rises as they enter with their arms balanced with the filled jars. "What took you so long?" she asks them, taking the jars from Zina.

Zina frees Camille of her load and reports, "A long line and then the barrel was empty and we had to wait." She leans her head toward the entrance. "I saw them coming with dinner, Mother."

"Good." Mayme puts the file into her purse. "I'll do your nails right before bed, Camille. We can wash now."

Her younger daughter stands as Mayme wipes a washcloth against her face. "Ow! It hurts." She cries.

"It doesn't hurt clean faces." Her mother scrubs her neck while Camille wrinkles her cheeks, causing her eyes to become little slits. As she rinses in the basin, the trays are carried in by the porters. Mayme's man hands her a hot loaf of bread under a towel. The little family sits in a circle on the bottom bunk eating the stew. Tearing the loaf into small chunks, Mayme distributes them to the girls, then places the remainder in the *sundoot*. Bread at the old house went stale sometimes, and Mayme cut it into small bits for the birds. Standing on the balcony, she threw them high, imagining the birds would catch them in flight. Later she saw sparrows pick through the stones and carry off piece after piece.

"How far to America?" Camille asks while Mayme braids her hair for the night.

"We are going to France first, and then we are going to wait for your father to write. Then we go to America."

"How far to France?" Camille turns her head toward her mother.

Mayme grabs her by the shoulders and puts her back in place. "Hold still and let me finish." She pulls Camille's hair around into the plaits. Camille wrinkles her face in pain. "Now." Her mother sits her down finished. "One more week and we'll be in Marseilles." Zina returns from using the slop jar and sits on the bed beside her sister. "Where will we stay in France?" Zina asks.

"I know a hotel where they help many Lebanese. It's not very fancy or very expensive, but we won't be there too long." Mayme folds their dresses and puts them in the trunk, then turns back to the girls. "Who has potatoes?"

Both girls curl their hands into fists and places them on their knees. Mayme counts out. *"Hroonkus, broonkus, tal en nazy, ounie, oonkus. Sha, sho be kasha, sho be shir, il asfooti,"* and on until Camille's potato is eliminated. She keeps the hand behind her back, then switches it with the one in the front. "No cheating or you'll go to bed now," Mayme warns her. Camille giggles and thrusts the hand behind her back again. *"Hroonkus, broonkus, tal en nazy . . ."* Zina wins the game and becomes the leader for the next round.

When Camille's turn arrives she can't remember the rhyme and mixes the parts up. *"Il asfooti, il asfooti, tal en nazy."*

Zina rolls her eyes. "Mother."

"You could teach her right, Zina."

"Listen." She grabs her sister. *"Hroonkus broonkus tal en nazy ounie oonkus."* She repeats it very quickly.

"Slow down, so she can hear you."

Zina takes a long sigh, *"Hroon-kus, broonkus,"* she recites slowly.

Mayme raises her hands up. "You are ready to be somewhere else, aren't you, girls? Why don't you say a silent rosary tonight."

The sisters roll back and crawl under the blanket. A small whisper comes from Camille as she counts her beads: *"Hroonkus, broonkus . . ."*

Mayme gathers their underclothes to wash. From across the room she can hear Souad crying. She drops the laundry into the basin and walks over to her friend. Souad looks up at her. "He's so sick, Mayme, what if he dies before we get to America?" Mayme glances behind her and notices the empty bed.

"Where is he, Souad?"

"They put him in the ship hospital. His fever is high, and they said he has to be quarantined. They won't even let me in."

"The doctors know what they are doing. They will help him now. You should pray for him." She sits beside Souad. "Where's your rosary?"

Souad wails, "I won't pray anymore. I have prayed enough, and look what I have. My little Hanna dead from the flu, I haven't seen my husband in four years, and now Yousef. I cannot ask anymore." She places her head into her hands.

Mayme puts her arm on her friend's shoulder. "Don't worry. He understands."

As Mayme returns to her bunk, she listens to the other voices in the room. A mother sings a lullaby to her children, the players of a poker game shout their bets, other sick ones moan, some people are praying, crying, snoring. All together in this one room, each family has its own little world as if they were on different islands in the same sea. Mayme worries about all of them. She would make a good nurse, like the people who worked for Mrs. Bayly. They talked to the sick people, washed them, put needles in them. Mayme watched them in their uniforms—some were white, pure white with round hats, and others were gray. She didn't know why they were different. They spoke to her only when they dropped off their stockings to be mended. All the other times they talked to the patients. Maybe they cured them with their conversation. One special nurse wrote letters for them and another cared only for the children. She showed them how to make dolls from handkerchiefs. Mayme hopes one of her daughters will become a nurse or even a doctor. Not Camille, though; she can't pay attention. Mayme looks at her youngest daughter asleep, breathing with her mouth open; Zina lies beside her with her arm thrown across her sister. Mayme teeters a little, then sits down. She will be glad when they are off this boat too. She takes a deep breath and falls onto her bed.

Hotel Splendid

◆

M a y m e
1920

H o w   m u c h?"   M a y m e   asks the front desk clerk at the
Hôtel Splendide for the second time.

"Eight francs," he answers in a loud voice. The lobby buzzes
from the traffic going in and out. The last time she was in Marseilles, Mayme enjoyed the quietly busy hotel. Now Arabs in burnooses shout across the room at one another, Druze in their dark
clothing pull along screaming children. Mayme's girls sit on their
trunk with their chins resting in their hands.

"You might share a room," the clerk continues.

"Mayme drops her shoulders. "Then how much would it be?"

"Six francs."

Camille jerks on her mother's skirts, "Mom, let's eat."

"I want a room." Mayme opens her purse. "Just one for us alone."

"As you wish, madam." The clerk turns the ledger toward Mayme, and she carefully prints out her name, the only thing she knows how to write. She climbs the stairs to a room on the third floor. Behind her a man carries the *sundoot* on his back, and the girls follow.

The next day when Mayme sets out with her girls to register their address at the Lebanese and American consulates, Zina dawdles. Mayme tugs on her older daughter's arm, but Zina stops and stands in the street. What now? the mother wonders when Zina begins to cry. Pulling her daughters away from the traffic, she stoops to look at her. The girl is hot and her face is swollen. Leading them to a small park, Mayme places Zina on a white iron bench. Her daughter swoons and collapses on Mayme's lap. "Camille," Mayme hisses. Taking the scarf from her head, she hands it to the child. "Put water on this." She indicates a fountain in the middle of the square. Camille runs to the edge and dips the scarf in, and when she returns, they try to revive Zina, but the sister will not waken. Mayme props her against the bench, then, kneeling down in front of it, she pulls Zina onto her back.

Mayme hopes she remembers Marseilles well enough to find the Lebanese doctor who gave them their medicines when she and Shebl went to Brazil. Many new things have been built since Mayme's last stop in this city, but the port district and the neighborhood where the Lebanese and Syrians keep their shops are little changed.

Motorcars occasionally chug by, but the peddlers still use push-
carts. Passing a street of brown row houses, she crosses through
the old neighborhood where leather goods and glass are made in
large flat buildings. A new automobile garage has been built and
almost makes Mayme lose her way. On the next street, she spots
the old convent that has been turned into an orphanage. Dr. Halim
told them stories of the Italian children who had been left there.

The number of people in Marseilles seems to have multiplied by
thousands, but Mayme pushes through them until she sees the gate
of Dr. Halim's house and the long pathway to his door. Mme. Halim
answers the bell and takes the sick child from her mother.

Zina has contracted the German measles. Over Mayme's protests about the costs, Dr. Halim orders a car to take the child to
the hospital. The law requires quarantine of all patients with this
sickness, he explains. After he gives Mayme the address of the
hospital, the woman offers him some money, but he shakes his
head. As the car drives away, Mayme leads Camille back to the
Hôtel Splendide.

Every day Mayme leaves Camille with the neighbors and walks
to the tramway to visit her daughter in the hospital on the other
side of the city. German-measles patients are allowed no visitors,
so the nurses do not permit Mayme to enter Zina's ward. The door
is sealed and the window is nearly covered with newspapers. Raising herself onto her toes, Mayme can see the lines of beds through
a small newspaper frame. In the fifth bed on the right, Zina lies
against a pillow, her head shaven and her face pale. Mayme watches
her daughter for more than thirty minutes, then leaves.

Walking instead of spending more money to ride home, Mayme
realizes she must contrive ways to pay for the doctors and the pas-

sage to the United States. She feels as if she were in Batroun again without a sou to her name. But now she has no village to return to, her jewelry is nearly gone, and the room is very expensive.

When she reaches the hotel, she looks around the lobby. She is greeted by several people who seem to be standing around waiting for someone. Apparently the hotel is booked solid and these people are hoping for a room to become vacant. Mayme approaches a group of young men and introduces herself. "Are you guests here?" she asks. Mayme explains that in her room are two couches and some floor space if someone needs quarters, temporarily. By the end of the week two men are living with her and her daughter. She strings a curtain between the kitchen area where she places the two small beds and the living room that she is sharing with the boarders. They pay three francs apiece and Mayme earns extra money by running errands, doing laundry, and shopping for other Arabs.

By the second week, she can converse with the merchants in their street dialect. For most trips Camille accompanies Mayme, for she doesn't want to leave her alone. She has heard from the grocers that small girls are being abducted and never are seen again. Mayme is relieved that her lodgers do not linger in the room during the day. In the evening she and Camille sit behind their curtain folding laundry and praying for Zina's recovery. That same week the tram workers go on strike. Every day Mayme walks across Marseilles to view her daughter through the newspaper window. The round trip takes three to four hours.

At the end of the week, Camille has the German measles too, and this time, Mayme accompanies her to the hospital, but she is forced to leave. She stands in front of the building for a long time, then walks home. When she returns to the room, the boarders are sitting on the floor eating. Their clothes lie across the back of the couch; empty wine bottles sit on the table. She shivers and flees to a nearby church, a Roman Catholic one. Mayme lights a candle under a statue of Saint Anne. She had prayed to Anne for years to grant her children. Anne gave birth to Mary at the age of eighty, the story said. *Protect the children you gave me,* she whispers. The small flames flicker in their tiny dishes. Resting her head against the pew, Mayme prays.

Camille does not stop crying just because the nurse tends to her in her own cubicle. She wants her mother and she twists and turns and weeps. The girls have never been separated from their mother or one another before. Camille can't understand what they are saying to her. She shouts in Arabic, *"Oomi"*—Momma—and screams when they cut off her blond hair and shave her head. She hates the smell of the hospital, especially the sheets when she turns in her sleep. The nurses who coo at her also stick needles into her behind. She will tell her mother. For two days, she stays in the bed, twisting and crying, and itching.

The afternoons in the hospital are the quietest. The children in the wards play or sleep and the doctors have finished their morning visits. Camille crawls out of her bed. They put a heavy cotton gown on her. In her bare feet, she tiptoes down the hall, peeking into the doors. She hears many other children crying. Maybe they stole children, hundreds of them. Reeling from her fever, she creeps toward the large covered door. She stops and listens. *"Oomi!"* she hears someone shout.

"Zina!" Camille runs to the door of the ward.

"Zina!" She bangs against it. A nurse rushes to the door and opens it. Camille speeds by her and stands in the middle of the room searching for her sister. She hurries to the fifth bed. Zina jumps up and hugs Camille. The nurses babble in French beside them. Zina looks at them and says carefully, *"Soeur."* The next day after lunch a nurse escorts Camille to her sister's bed; they play during the day and sleep apart at night.

This scene is described to Mayme as she frowns at Camille's shaven head. The golden hair is gone, and from what she can tell, it is growing in black. "Mrs. Nader, your girls will be out in a few weeks."

"Merci," Mayme answers and leaves the hospital. She travels back to the Hôtel Splendide. Two more men have joined the other boarders. Every time she turns around, she sees another face. This time the room is unoccupied except for heaps of sewing and darning waiting for her on the sofa. She piles everything on her lap, rubs her eyes, and starts her work. Apparently Souad's son infected her daughters, but as she surveys their small room, the dark worn wood, the frayed rug, the torn mattress that has lost part of its stuffing, she blames it. The girls have little sunlight, no place to walk where she can watch them while she works—just more dust.

"Are you really mad at us?" Zina asks as her mother leads her off by the elbow.

"Furious," her mother replies, smiling. The girls have been home a few days.

They follow their mother to behind the church where there are benches under willow trees.

"You're going to get a terrible beating." Mayme stops and motions for each girl to sit down. "Here's your beating!" She laughs as she reveals a melon hidden in her coat. They relax together and slice the melon, where no one, especially their boarders, can see them eat this special treat. "We are moving next week."

"Are we leaving?" Zina asks.

"Only the hotel. Your father sent a little money and will send more, but in the meantime, we will live in our own room. With no one else around. I will show you the building on our way back to the hotel."

"When will we go to America?"

"First we move, then we wait for the money, and then we have to have you examined again by the doctor."

Camille grimaces at the mention of another doctor. "I am not sick."

"You said your eyes hurt." Her mother pats her brown short hair.

"They don't." Camille turns her head so her mother cannot look at them.

"Even if they don't, little miss, everyone gets examined before going to America."

My dear husband. It feels like we are going to live in Marseilles forever. Camille's eyes are bad. She must go to the doctor every day. He treats them by rubbing them with stones on the eyelid. It is expensive to see a doctor every day. Now we have no money and she cannot pass the exam. I am sewing and working for people in the building. In three months, you can learn a city pretty well. . . .

"What's this disease called again?" she asks the doctor.

He replies with a long word Mayme doesn't understand. "It's common and apparently a problem in America. You can't get in with it. They check everyone's papers."

"Are her eyes getting better?" Mayme asks.

"Not very much. She will need more treatment. Maybe another month."

Another month. Mayme writes again to her husband. She doesn't know how long they will be in Marseilles, but she cannot get both girls approved for travel. The tickets for open passage rest in the drawer at the consulate. They will give her visas as soon as the health papers are handed in. Mayme reports this to her friend Nadia as she accompanies her to the stairwell. They have visited with each other every week since Nadia came last month. Her husband is on his way from Cuba to meet her. The women share their loneliness. "Mayme, I hope you get to go to America soon."

"Thank you, Nadia. I don't know how long it will be with Camille's eyes in the condition they're in." She sighs. "Shebl thinks I should leave her with friends and go on ahead with just her sister."

They arrive at the door, and Mayme holds it open for her. "But I couldn't do that, of course. I'll have to think of something else. Or wait."

"Like the rest of us. See you tomorrow or the next day?"

"Bon," Mayme answers and slowly creeps along the carpet to the apartment.

At the table Zina is practicing her writing. She writes her name in Arabic and then in French. Mayme considers the words. "That's good. Is that your name?"

"Yes. The nurse taught me how. I like French, although the letters are funny."

"It looks like Portuguese. They write in the same direction too, not like Arabic." Reclining on the couch, she slips off her shoes. "Where is your sister?"

Zina glances up. "She went out into the hall with you."

"She wasn't with me." Mayme rises quickly. "Camille, are you

in here? Come out right now." She checks the closet and under the
bed. Mayme runs to the door and surveys the hallway. "Camille!"

She turns to Zina. "You stay here in case she comes back. I
have to go look for her." Mayme puts her shoes on and darts from
the apartment. She bangs on the door of a neighbor.

"Have you seen Camille?" she cries. The man shrugs and asks
his wife. They haven't seen her, but both will help search. Standing in front of the apartment building, Mayme looks up and down.
Many children loiter around the stairs and banisters, but Camille
is not with them. Mayme stops a police officer and babbles to him
in French and Arabic. He waits for her to repeat the problem and
she slows down and says, "My daughter, lost." He whistles to two
younger officers, who go back with her to the house, where she has
the passport picture, but her hair is brown now. Lifting her hair,
she repeats, brown. Bad leg, she says, smacking her left thigh.
The police assure her they will watch for her, but she might wait
for the girl to come home. Mayme follows them, pulls at their sleeves.
They shake her loose and motion her to be calm. Mayme races
away—to the park, and the school, and the stores. No one has
seen her daughter. Mayme shoulders her way through crowds of
people, into alleys and the small streets.

Her heart beats inside of her head, and her warm breath steams
her face. She asks her regular merchants; she cries to the priest of
the nearby church. Slowing down, Mayme catches her breath, leans
against a pole, and gasps and cries. Tears fall to the edge of her
chin, but she has no energy to wipe them away. When she returns
to the house, another neighbor approaches her. She reports, "Mayme,
I saw her on the Rue Bernard."

Rue Bernard is where the Hôtel Splendide is located. Mayme
hugs her purse and flies down the street for half a mile. She stops

at the hotel. The desk clerk remembers her and her children, but no, he hasn't seen her. Searching the hallways, she bangs on the door of their old apartment, checks the lobby. No one has seen her. By the time Mayme leaves, traffic has lightened, but the sky is dark. She drags herself along the street toward the train station. Pausing in front of their old church, she slowly climbs the stairs. If she prays hard, begs Saint Anne again . . .

As she nears the altar she sees Camille kneeling near the offering candles. Her little hands are pressed together and pointed straight to heaven as her mother has told her to do. Mayme seizes her by the shoulders. "Where have you been? Why did you leave? I was afraid something had happened," she shouts.

"I came to light a candle. I had my own money," Camille says frightened of her mother's sweating red face.

"Why? I would have brought you later."

"You will go to America later without me as Dad told you to. Don't leave me, *oomi*." Camille buries her wet face in her mother's skirt.

Her mother pets her head. "I wouldn't leave you. Where did you hear such a thing?"

"You told Aunt Nadia."

Mayme nods. "Don't worry, little miss. We are doing all of this together."

Camille hugs her mother's leg, and they stroll back to the apartment. On the way she gets a big piece of fruitcake for their dessert. Mayme knows of times when people had to choose between their husbands and children or their parents and their country. She hardly knows what it is like to be with him anymore. It hasn't even crossed her mind to leave the little girl. No one is going to be left anymore. Only one Camille and Zina remain and she will guard them. What would Saint Anne think, after all? She gave her the daughters, and if they have to spend another six months in Marseilles, they will—although she really doesn't want to be away from her husband much longer.

Nadia heard about a doctor and made the appointment for Mayme. "He is old and doesn't have many patients. Go to him." Mayme places a pink ribbon in Zina's hair and walks her to the office, only three blocks from the house. She instructs Zina on the way on what to say, how to act; Zina nods and accompanies her mother silently.

The doctor holds a light up to her eyes, one to her ears, listens to her heart, then nods his head. "What's your name, darling?" he asks Zina.

"Camille." She looks at her mother and smiles.

The doctor lowers his head and writes in a shaky hand. Mayme tries to make out the letters. She squeezes Zina's hand.

The doctor hands Mayme the completed health forms and sends them on their way. When they reach the street, Mayme sighs and smiles.

"How did I do, Mother?" Zina asks.

"You were perfect," Her mother answers. "But don't tell anyone or we won't be able to see your father."

"I know."

They stop at the consulate and present the completed papers.

"So, Mrs. Nader, are you ready to leave Marseilles at last?" the man at the desk queries.

"*Oui*, as soon as possible," she responds. She wiggles her leg as the clerk fusses with the papers. Sitting in a wooden chair, Zina pages through a newspaper.

"Mrs. Nader," the clerk calls.

Mayme lifts her head and sees him examining the papers closely. She waits at the counter. The man lays out the papers, one by one on the desk in front of her. Mayme watches his face and tries to form questions in her head. Leaving the magazine on the bench, Zina joins her mother. "Mrs. Nader." He points to the first paper. "These are your health papers." She studies the form, and he places his hand on the next one. "This is the visa for you and your children." He raises her passport and opens it to a blank page. "The purser will stamp all of these and your passport right here. Make certain everything is stamped by the time you get to Ellis Island." He puts everything into an envelope and hands it to her.

Finally, he smiles, "Everything is ready, Mrs. Nader. With your passage paid, you can go to America."

She puts the envelope in her belt and closes her jacket. *"Merci, merci."*

The new dresses that Mayme makes are trimmed in a very delicate lacing that she could have made herself if she had the time. But she buys it in the market and has enough left to decorate the bodice of her polka-dotted dress. The girls sit on the velvet sofa of their room, their legs hanging a little high off the floor. Mayme kneels and looks at Camille's eyes again. No doubt about it, since the treatments have stopped, her eyes are more inflamed and liquidy. "Do you understand what you have to do?"

Camille nods her head. Her mother pulls at one of her ribbons to make the bow tighter. "Are you afraid, little miss?"

She shakes her head back and forth and bites her bottom lip.

Mayme walks the length of the room, and both girls stay quiet. Someone bangs at the door. "Your car is here, Mayme."

The girls cling to their mother's skirt as she pushes her way up the gangplank. The whole world is traveling on this boat, she thinks. Women dressed in dark skirts with red embroidered flowers along the hems hold the hands of blond children. Large dark families and sleek well-dressed couples all force their way onto the ship. At the top, two desks stand. At one a doctor reads papers and quickly surveys the passengers; at the other, the purser stamps papers and directs people to their quarters. As the passengers press through the line, a woman falls into the water. She screams, the water splashes, and boatmen rush to the side. At this moment Camille slips away from her mother and sneaks under the gate.

"Stop that girl," an officer shouts. Camille rounds a corner, out of sight.

Mayme announces, "I must get on, that's my little girl." Mayme is led to the front and passes through the gate.

On deck, the struggle to move doesn't diminish. Mayme and Zina thrust their bodies against other families. Children wander away from screaming parents. Mayme peeks around trunks and between people as she makes her way through. Suddenly, she feels a tug on her skirt as she descends the stairs to go to their quarters. Camille grins at her mother, and they say nothing until they reach their room.

The bunks are enclosed in individual rooms and the entire deck is cleaner than the last boat. As they hunt for their number, Mayme notices toilet facilities. She clutches her daughters' hands and they settle in their room.

When they arrive in New York, they must wait a day on the docked boat until it is their turn to be processed. The passengers in third class roam around. Mayme rests; she is grateful the boat isn't moving anymore. Their quarters have no windows, and she can't raise herself to go to the deck. Others say they can see New York from there. She doesn't want to see it; she isn't sure it is there. Mayme puts her hand on her heart. Why is it beating so quickly? She has to comb her hair. They have prepared their clothing for Ellis Island and the train. The girls are playing *bustra* on the other bed with a deck of cards they borrowed. Zina wins game after game.

Camille pouts with her lower lip pushed out. "That's a lovely face, Camille," her mother comments. "I hope it stays that way for your father."

Rising, Camille gazes in the mirror, then pulls her lip in. Zina approaches her with a brush. "I'll do your hair."

"No!" Camille screams and withdraws her head. "You hurt."

Mayme says sleepily, "Let her do it. Zina, be gentle."

Mayme hopes they will have long hair again as in the old country. Her hair reaches below her waist when it is combed out. In Marseilles, the French women kept theirs short, around their face in curls. But not Mayme; hair is a gift from God. She will brush hers a hundred times before she goes to bed.

Ellis Island has three buildings that everyone marches through. Each family presents the papers first and barely speaks. Some tell stories of people they know who were deported before they even put a foot on New York soil. Mayme says nothing and tries not to listen to these tales. She wants to put her hands over her ears and shout, *shut up shut up*. Camille and Zina stay near her until they reach the examination room. Mayme signals Camille with a shake; Camille releases her hand and wanders down an aisle past empty benches. Her mother doesn't look back as she presents the papers to the officer. The bored clerk writes the names down incorrectly: Magda, Nina, and Caroline. Mayme studies the paper as if she could read it. "Where's your other daughter?" he asks.

She screws up her face at him. A person in the line translates it into French. Mayme searches the room with her eyes, then points to Camille at the door. The officer directs someone to bring her. Camille drags her heels as she is brought to the front. She stands at the desk and the officer glances up. "You're a pretty girl; stay with your mother." He pats her head. "Go on." He hands everything back to Mayme. She rushes back to the boat.

A Syrian family going to Cleveland, Ohio, offers Mayme a ride in a car to Newark, New Jersey, where they must catch the train. They tell her that Uniontown, Pennsylvania, will take one day to reach and she will depart before they do. Mayme smiles at the Syrians and accepts their offer. More than half the day is spent going to the island of Manhattan, getting a car, and waiting for the train. Three times Mayme does not know where she is. Everyone moves so quickly. She is relieved that she has this family to guide her through the streets. Once they are all seated she tells them about her husband and brother and their stores. Mayme talks a great deal to the Syrians and to her daughters. Their father will be so happy to see them. He will think they are very pretty. It is important to learn English right away. They will go to school as soon as possible. The girls lie against the seat, their ears full of the roar of the train and their mother's chatter. Father, uncle, school,

English, store, money. Mayme looks at their sleeping faces. She pulls out her rosary and rubs the beads between her fingers.

Outside her window, green soft hills and trees whose leaves seem fluffy pass by. Motorcars creep along roads near the tracks. She leans back. But now they are on the train. Going home. Mayme runs her hands along her face, outlines the crevices, massages her high cheekbones, strokes her hair off her face. The land is soft, but her face feels rough, like cedar bark. For the first time in a month, her stomach is calm. Being ashore steadies her. She brushes her hand along the wooden edge of the window. When they enter a tunnel, her face appears in the glass. It seems as small as Zina's; her eyes are very close together. She tucks a stray strand behind her ear. They return to light and to fields where black-and-white cows graze. So much grass for them and so soft and clean. They do not need to push aside rocks to get their food.

Covering her daughters with their jackets, she lays her head against the pillow once more. The sound of the train reminds her of a song. Which one? Not any from church, nothing her mother taught her. No, it is more like a prayer, a litany, a story of a life. Mayme unlaces her shoes and closes her eyes and lets the rosary fall against her polka-dotted dress.

◆

I l C o n t e
d i   A v o a

◆

C a m i l l e

1935

Traditionally Camille is one of the seasick. In 1920 on the first boat from Beirut to Marseilles (did it have a name?), she felt her stomach rise to her chest, to her throat and mouth. Her skin gathered beads of sweat and her breathing roughened. She held on to the door, or the bed, or her mother's hand.

Everyone seemed to be sick then. The third-class passengers were crammed in the bottom of a converted troop ship and shared bunks. Each family built a little house by hanging clothes from the beds, stacking trunks to form a wall, and turning their backs. For thirty days they squatted to relieve themselves where they could not be seen. Camille slept next to Zina, in the crack between the bed and the wall. While she listened to her sister's breathing, her face wept from dizziness and heat. She did not roll over until she needed the basin, which she sometimes missed. Her mother bathed her while she cried. "Don't worry, Camille." Zina offered a newly rinsed towel to Mayme, who placed it against the little girl's forehead. "Now lean back and rest." Camille closed her eyes and imagined walking—walking from one end of Abdelli to the other. She pointed; *This is the house in which I was born.* In this dream, her leg had no injury and she was able to go fast. She breathed harder and harder until her face grew damp, and she cried into the wet cloth her mother had placed on her eyes.

All the passengers took turns, it seemed: heaving in the night, clacking down the hall, rushing to the rail or the w.c., or holding the child who whimpered. Eventually, the noises and smells receded behind conversations with one another, the squeak of the wheels of the food carts, and the moaning of another who had caught the German measles.

After her first boat trip came her first train ride. She hadn't known what to expect, and the rushing of the train frightened her. The boat had been so slow and seemed to move mysteriously from one land to the next, but on the train the world passed by in a jagged blur. At first she couldn't bear to look out the window; she didn't lift her head. Leaning against Mayme, Camille drew her legs up to her chest and crossed her arms tightly. Her coat, placed over her backward, served as a blanket, and the three golden buttons on the sash jiggled back and forth. Eventually she brought her hand out to play with them, but she let the arm fall into Mayme's

lap as she dropped off to sleep. When Mayme rose, Camille bolted
up and stared as her mother swayed down the aisle, holding on to
the seats for balance. She was gone for hours, Camille thought,
and Zina was asleep. The little girl scooted over a seat and saw
through the window corn growing nearly to the horizon. Leaning
forward to look out the other side, she discovered small green hills
with fences that went up and down them so uniformly they seemed
to have grown out of the ground.

Camille was nervous on that first train journey—leaving her home
and her country, and meeting her father and her Uncle Elias made
her cling to her mother in a way she never had in Abdelli. When
she needed to be with Mayme, Camille would whisper, *Comb my
hair, please.* Mayme separated her legs and Camille stepped in.
After a few strong tugs on the knots, Mayme's stroke was soft and
comforting.

After a long night and part of the morning on the train, Mayme
took the girls to the rest room with her. She first lathered her own
hands, then she quickly washed Camille's inside of hers, jumbling
them like dice. Her mother was being so rough and determined,
Camille wanted to pull away. Mayme tied her daughters' dangling
hair with two ribbons and then combed back her own, placing a
small round hat on her head. Mayme led Camille and Zina to the
passageway, where they stared at the brown wood door. When they
stopped, Camille was tossed against the wall. A porter offered his
hands to the little girls as they stepped onto the wooden box, then
down to the platform.

As soon as Mayme descended, she fell to her knees and kissed
the ground, crying aloud. She rose, then ran across the platform to
a line of shouting people. Zina gripped Camille's hand. Through
the shifting legs, Camille witnessed Mayme fling her arms around

a man dressed in gray wearing a gray hat with a white band. His teeth gleamed under his thick mustache. They turned and came toward the girls. Mayme's face sparkled with tears. Backing away, Camille almost tripped onto the track, but the man's long arms reached down and rescued her. She wiggled away from him and hid behind Mayme's legs.

"Say hello to your father, honey," Mayme prompted her. *Father.* The word to her was like ocean or sky, something that was vast and undiscoverable—heaven, hell. Camille shrank away, but Zina kissed the man and let him pick her up. The little girl lagged behind as he led the way through the crowd.

That was fifteen years ago when Camille was a six-year-old girl from the *old country*. The train station in Uniontown was no longer used. Since then her father had moved his business from there to McClellandtown, Zina had married, and Uncle Elias had become a priest. Those hills that had looked so green to her on the train became Camille's territory.

Behind her home in McClellandtown, she ran through the woods until they opened to a grassy meadow. Lying atop the hill with the blades sticking up around her, she sang, flopping one leg over her knee and jerking it up and down to a rhythm. A bird called from a high branch, and Camille searched for it. The sun burned through the tops of the branches, and when the bird flew away, his wing threw gold back to the sun.

Sometimes Zina joined Camille in her outdoor games, but the older sister was more serious. She read and wrote a great deal. Even at night when Camille tried to sleep, Zina's light kept her tossing and covering her head. She warned she would tell. Zina had been scolded for reading that late. Zina took her sister's arm and read to her from the novel. Outside their door, their parents

recited the rosary. Through the window they heard crickets and
frogs filling the night with chirps and bellows. The sisters whispered and they made a tent by draping their blanket over the head-
board. Camille held a flashlight and Zina read. Eventually they
fell to sleep with the lamp shining between them.

Her father's business changed with each new idea. He and Elias
planned a conversion from general goods to a confectionery; a restaurant, then a dry-goods store. But no matter how successful or
unsuccessful they were, the Nader house was always busy. Elias
had many friends, and he gave parties that would last late into the
night. The guests often were invited to stay, and they were given
the girls' beds. When the girls rose in the morning, they found
their father in his brother's room and overnight guests in the halls.
Mayme's face was heavy from fatigue, and she spoke briefly to the
girls as they performed their chores and dressed for mass. They
left the house alone and walked over the hill to St. Francis's, long
before anyone else arrived. When the bells rang, their mother,
father, and uncle slid into the pew beside them.

After Uncle Elias went to the old country to become a priest,
fewer men spent the night in the store. Many things changed. The
business concentrated on dry goods, rather than Elias's special
confections. A seamstress was hired to make the dresses, and she
had books of patterns and pictures Camille could choose from. She
missed Elias, who could fashion her a velvet dress from his imag-
ination—the skirt flared into folds and the top with its wide strip
of lace resembled a bolero.

Zina went to Lebanon with Elias, intending to become a doctor.
Instead she married her first cousin Boutros, Rachid's oldest son—
as was expected—and abandoned her studies. Camille was anxious for her sister's return. Her father's health was declining, and

Camille spent all her time working in the store, driving the truck, and serving in the beer garden. It was a dreary life and very lonely. She could barely remember her trips to the meadow. And when her sister came finally, with her husband and daughter . . . these are the things Camille is not putting in her diary.

She lies across her bed in a cabin she shares with her parents on the ship, *Il Conte di Avoa,* and writes the word "Escape" at the top of a blank page. They are going to Lebanon. Camille has left McClellandtown at last. Maybe forever.

"Go and catch a falling star . . ." What was the rest of it? She had heard it recently, though she could not remember where. Ummi? *Go and catch a falling star.* Perhaps she had learned it in school and just now remembered it, or maybe Zina had been reciting it to the children. *Go and catch a falling star.* Her sister wrote stories more than poetry—little stories of young girls traveling through many countries. She inserted French words into her dialogue and described Marseilles and Paris. Her high school teachers had encouraged her to send them to publications. She chose the *Syrian World* in New York City. Camille might submit some poems there someday, although she never wrote any of her own. (Go and catch a falling star.)

Right before Camille left McClellandtown, her cousin Nora held a party for her. Camille stood at the door surprised by the number of guests, the large cake, her name printed in icing.

Of all the parties they had held in Uniontown and McClellandtown, that was the only one given for Camille. The night she graduated from high school, she walked alone up the long hill to the auditorium carrying her gray gown and cap over her arm. The white taffeta dress had been worn by her sister four years before. Zina was an academic student and attended every day. When she graduated, her party filled every room in the house and part of the store with visitors.

The diary was a gift from Uncle Elias. Camille promised to write in it every day. It was a small book that closed with a zipper. She started that night: *July 25, 1935. Dear Diary: This is a funny time to begin a diary, but a farewell party was held for me tonight. My cousins Rosie, George, and Nora Nader held a party for me in Nora's house. Everyone from our town was there. Also Johnny Hannah, Tony Hannah, Sara Rogers, and some outsiders. I had a good time and received some presents. There was a very large and beautiful cake. "Bon Voyage Camille" was inscribed upon it. Punch and other liquors were served. I had on a black dotted satin dress with a Queen Elizabeth collar. Very slenderizing. No one from our family but me went.*

Shebl, Mayme, and Camille went to New York ten days before their ship was scheduled to leave. When they boarded the train in Connellsville, their new station, the porter told them short-distance passengers had to stand because the train was so full. By explaining that her father was sick, Camille secured herself, her mother, and her father a back row with seats facing one another. Here she saw the sights she remembered from when she first arrived in America and crossed Pennsylvania fifteen years before. But this time she was not nervous and she leaned toward the window when the train curled around a horseshoe bend, and she was not surprised when farmhouses seemed to rise up as the train descended the hills of the Alleghenies.

They visited friends in the Bronx and Brooklyn before they embarked—all people from the old country. Camille looked at the women who ran these households, and they resembled each other with their long lined necks, sharp chins and noses. The women's eyes were underlined in gray shadows like Mayme's, and they wore rouge smeared in circles over their sleek cheekbones. They looked distracted, as if they were always remembering something important, someone to look after. Gold chains lay against their olive skin like string, and their bangles sat in little fallen rings by the sink, on the table, or tucked behind the juicer on the counter. A smell lingered in the houses, a mustiness, no matter how big or small, as if everything were just brought down from the attic and set out for display.

In Torrington, Connecticut, the family stayed in a large house that had a flower garden. Camille couldn't imagine all that work put in digging and weeding for something that couldn't be eaten. Her feet had sunk into the muddy ruts of their vegetable patch behind the store in McClellandtown as she tended the tomatoes, scallions, beans, and squash. She was proud of the rows of food that would be picked and put in mason jars on the pantry shelves. Humming, Camille picked, seeded, hoed, and tilled. She stuck her hair under a cap and wore heavy overshoes. The dirt smelled wonderful and felt like flour in her hands. She let it cascade to the ground.

To walk among the flowers of her hostess, Camille put on a sunback dress. She felt an urge to recite Ophelia, but she could only remember Portia. Too sad, *quality of mercy* and all that. A stone path curved through the garden of flowers to a trellis wrapped in roses roofing a wooden swing. She removed her hat and fanned herself. Peonies covered with ants swayed near her legs. She liked the high flowers: peonies and irises. She wanted to fill her arms with them and lay them across her bed—a purple-and-white blanket. Maybe not—too much like a coffin.

The host ran out to talk to her, to see if she needed anything. She practiced a distant smile. Would you like to go to the church with us? "Yes, I would love to see it."

They departed from the pink house and the older women dressed in black as if the garden had never existed. Camille watched them walk together whispering out of earshot of the men. Her father marched along with them, looking healthier and brighter. The sun was strong and Camille thought, *Tomorrow will be August; I leave in August.* They stopped on the street and talked to a few people, who were introduced to Camille. Most turned to her father and said, "Your daughter is lovely." A thought he probably did not have or believe. He responded, "Yes, she is a good girl. We're taking her to Lebanon with us."

"To get married?"

Everyone smiled, even Camille, who was wishing she had worn a brimmed hat in the hot sun—her linen beret barely covered her head. A girl at twenty-one hears that question and others: Not married yet? Why isn't a beautiful girl like you married? Everyone had plans for her, but she didn't think about them. She wanted to leave McClellandtown, that's all she knew. Too old, too tired, too fat, too lonely. *The quality of mercy.*

Zina, Boutros, and her parents also had talked together about Camille's marriage. Everyone in Lebanon had agreed that she should meet Jean or one of Boutros's other brothers. Tall, dark, and handsome, her sister winked. Jean wears a thin mustache, just back from Brazil, devoted to his mother.

Go and catch a falling star. Camille does not want to write in her diary now. She releases the bedspread from the little ball she had gathered in her fist and pats it smooth. Rising from the bed, she examines her face in the mirror, then goes on deck. She leans against the rail with one hand and gazes out to sea. The wind whips her hair around her face, and her white skirt clings to her legs. The water tosses tiny blue currents. Is this a scene she saw in a movie, or a passage from a book by Henry James? Camille wonders how she looks standing at the rail next to a life preserver that reads *Il Conte di Avoa.* Is her face turned just right? Does her white chiffon blouse flutter enough to show her figure well? She pushes her chestnut curls off her wide forehead and looks toward the water.

Zina is the one, Camille thinks, who always strikes a pose. She stood in a doorway, one hand on the frame, as visitors arrived. Before serving dinner she paused with the steaming platter in her hands, until the guests looked up at her and exclaimed, "Oh, that looks wonderful!" Camille stayed in the kitchen until everyone was seated, ran out after they had begun eating, wiping her wet arms on her apron.

On the *Conte de Avoa,* Camille travels without her sister, and although her parents are aboard, she feels luckily alone. Camille looks down at her short stocky thumb curling around the ship's banister. Her hands are prematurely wrinkled, like those of the field workers who bought tobacco in their store. Their tanned, lined hands dropped change onto the counter. Dirt filled their nails. Camille examines her small hands and thick fingers. As a child she sat on Uncle Elias's lap and placed her palm against his. He closed his long fingers over hers, and she wiggled to free herself. They haven't grown much since then, it seems.

Zina and Mayme have long slim hands that fill gloves to the tips.

They wear rings with large stones. When they brush a hair away from their faces, their red nails shine like jewels against their cheeks. "You have your father's hands," Mayme said once as Camille swept the emery board upward. Yes, she knew, and she understood why they looked so old too. She massages them with heavy creams, but just the same, the skin cracks around the nails.

From her other hand, a hat flops against her hip. What Camille likes about standing on deck is she can hear no one. The water rushing beside the ship and the drone of the engine drown out conversation. Some people stop to look at what she sees—the table of water, the wall of sky—or they bend and watch the ocean rise to let the ship through.

Camille takes out her handkerchief and pats the droplets forming above her lips. Maybe she is a little dizzy. She backs away from the rail and sits in a chair and shuts her eyes. People pass and she hears their voices but keeps her eyes closed. (Get steady, girl, you've been doing well so far.)

"There you are!"

Camille lifts the brim of her hat. "Hi, Mary." Her companion stands before her.

Mary sits in the striped canvas chair beside her. "I expected to find you in your cabin, writing letters."

Camille had met Mary d'Orsi at the beginning of the trip in the dining room as they waited by the maître d's desk. The d'Orsis invited the Naders to join them. Mary stuck out her hand and introduced herself. After dinner the two girls strolled the deck together four or five times, eyeing each other's clothes and imagining that each time they walked into the dining room, they created a stir.

"I saw your parents; your mother looked a little sick."

"*Mal de mer*, of course. It was too hot in the cabin, so I came up."

Mary nods and leans back. Together they survey the passengers. Women walk by in bathing costumes, and the girls glance at each other. Mary giggles and lifts her book to cover her face. Pulling her skirt over her knees, Camille turns her head. The deck is crowded with "hat-wearers," she observes—men in ribboned white fedoras smoke pipes, women's large brims bounce like gulls practicing flight. Camille's hat has a small round crown and barely shades her face. Occasional laughter in French, Italian, and Greek streams by; a shriek draws her eyes toward the swimming pool and a young man whispering in the ear of an older women in a long gown. Arrows of sun bounce from the jewelry of two people standing near the rail and flashes on Camille's face. For a moment, she becomes hypnotized by the spark. "What are you thinking about, Lily?" Mary leans forward. "Robert, I'll guess."

The two girls spent the previous night dancing to a live band in the lounge. As they waited for the perfect table at the edge of the dance floor, Camille shifted from one foot to the other. She became very warm as the couples floated by. Camille and her sister had learned to do Brazilian dances and all types of waltzes and steps, but they were not allowed to go to the "balls" sponsored by their high school.

"I would have believed you were the most popular girl in school." Mary holds her knee.

"Why?"

"Oh, I don't know. You dance so well and you dress grandly, and you write so many letters."

Camille lowers her eyes. She graduated high school four years before as a commercial student. She had imagined herself as a nurse—like Mrs. Bayly on the *Ship of Hope*—but for that she had to have an academic record, something she could not achieve when her attendance was reduced to three times a week, then once a week.

"What did you do instead? Work?" Mary has already told Camille about the private Catholic school she lived in for four years.

"I drove the truck—the delivery truck for the store." In the winter, Camille wrapped her legs in blankets because a draft blew up her dress through the missing floorboards of the cab. Wool stockings barely protected her. Underneath her coat she had layered two sweaters and two large scarves. Frost shaded, then coated the window and she had to scrape it inside and outside as she bumped along the dirt roads of Fayette and Greene counties. The truck whined and she shifted and pulled it up a long hill. When the cattle grazed near the houses, she knew the farmer expected a rough winter. A gust rattled the windows, though she cranked them shut. She spoke aloud, recited everything she knew: the Pledge of Allegiance, the Preamble, the Declaration of Independence, and poetry—her favorite. Occasionally she let the truck veer on the empty road as she rubbed her blanched hands together. And Camille cried—when she couldn't move her feet anymore; when she needed to go to the bathroom, but couldn't bear to undress in the cold air.

She would have preferred going to school, being with boys and girls, staying warm, but she forgot that when the mountains floated blue beside her on a dewy morning or she had to screech to a stop because a calf had wandered to the richer grass beyond the fence. Poetry rolled out of her like her own name, the names of her family, the places she lived. In the crisp cool morning of a Pennsylvania sunrise, she spoke it with the windows down so she would not fog them: "Gather ye rosebuds while ye may, / Old Time is still a-flying; / And this same flower that smiles today / Tomorrow will be dying."

"You are my best friend now," Camille tells Mary d'Orsi, a girl whose hair is short and who wears a black camisole under a white blouse. *Best friends*, a phrase Camille associates with the girls at school who dressed nearly alike and fussed with each other's hair in the powder room. They ran together in the halls and shared lunches. Camille imagined long passages of love covering pages of her autograph book by some devoted best friend.

"I know you'll write to me." Mary pulls her glasses down onto her nose and laughs. "You love words—a real four-eyes, like me."

"Do you know," Camille sits up, "what my very first English word was?"

"Mother?"

"Huh-uh, listen, this is funny. My sister went to school long before I did, so I got to play all day long with these girls Jeannette and Annie, the Esper sisters. We were the Nader sisters, they were the Esper sisters. We played in the field, on the roads, and in the store, until we were chased outside."

She crosses her legs and covers her mouth. "This is so embarrassing; I can't believe it."

"Go on." Mary looks off into the crowd.

"Yes, there were these pilings, you see, with a word painted on the side of them. I said, 'Jeannette, what is this word, I want to learn English.' She said, 'Fuck.' Then laughed, and Annie laughed too. I didn't know why. I repeated it all the way back to the house so I wouldn't forget it. I knew how to spell it and I practiced how to write it. Then my sister saw it in my notebook and screamed; she told my mother and my father. I got a good beating."

Mary stares at Camille. What's wrong? Camille's face reddens and begins to feel warm. She had covered her mouth and whispered the word. Maybe she shouldn't have said anything, or have called it the F word as the other girls did. "Why, I didn't know English wasn't your original tongue." Mary's eyes examine Camille's face. "We had a girl in our school from the 'old country,' and she sounded positively foreign, like my papa, but you, I don't know, you seem straight-up American to me."

Camille flops back. "I came over when I was very, very young." Camille's stomach seems to rise against her dress; she feels as if it will break through. "I have to go down and lie down—I suppose I have a little *mal de mer* myself." She pats her waist. "See you at dinner."

"Definitely." Mary stabs her hair with her sunglasses. "And then we'll go to the dance, if we can."

"Definitely."

The cabin would probably be empty. Her parents go to the salon to play cards or eat. They have some friends on board as well—others going back to the old country. She opens the shutter on the porthole which looks out onto a deck. They never had quarters like this before: four beds and a desk and two chairs.

Maids and porters see to their room every day. When Camille enters, she finds a dark-haired, dark-eyed woman pulling the sheets on the bed. Camille tries to talk to the woman as she cleans. Is she Italian? The maid does not answer. Camille watches her until she leaves. The cabin is boring. Camille stands quickly. She doesn't feel very sick or tired. She pulls her skirt down and brushes her hair. After rummaging through a drawer she finds a rosary and wraps it around her wrist like a bracelet and puts the cross inside her closed hand. *The church is called a chapel*, she told her sister in a letter. It is quite small but very beautiful. She places a lace veil over her hair and enters. A few passengers sit in the light wood pews with a cross carved into the side. She genuflects in the center aisle and sits at the end of a row. Camille drops her head and counts off the beads with prayers, alternating between English and Arabic. When she reaches the mystery of the visitation, Mary to Elizabeth, she notices her hands are gloveless. Slowly she withdraws them from sight and places them in the folds of her skirts. The air becomes heavy and enclosing. She glances around: most of the people are gone, except for one young man near the front who holds a book between his hands. She forgets her prayers and continues to stare at him as he rises and turns, catching her eye. *What's wrong with me?* She drops her eyes again, looks at the darkness between her body and the pew in front. She feels him pause beside her, then move on.

The girls meet again at dinner. Nothing is changed; Mary talks on about how wonderful the pink accessories are with Camille's white dress. She saw Bob and he wondered if Camille would be at the dance tonight and Mary said of course. Camille smiles and drinks her water.

The next morning Camille stands on deck for at least half an hour hoping Robert will appear. She has washed out the striped sunback dress that he complimented the day they met, curled her hair, and put on her white open-toed shoes.

Camille leans against the rain with her face toward water and lifts her head in the breeze. As lunchtime approaches, fewer passengers stroll the deck. Two older French women knit and chatter near the door. A dog scoots by and the women pause, watch it turn the corner, then return to the handiwork and their conversation. Camille hums "My Bonnie Lies over the Ocean," but can't hear her notes for the water's roar. When the man she saw in the church walks toward her, she is examining someone at the other end with a gray hat who may be Robert.

"You don't know how hot August is when you stand on deck." He watches the loose strands of hair blow around her face. Camille's cheeks feel warm, and she pushes her hair behind her ears.

"No, but the cabins are hot." She doesn't look up at him as he speaks.

"Do you have a fan?"

"Yes, yes we do, but unless I sit right in front of it, I don't feel any cooler."

"I am Joseph Maese; I hope I am not bothering you. Were you waiting for someone?"

"No one," she says quietly. "I am Camille Nader; I am traveling with my parents."

"Where are you going?" Joseph moves to her other side to get a glimpse of her face.

She raises her head. "Beirut, Lebanon. My father is sick and is going home."

"To either heal or die." He glances down. He holds a book in one hand and rubs its leather cover with the other one.

His comment startles Camille. For the last few days, in the salon and the lounge, she has chatted about clothes and France and food. Mary and Robert and Richard laughed as she told stories of her cow and her delivery route. (Never at a loss for words.) This man has light brown hair and copper face; his gray eyes stare steadily at her through his round gold-framed glasses. He wears a brown suit, a little formal, she thinks, for the morning.

The boat rocks, and he puts his hand beside her arm on the rail. "Where are you going?" she asks.

"To Khartoum. Do you know it?"

"Yes, of course, the Sudan." Straightening her back, she crosses her arms over her chest. "You connect at Cairo, I would imagine."

"That's true." Joseph pivots and points toward the chairs the knitters had occupied. "Would you like to sit down?"

Camille steps over and sits upright in the chair closest to the door and holds her purse with both hands. After he joins her, he places the book on the table between them.

She twists her head to read the title. "I read *The Canterbury Tales* in school, a long time ago."

"Did you like them?"

"I am afraid I thought they were quite long, and I don't remember them; I suppose I should try again." She rests her back against the canvas sling.

"You would like them; they are better when you read them as an adult. Some are quite funny." He opens the book and searches until he reaches "The Monk's Tale" and begins to read.

Camille remembers well the week the junior class studied *The Canterbury Tales*—the monotonous voices of her peers reading the lines like a foreign language. Their book *British Masterpieces* was too thick to read without holding it open with both hands, and the illustrations were flat gray portrayals of a medieval priest, maiden, and clerk. She wasn't quite sure what it meant to be a clerk in Chaucer's time, but she knew that it was not a job for women. All clerks that she knew were women, and she was the main one at Nader's Dry Goods.

British Masterpieces sat like a rock on the end of the shirt case. All week long she stayed in the store and worked around it, dusting the boxes, refolding the towels, and ironing the shirts and pants to perfection.

Shebl returned from the wholesalers in the middle of the week. "Unpack these, price them, and put them on the shelves." White towels, fifty-nine cents; white sheets, three dollars. Two tall piles. She worked all evening and afternoon, writing as neatly as possible on the little white tags. She looked up to find him staring at her. He was drumming his fingers on the top of her English text. She scrutinized the table—everything looked perfect.

"No." He pushed the neatly arranged pile over, sending all the sheets onto the floor. "Five fifty-nine for the sheets," he shouted.

Bending, she gathered them as they lay by the toes of his black shiny shoes. He did not move as she picked them up. She rubbed her glasses and she started to mark them all one by one.

She would not be going to school the next day either. They had already sent a letter home with her asking about the absences. Since Zina left, Shebl was not very interested in the school. He said nothing to Camille, and she stuck the letter in her book and pushed it across the table. For now she was trying to figure out the store's account. The bank had sent a statement, and Camille sat down with the ledger as usual. Placing little marks under "Debit," as she was taught in accounting class, she saw that everything matched: gas, oil, milk, salaries, merchandise. Yet forty dollars was missing. She added the columns again, looking at the statement and listing everything on a separate sheet of paper. Two hundred and twenty-two dollars was her sum, but the bank showed one hundred and eighty-two. It was hopeless. She would have to ask her father about it.

Shebl glared at her across the table after she told him. Her voice cracked as she said, "I don't know what happened to the money."

"I know where it is, girl," he whispered. "You have it."

Camille jumped up. "What?" Blinking, she tried not to cry, "What would I do with it?"

"Where is the money?" he shouted at her. "Where is it?" Grabbing her by the shoulders, he shook her. Her glasses flew off and tears streaked her cheeks. She could not speak.

Mayme shouted, "Leave her alone, Shebl, she will tell."

Camille turned toward her mother and put out her empty hand; she opened her mouth. Grabbing his hunting gun, he leveled it at Camille. "Tell me where the money is." He pressed forward and put the barrel on her chest, and she backed into the wall. "You are nothing but a gypsy with your American friends and ways and your disgusting clothes." His eyes turned to black studs riveting her to the wall. Her chin dripped with tears and her breathing became shallow.

Mayme yanked the gun from her husband's hand. "No!" she screamed.

"You are as bad as she is," he yelled at his wife. Then he spit on the floor and walked out of the house.

Camille sank to the floor and cried into her apron, but the voice continued around and around her head. She could not stand his voice after that.

When Zina and Boutros arrived from Lebanon that spring, Shebl and her brother-in-law investigated the problem. The check for forty dollars had been written by Zina in Lebanon. Of course, why hadn't he thought of it. Zina, Boutros, and Shebl laughed.

That year her father's stomach tore up inside and bled. Rumblings in the night. Camille slept with a wet cloth over her eyes. She often imagined herself with severe headaches and excused herself from the dinner table. Then her sister called out, "Come back to do the dishes." Camille stood in profile, then walked away.

The dirt road to the high school passed in front of the store. Letting the door slam, Camille began to climb the path she knew so well. She wasn't particularly fond of the school, but the walk passed by the house with the low white corral fence near the road. The front lawn was flowerless and neatly trimmed; the house stood alone. At Christmastime, a candle burned in each of the sixteen windows, clearing a circle in the frost on the glass. Sixteen perfect stars. Lights that radiated around baby Jesus. Now in February only a distant glow shined from an upstairs window. Camille crossed the road and looked up, but she could see no one up there. She never did—not around the house or the new dairy buildings at the foot of the hill. A steeper hill rose from the creek. Jerseys and Holsteins climbed out of the water and walked parallel to Camille until she reached the top. The wind scrambled her hair and dress. Pulling her coat around her, she hooked the collar and shoved her hands into her pockets. The patch of woods across the valley where they had picked their blueberries as children looked brown and thorny without leaves. A gray sky settled on the mess of trees and shrubs across the silent highway, as if the whole world were deserted.

Camille inhaled and then curtsied to the valley and began to sing a song she was teaching Zina's daughter. "I am always chasing rainbows . . ." Her voice held the last note, and she cocked her head slightly. What was the next line?

This was silly; she knew the song. A line of geese overhead curled into a vee with one side shorter than the other. Camille

lifted her head and watched them. *I'm always chasing rainbows.*
She lingered for a minute more, then stomped down the valley
toward the school. Inside her coat, her body sweated; her face felt
cold and she breathed little clouds. Leaning against the blond bricks
of German Township High School, Camille closed her eyes. What
had the science teacher taught them about condensation? She
couldn't remember anything: songs, science, poems. Another
headache. She would go directly to sleep after the dishes; she didn't
care what needed to be done. They could take care of their own
children and the store. (They would pay back what they borrowed,
her mother told her.) Camille placed her hot hands on her face and
warmed her cheeks. On her return she wondered if her left leg
didn't drag a little.

Camille wiped her hands and opened the jar of Pacquins she
kept beside the sink. "If you wore gloves, your hands wouldn't be
so chapped." Her sister stood at the entrance of the kitchen with
her hair rolled and tied for the night; her tall thin frame was a little
puffy at the stomach. "How about some Turkish coffee?"

Camille wiped the already clean table. "No thank you, I don't
like it, it's too strong."

"I want a cup, and so does B. Maybe Mom and Dad too." She
left the kitchen.

Camille pulled the brass urn from the shelf over the sink, mea-
sured the dark grounds into the bottom, then poured water into it.
She watched the coffee through the narrow mouth of the pot. Boutros and Shebl were playing backgammon in the parlor. Their voices
rolled with the dice and mingled with Mayme's quiet conversation.

The women worked on something colorful, she imagined: a border on a pillow looped in pink and blue flowers or some embroidery
on a white blouse, golden angels or an ocean with tiny sailboats

lost in the blue lines. When the coffee boiled she lifted it from the fire, then lowered it for the second boil, measuring the sugar she would add before the third.

She sat with her mother and sister and worked a pattern on a tablecloth, but could not concentrate. Zina laughed, reminding Camille of their childhood nights trying to learn Arabic, how she always looked off into another part of the room, as if another world was there. Her mother added more stories of her daughter's capers and near-disappearances. Camille listened as if they spoke of someone she didn't know. She glanced at each item in the room: chair, window, vase.

A man she had been introduced to at the church dinner visited her one night. He was very polite and called her Miss Nader. They stood in the store as he asked after the health of each of her family and she replied. He complimented her dress and hair, and she smiled and looked down at the blue skirt she wore. The man drifted around the store as they spoke, looking into the cases and on the shelves. He had a business himself, something to do with automobiles.

"That's a beautiful necklace." He pointed to a string of clustered beads in the showcase near the register.

Camille glanced down at a set she had admired for its bluish tint. She pulled them out to show him. He held them up to the light. "They would look beautiful with your eyes." He slid a small framed mirror to her. "Here, let's try them." Camille watched them dropping onto her blue blouse. He lifted the bottom of her hair and fidgeted with the clasp.

"What is going on here?" Boutros entered from the back, shouting.

Camille froze, continued to stare at her neck.

Boutros approached her friend and pulled the necklace from his hand.

"But Mr. Abi-Nader, I want to buy her this necklace."

"You will buy nothing." Boutros pushed the man's shoulders. "Get out of here and don't return."

"Stop," she screamed. "He was only trying it on me."

"Of course." Boutros turned at her. "What next?"

"Mr. Abi-Nader—" Camille's friend held his hat.

"Get out of here and never come back again." Boutros shoved him through the door and shut it.

He had no right, she thought. Sometimes when she was busy in the store, Boutros came up behind her and pushed his body against her, put his hands on her arms, shoulders, and neck. Once Zina walked in and nearly lost her baby in her convulsions. She called Camille horrible names. (How many times.)

Zina's return had not brought relief for Camille, only more work. Camille cared for her sister's children, worked in the store and beer garden, cleaned the house, and Boutros shouted at her too. His voice blasted, "The dresses all need to be ironed again," or "Bring me some water." He assumed control of the business and of Camille.

Mayme and Shebl had become residents of their bedroom. Since Shebl's ulcer was perforated and he could barely participate in the work, Mayme cared for him and watched her children through the door, and listened through the walls. She had nothing to say.

When her Uncle Elias came to visit from his parish in New Castle, Camille cried. "Why are Zina and Boutros like that, Uncle?

They took all my money, they tell me what to do, day in and day out. I am not allowed to have friends to the house, especially boys. I want to be something other than a servant. My sister screams at me—cook, clean, fold, press. She doesn't think I am worth anything. She forced me to take dressmaking. I am a miserable seamstress, but I go to be away from them. I wish we were alone. I wish you were with us."

Elias sat in his priest's robe. He wore thick glasses to read, and his once bushy red hair had turned all gray. Camille loved him more than anyone in the world. Years ago he had taken her out in her pajamas to look at the northern lights; she thought they were always in his eyes after that. When an eclipse came, he broke Nehi bottles for them to look through. The broken glass was a jewel to her, a way into the secret of the heavens. The science teacher told the class no one could look directly at the eclipse. Oh, but her uncle knew a way you would not, could not, go blind. Was she bragging that they had soda pop in her store?

Or had she said beer garden? Yes, the Naders had one, and Camille worked in it, though she told no one. After the dinner dishes were done, she waited on customers until closing at two in the morning. Back and forth from the tables to the icebox. The customers were a quiet card-playing crowd who talked politics and related stories of the old country. She sat at a table near the kitchen on quiet nights and read her lessons. Sometimes she felt each second of the clock move from one eye to the other, and she fell into a daze. They called her Lily. (Lily!)

Camille cried in her sleep. Poetry flew from her head when she tried to recall a line or a verse. Her cousin Nora was engaged; the Esper girls married. Camille stood in the store during supper waiting for customers, and she caught her reflection in the window of the front door. Everything behind her faded, and her figure, isolated, hung in the dark.

"Go to Lebanon with your parents," her uncle advised.

"Ummi, do you think they would let me?"

"Your mother will need help; your father is very ill. I don't think they will have a choice."

It was a wonderful idea, and Camille stayed awake the entire night dreaming of her escape. When she milked the cow in the next morning grayness, she curled her back, then released it; she tried to remember where she had put her glasses. She spoke softly to the cow (had she seen them?); she stroked its bristly hide as she worked. Before Camille went to fetch the water, she stared into the eyes of the animal. "God grant you a pleasant day, my dear."

Camille spends the entire day and evening with him, Joseph Maese, a literature professor at the American College in the Sudan. When he stops and points at a fin rising from the current or at a constellation, he reminds her of her Uncle Elias and the northern lights. She tells him about her uncle and his long career as a playwright, costumer, salesman, rubber trader, actor, and finally a priest. As the night breezes cool them, she pulls Joseph's brown striped jacket around her shoulders while they walk the deck another time and another. And the next day and the next. *August 14, 1935. Parting today, kissed on the gangway.* He promised he would write.

Two days later their ship approaches Beirut. Camille stays in her cabin, staring into the mirror at her round face and crown of brown hair. She raises her brush but then drops it. Camille rocks and then steadies herself until she is able to sit down. *(Go and catch a falling star.)* The porter knocks on the door. "Miss Nader," he calls, "may I get your bags now?"

Camille blinks. "Yes," she whispers, then shouts, "Yes, come in!" As Camille follows the man out of the room, she remembers finally the whole poem to the very last verse. "Though she were true, when you met her, / And last, till you write your letter, / Yet she / Will be / False, ere I come, to two, or three."

◆

CHAPTER TWELVE

Sunflowers

◆

C a m i l l e

1937

G et with child a mandrake root. Camille writes looking from her father's house into the shadowy valley.

*8 July 1937. Dear Sis, Thank you for the pattern you sent along. I don't get into Beirut much, but would like to. They are hard to find. I appreciate having such grand outfits to make. I wish I could sew as well as you do. Mother will help me. She needs things to keep her busy; she misses Father so much. I have been ill and I am showing quite a bit now....*What can she put in these letters now?

Nothing happens except for the swelling of her body: stomach, hands, feet. The constant nausea, the fights. The whispering in church. Like the roll of a drum behind her, voices ra-tat-tatting; faces hidden behind hands, and women pointing with their eyes. She and Jean don't dare arrive late or sit too close to the front or back. Bodies shift around her to greet her husband and to turn away from her and Mayme.

The thing I dislike about being pregnant is not being able to work with Jean (I've started to call him Johnnie and teach him English). I miss going into the fields.

When she came to Abdelli, the fair girl from the States worked like a boy in the fields: planting tobacco, plowing and hoeing the ground until the sun paralyzed her and she stood dripping with perspiration, unable to move.

"Take her home, Jean, put her to bed, she's ill," a brother's voice commanded. Stopping on the road, she vomited and fell near his boots. His arms circled her and held her. "Should I carry you?"

"No, I can walk." She leaned against him. His clothes were soaked through too. She was afraid he was too thin to support her, but she fell into his arms and he squeezed her.

Standing on the balcony, Camille watches them work the hard dry ground. Jean hoists a basket onto his shoulders and walks it to the cart. Camille does not want to move, although she knows she must go to her mother-in-law's house; she must help her to thank her, she has been reminded. For what? Camille wondered. "We fed you after your father died." Oh, yes. A week or two of lentils and rice on three plates, delivered by a grandchild. Some bread, dates, yogurt.

She returns to the table. *I don't have to take the medicine anymore*, she writes. What else? Details of the planting seem dull. What should she really say? That the fights with Elmaz were subsiding, that when she enters her house, she reports directly to the kitchen? That their mother has not left the harra since their father died? That Mayme prays day and night—crying and shaking in her bed? Camille rises and walks across the parlor; above her the white painted clouds of their fading mural flake away. The chandelier has been replaced by a lantern on a long cord. She enters her mother's room and finds a sleeping Mayme throwing her body back and forth, knotting the sheets. "Mom." Camille touches the thin bony arm. "Mommy." Mayme sinks back quickly, becomes quiet again, breathing through her mouth.

Back at the desk, Camille seals the letter and places it inside her diary. Her script, the Palmer method learned in the fourth grade, fills the small lined pages of her diary. When she first got it, she described in great detail what she wore and ate, and whom she met. The longer she lived in Lebanon the fewer sentences she wrote; they finally became abbreviations and thoughts, dropped onto a page, underlined by a prayer. *Mary pray for me. Jesus, Mary, and Joseph.* That's not what she wants to write. *People die, people marry.*

Washed a large wash, received patterns, letters, etc., from Sis, all grand. Soldier came to vacation at Shiban house tonight. Jesus, Mary, Joseph, have mercy on us.

In March, while she was sick, losing blood and dizzy, Jean wrote in her diary for her. His looping Arabic curled half on and off the lines. She could barely read it. Laying down her pen, she flips to the pages written in English. If they had lived in Beirut, her neighbors would know English too. But no one in the village speaks it well. Even her father returned solely to Arabic. English belonged to the sisters and for a while, her diary. (Oh Sis.)

Before Shebl died, every evening he and Jean discussed the possible crops and yields they would get if they started to work the land right away. Tobacco would be the highest money-maker, then olive oil, and figs. The two men had lived in countries where plows ripped through hillsides and corn reached the edge of every road. Shebl described the American farmer circling the fields on tractors, filling in the creeks and setting fences—no waste—corn, wheat, potatoes, and beans as far as he could see. Jean reminded him of Brazil—the rubber and coffee plantations of Brazil—hillsides of leafy shrubs. They brought with them to Abdelli an imported enthusiasm. Rachid said no one would be interested in the land. His sons schooled in Beirut.

Jean would work it alone, he declared, and when everyone saw how successful he was, they would help. Shebl cheered him, and Camille volunteered. She wanted to work outside, not in the kitchens. Standing next to Jean, passing bushels to him, she could get to know him better. After a day of working, they walked back to the house together. "Did you know when you were born two thousand people lived in Abdelli?"

"Really?" She leaned against him as they sat beside a brown creek. "How many now?"

"About seven hundred."

"What happened to them all?"

He massaged her arms. "Emigration. Like you and your father and me, and others who had no money here; who knew that the cash flowed in the Americas."

"Why aren't we rich then?" She looked up at his chin. He was closely shaven, and some powder lightened his jaws.

"We will be. I will get this land into high production soon." He would do what he had to. Camille trusted him, and if they did marry, she would be safe.

After the harvest, Jean moved to Beirut to work in a bicycle shop. Camille was pleased, because Beirut was the only place in Lebanon she really liked. When she and her parents entered the harbor two years before, the city hadn't looked anything like she remembered. The coast had filled with apartments and hotels. Restaurants lined the shore, some built out into the water on little piers. Large private boats with tall masts stood—their shadows like the crosses of telephone poles fell across her path as she was pulled from the craft that brought them from the ship. Camille, Shebl, and Mayme waited on the dock and stared into the crowd. Everyone looked so sunny to her. Women with large-brimmed hats and thin dresses pulled old parents toward them. Motorcars waited in the street. She could be in France.

While her father talked to customs officials, their luggage was placed beside them. Mayme led them through the crowd to the end of the dock. Walking into the street, Shebl looked both ways. When he returned, he picked up the baggage and carried it to the corner, then waved for a taxi. They wound through the narrow streets, looking for a hotel. Camille stared in front of her. The buildings' shadows overlapped. The sunny shore lay at her back as if she were traveling through a tunnel and would emerge on the other side of the mountain and would soon be surrounded by green pasture with the black-and-white cows from the Pennsylvania hills. Instead they entered a darker building, a hotel Shebl remembered. Both rooms smelled of urine and alcohol; Mayme wiped the furniture with a damp towel before she allowed anyone to unpack. Shebl made calls from the lobby. The family would come the next afternoon. In the bedroom away from the excited conversations, Camille wrote: *Landed in Beirut. No one met us. Lots of trouble, slept in an awful hotel.*

When the family arrived the next day, Jean was with them.

Friday, August 15, 1935. Folks arrived in the afternoon. He answers description. No like him. Squinting his eyes, he held a cigarette between his thumb and forefinger, and his skin shone in a dark glaze. Someone might say Arabi instead of Libnani and Jean would mind very much.

The family went to live in Abdelli until Shebl's condition became worse. When he had to return to the hospital, Camille returned with him to Beirut and stayed with her cousins. They took her to the American University, where she sat in the rooted lap of a large tree. They pointed out the cinemas that specialized in films from Hollywood. Gary Cooper's name was on the marquee at the Ciné Clemenceau. She toured the *hamra* and its French boutiques, and the *bourj*, which served as a central crossing place and harbored the entrance into the souq, the open market.

But usually in Beirut, she strolled as if she carried a parasol and had nothing to do. She watched the Muslims in striped galabiyas remove their shoes outside the mosques. The archways under which they passed were layered in gold leaf. The domes were golden or turquoise and mother-of-pearl. Other women in the street wore veils, the Druze in black, the Arabs in crimson and yellow. Even with their many folds and veils, she noticed their hips swayed when they walked. In the market women supported all manner of merchandise on their heads. Camille was hypnotized by their fragile balance: ceramic jars, baskets, chairs.

Because nothing more could be done by the doctors, her father returned to the village. When he died, he left Mayme and Camille alone in that harra again as he had many years before. After twenty years away, she and Mayme sat in their near-empty house again, and the dust rose on the road and the rocks tumbled, until Jean entered and knelt by Mayme's side. "I'll take care of you. Don't worry. I loved Shebl a great deal."

As Camille's betrothed, Jean became the man of the house. He took care of Mayme and Camille and the harra. In the morning he cleared the land for a vegetable garden; in the evening he opened the door for evening guests. They were seen sitting together, the three of them, eating dinner. His brothers asked him questions about his cousin, teasing. His eyes did not squint, but sharpened.

Camille hoped he did not feel sorry for them, because she was beginning to like Jean. As they strolled to Tula he asked, "Why didn't your mother give my uncle a nicer funeral?"

"She needs the money."

"What's more important?" He put out a hand to help her cross a creek.

"Going back."

He shook his head. "It wasn't right. He was such a good man."

A good man. That's all he needs to be, Camille began to understand.

The sun dropped into the clouds, and Camille shuddered but didn't turn away. What she really wanted was the light on her face as she sat in the lounge chair on the *Conte di Avoa,* or from the *roojme* on a quiet afternoon, or on the boardwalk in Beirut: the sun, bathers on the beach, a ship nearby.

Years in Brazil on the water filled the stories that circled them as they walked. "In many ways we are both citizens and foreigners," Jean told Camille.

"Do you feel you belong more in one place than the other?" she asked. In McClellandtown she could walk away from the house and away from family's eyes. An occasional customer might pass and greet her, but Camille cut across empty fields and tramped over the wooded hills.

"Oh, I belong here, with my mother," he answered. "In Brazil I was always sick and traveling; when my brother left, I became very lonely. I speak Portuguese quite well, you know." They linked arms as they crossed a street in Beirut, then released them on the other side. Selma and her husband stayed behind them as Camille stopped at a market to buy a nougat. Jean translated signs and sentences into Portuguese, and Camille repeated them. She imitated her father's voice. Jean laughed. He knew many languages and loved to read in Arabic, especially history. "I like to understand how governments work. For instance, it's important that we keep Lebanon for the Lebanese. We are not Arabs, you understand." He told her what he knew about the United States and Abraham Lincoln, his hero. "I would have liked to be a lawyer, but it's too late for that. We must get my brothers through school. Did you know my brother will be a priest by next year?"

Later Camille placed a plate where he sat at their table. "I would have died without you. I think my life and my mother's would have ended if you hadn't come."

Best friends. Camille had bought an autograph book in high school at the five-and-ten in Uniontown. Its pink pages were covered by heavy brown cardboard and tied with a black ribbon; gold letters spelled out *Autograph* in elaborate handwriting that Camille imitated on the first page. She had written a poem inside: "To keep my friends / Is my delight / So in this book / I pray you'll write."

Then signed it Camille Nader. The other pages stayed empty. The week after she bought it, she missed school because her father had to go to the hospital and she had to watch the store. Later, hankies were stacked on top of it until she packed it for her trip to Lebanon. She tapped her fountain pen and turned to the first empty page and wrote: *Mrs. Jean Rachid Abi-Nader, Abdelli, Batroun, Lebanon.* She pulled at the page to rip it, burn it, hide it so it could never be found. Instead she placed it in her drawer, knowing she would marry him, as everyone knew. Since her father's death, they no longer teased her or him. The question no longer slid across a table like a long knife: "When are you going to marry?"

She would have married Joseph Maese the first day she met him, if he had asked. (He promised he would write.)

After they were engaged, the days were spent sewing the satin-covered buttons up the sleeve of her wedding dress, tatting the lace for the upper arms and bodice, getting fitted for the veil and skirt. With his sister, Selma, and his mother, Elmaz, in attendance, Jean stood nearby. Camille thought only of Jean. (Best friends.) He sliced the air with his hands as he spoke quietly to her.

In the diary she wrote, *"February 4. Thursday, exceptionally beautiful day. My wedding day. Mom, Selma, and Emira helped me dress, then many others arrived. Sat in the salon until mass time, nuptial services and mass and communion. Visited Dad's grave on the way back. Many people. Maron left today; Nader arrived in the afternoon. Jesus, Mary, and Joseph.*

February 5. Fine weather. We spent a hard night because we were

dumb and I did not respond. Broke through early this morn after
Mom explained. Still no response from me. Spend day with people
going in and out as the custom. Selma did not come up all day and
night. God have mercy.

What she did not describe in her diary were the fights that started
the morning after her wedding and lasted into the day. Camille
could not accept this custom of hanging the bloodied wedding sheets
for the town to see. She explained that to her mother. "I don't want
to. Can't you tell them that?"

"I can't help." Her mother shrugged.

"Well, I will tell her I won't do it."

"You know what they will think," Mayme pleaded.

"It's dirty, it's sickening! They can't examine me like that."

"You have nothing to worry about, you're a clean bride. What
will they think?" Her mother held her by the shoulder.

Camille looked into her mother's face. "I am tired of caring what
they think."

Camille couldn't imagine her sister on her wedding night covered in white silk lying still, as Camille had, while her husband
stroked her skin and covered her face with kisses, touched her
breasts, her stomach, and pushed himself into her. Camille didn't
know what was expected of her, but Zina probably did and then
collapsed into silence until morning. Jean had kissed Camille in a
strange strained fashion, asked her to take off the outer coat of the
peignoir. She laid it across the chair by the bed and watched it as
her husband sweated and panted on top of her. Inside her muscles
contracted. A rocky boat, a very rocky boat. She didn't feel ill but
hurt. Hurt and very tired. *Nothing is ever as easy for me*, she wanted
to write in her diary, but she didn't. How did she get so tired?

She thought it would all wash away, wash away with the early-morning rain. Wash away, as Camille did when she cleaned the sheets so they could not see the stroke of blood like a number seven in the center, as if he had cut himself shaving and dabbed his neck. That was all there was, no puddle as everyone expected. She washed it away and laid it in the sun.

Could she ever explain why she didn't want her sheets hung from the balcony? Her sheets. Her wedding. Her language. No one would understand except for Jean. He agreed, although it didn't help. It was between Elmaz and Camille, and no one could say anything that would help and no one did. Selma, his sister, walked into the house. "I smell a groom," she said. Camille guarded the kitchen, the table, the quiet which ended when the sheets were not hung. (Where are the sheets; where is the blood? Certainly their young spirits don't make them shy.) Looking at the balcony in the east, the railing in the west. The doors were closed and the rooms were empty. She opened and closed her hands as they spoke to her. They felt a little swollen, and so did her feet. She would sit down soon, after they went away. The door opened again.

People came all day; some tried to reason with her. There was nothing more to say. Her voice deepening, her eyes narrowing, she knew no one would understand, so she said nothing. Wanting something of her own, needing to feel this way, Camille held her ground. The odd bellows of their voices rose in an erratic chorus. They sounded like the cows who called desperately to their calves. With their legs spread and firmly planted, they tilted their heads and released a call, each one different, as if they were names. Mother and calf moved carefully away from Camille.

Her mother-in-law stared at her. The bride crossed her arms over her chest. If she released them, her hair would rise at the nape of her neck and she would whirl around, grabbing everything, tearing the pictures from the wall, emptying the cupboards and throwing everything into trunks and leaving for Beirut. Away from all of it. In Beirut the ringing of the church bells is softened by the rushing of the water. The bride rides to the church in a carriage or white automobile.

(Jean and Camille received no gifts.)

Camille sucked her lips between her teeth. She would have none of their embarrassing tribal rituals. Never. They were convinced she had entered the marriage a soiled bride. (She's really an American; having Jean live with the two women was a mistake, Elmaz. She trapped him. You know, she received letters from a lover.)

"Letters? What letters? Tell me about the letters." Camille finally spoke.

Her aunt drew back. Camille dropped her twisting hands and let her shoulders fall. "You know what I am asking."

"No, Camille."

"How many letters?"

"Four or five, maybe, from Khartoum," Selma answered.

"You had no right."

Selma had intercepted them to protect her brother, to see the marriage would happen.

"How many letters?" Camille had to know.

"Who remembers? That was three years ago."

Mayme rose and told them to go; it was time to leave the bride and groom alone. She twisted her wedding ring around her finger. Around and around. Joseph Maese had kept his promise.

Being pregnant in her first month was in her favor, Camille had thought—not like Mayme, who had waited eighteen years for a firstborn. Perhaps her luck would change; perhaps she carried a boy. But the voices rose again and pierced her: *She was pregnant before the marriage, that's why there was no blood.* (It's not true, please listen.) *They all know he was living with you.*

She tried to get away from them, away from the voices, but she became ill all through spring. At the beginning of summer, she was back on her feet.

Dear Sis, I think I'll be all right now. I have a little cold, but my stomach has settled down. . . .

"You miss your sister, don't you?" Jean asks Camille as she sits at the desk and counts the number of letters she has written.

"Very much." She places her pen on the half-written page and goes to get him some water.

His forehead is circled by a white ring where his hat has rested. "Perhaps you will see her soon—our whole family, you and me, your mother and the baby."

Camille smiles. He drinks the water in one gulp and returns to his work.

She knows how much waiting marriage involves. She sees her mother standing on the same hill she stood on many years before looking for her husband. But who does she wait for now? The only husband is her daughter's. Mayme walks to the field with bread and dates. Camille sits on the balcony in a straight-back chair and removes her shoes. Her red feet swell. She must wait too. In McClellandtown, she was anxious to leave. Once the plans were finalized, she packed, cleaned the store, the house, the yard; reor-

ganized the storage, patched, and ironed clothes—anything until
the day.

In August the village population increases: students come back
from school, some businesses are closed, and some keep country
homes there because it is normally cooler than the city. But not
this year. The rains unearth the mosquitoes and the hot August
sun hangs over them as if it would never move. Nevertheless, Camille
walks longer and faster every day, for a little exercise. When she
stops to rest against a rock, she swings at bugs landing on her arms
and legs. In the middle of the day, workers return home. The hot-
test summer to date. Damp. No breeze. Worse than Beirut. They
enter their cool stone houses and drink glasses of lemon water and
cool tea.

Elmaz tells Camille that being in the heat gave her the bad cold.
Camille's eyes are inflamed, her nose is dried, and she swoons
when she tries to sit up. Spending the week in bed, she fights with
the sheets. When a cart rolls by, she imagines piles of tobacco
leaves or baskets of olives load them down. She listens to the
neighbors talk below her window. The house seems insufferably
hot until a breeze rises again. Rising from bed, Camille tours the
harra opening every window, causing the papers to ripple on her
desk and the tablecloth to flutter. She goes to the balcony and
brushes her hair straight back.

"You're looking better." Her mother approaches.

"I'm completely cured, Mother." Camille smiles. They wrap yogurt
and place it in the sun, then walk to the ovens to bake bread. As
it browns, Camille dips her apron in the pail and dabs her warm

face. The hot oven air blows at her when she turns the loaves, but she carries seventy loaves of bread home with her.

On Saturday she and Jean pass the day traveling by foot to Gouma. Camille stops repeatedly and watches the valley. The thick vegetation resembles green clouds hanging over the town. Little white roads wind through the villages, and a cross rises between two trees. She cannot believe how shallow her breathing has become. When she pauses her face reddens, and she must bend a little to catch her breath.

"That little cold made me feel like a prisoner." She puts her arm through Jean's. "It's a beautiful day."

The next day, her own shouts awaken her. Alone in her bed, she sweats onto the sheets. Everywhere she lays her hand is damp. Camille tries to sit up by pushing her elbows into the mattress but cannot rise. "Mother!" Her voice echoes against the high ceiling. Jean and Mayme open the door and run to her. Camille falls into Mayme's arms, and Jean rushes out and yells through the window. When the doctor comes and gives Camille some medicine, Mayme lifts her head, but she falls back onto the mattress, crying. *I feel as if I am going to die.* Camille drifts to sleep bathed in her own waters.

When she opens her eyes again, Mayme, Elmaz, Selma, and other neighbors sit around the bed. Jean's voice comes in from the hall. She can't see anything else. She wants to talk to him but can't open her mouth. Maybe she isn't awake, for no one looks her way. Suddenly her stomach tightens and squeezes. She screams, and all the women rise and surround her.

The doctor is called in and pushes his way between them. What happens now? The door shuts, the room is quiet. Mayme is crying. (Brush my hair, Mommy.) Camille wags her head and shouts; she

cannot stand the pain. It hurts. It hurts. The doctor pushes her
legs apart, bends them, but she wants to shut out the air, the flow,
to let nothing, especially her baby, leave her body.

The doctor warns her to keep her knees up or he will tie them.
Lifting her body, Camille arches her back. She feels as if a tree
were splitting inside of her. (Too soon.) She cries. Winds of hot
breath—heaves of air—hate, hate—her back releases. She collapses as the doctor hands the tiny infant to her mother.

"Let me see," she whispers.

"No."

Mayme walks away with the baby.

The doctor plugs his ears with the stethoscope and rests the
metal cone on her.

"Please," she screams.

"No," he says. "It's very small—we have to get him warm right
away."

The doctor calls her husband. Jean stands beside Camille, takes
her hand. "The baby is too small; he won't live."

(I'm sorry.) "Call the priest."

"He's coming."

"Let me see him." Swinging her legs, she tries to rise. Her
husband is crying. She stares at his dark streaked face.

"I'm sorry." Crying, she puts her head into the pillow and then
vomits. She tries to cover her mouth to stop it, but it runs through
her fingers onto the wet sheet.

When she wakens, the room is quiet and the windows are closed.

"The baby died at sunrise." Jean sits at the bottom of the bed.
"They tried to keep him warm in the oven; they brought a wet
nurse, but he did not change. He lived ten hours." Jean's face is
expressionless. Approaching Camille, he puts his hand on

Camille's cheek. She swallows; she cannot speak. She flings her head back against the pillow over and over, until she falls help-lessly asleep.

They baptize him that afternoon in the parlor. Camille lies in bed listening to the whistle of her own breath and watching as neighbors and relatives stand around. "Doctor," someone asks, "is it a full-term baby?"

"No."

"Then how many months? We must know."

Camille does not hear the answer. Through her bedroom door, she can see her neighbors in the parlor examining the child. They want to make a judgment against her. They never believed her, not a word she spoke. (She is loose: God took it from her.) Camille tries to open her mouth. *Leave my baby alone.* She is crying, crying and shouting. No one looks at her. They all stare at the table. The priest enters and kisses his stole on both sides. Camille reaches out her arms. This priest lifts the baby, but she never touches him. They say it wouldn't be good for her. Instead she stares at the green walls, the ivory ceiling, the dark wood that frames the doorway. The picture of her mother and father reflects the curtains on the window in its glass. The chairs that held the village women circle her bed. Her white satin robe lies on a tall uncomfortable chair. When she closes her eyes, she rides a rocky ship. It has no name.

Camille opens her eyes to see Jean sitting beside her. She has been in bed a month now. "You know, I am very proud of what I have done here in the village. The olive press has been repaired, old carts rewheeled, and children are being sent to weed and pick as when I was a boy." Camille sits up and puts his hand in hers. He continues, "They can take care of it now." Brushing back her

hair, he tells her it is time to go to America. America. He suggests
new strategies for getting a visa: they need witnesses of their marriage, they need to verify his police record and find money.

Camille and Mayme are pleased. Since the death of the baby,
they see no one. Walks through the village are quiet and unevent-
ful. Rachid and Elmaz send no children with messages. The roads
in the mountains are covered with snow, and wind rattles everything around them. Since the American Thanksgiving Day (*but not
for us*, Camille writes), they do not take their long walks. The snow
mutes the rolling carts, the neighbor's voices, even the church
bells seem distant, muffled. Camille sleeps with Mayme while Jean
is away arranging passage.

When the boat signals the approach to New York Harbor, Camille
quickly sorts her belongings. She has an assortment of gifts for
Uncle Elias, Zina, Boutros, and the children. In Paris she wandered along a boulevard with large windows. Mannequins with a
bent arm or turned head wore satiny dresses. Camille saw herself
in the window facing them. Round and short, flanked by wooden
women. She bought a rain cape for her niece Adele, Vicks for her
husband's bad cold, and returned to the hotel.

Her sister has four children now, but Camille hardly knows the
last three. She found them blankets and nougats and she would let
Zina distribute them. Her sister wrote, "I am glad you are coming;
I have my hands full with all the children." Camille shrugged. She
repeated in her head what the doctor told her—that she would
never have children unless she had the operation.

She stands on the boat and it sways back and forth until it nearly tips, and Camille holds tightly until she cannot unclench her fists. She believes the doctor was wrong; she could have a baby. She tells Jean each night that she is ready, that she feels fine.

Tomorrow is Palm Sunday. If they disembark by eight, she can store the luggage, and they then can take the train to mass in Brooklyn. If they are delayed, they'll have to take a taxi. Camille plans everything. When they boarded, her mother cried for hours and has said little since. Camille asked her questions and Mayme answered yes or no. She lay on her bed with her rosary.

Camille walks up the gray wooden stairs to the deck. She walks around the hull and finds Jean staring at the city. The lights shine on the tops of the buildings and in some windows. Placing her hand on his arm, she greets him.

"Look," he says and points to the Empire State Building. The ship has stopped a quarter of a mile from the dock and the city shines like a scattered Milky Way above Abdelli. The light behind them casts their reflection into the water. Jean's tall frame stands beside Camille, pale and small. She lifts her head. She's here at last. Suddenly her heart is beating in her face. Jean turns. "It's beautiful."

Camille moves closer to him. "Yes, I have been here before." She watches his brown eyes fill with light. Soon he will see sunflowers.

♦

Sisters

♦

Z i n a

1940

W h e n   B o u t r o s   f i r s t   showed Zina the house, she liked
its sturdiness. The large solid stones forming its base have diamond shapes rising from each of them. A hand could run along the
facade, and a diamond would fill the palm. A nice stone—*houses
built the way they should be*, people said to one another in Abdelli,
thousands of miles away from Masontown, Pennsylvania, the small
town that would be Zina and Boutros's home. This house is like
Beit Shebl, her family's house, with its three floors and large rooms,

with a parlor and living room and dining room and kitchen that has space enough for a table; with its basement and attic and front porch. She especially likes the large stone railing in front where she sat the day before while hired men carried her furniture up the stairs.

As a girl, outside of Beit Shebl, she sat on a stone and watched the village. Her father teased her and called her a duchess on her throne. Below her houses rose from the blond Abdelli dust. Stone was placed upon stone, without mortar. Red tile roofs, iron doors and curled window gates, wooden shutters, and some houses, like her father's and her uncles', had shiny marble floors and stairs. "This is the way a house should be built," someone said, passing the half-finished structure. Someone else agreed, looking at the plans in a small dark dining room of a family home.

"We are ordering a chandelier from France," Shebl bragged.

"With how many crystals?" someone inquired.

Wagons loaded with slabs of marble and granite rolled up the rocky Abdelli roads. Oxen breathed little clouds on dewy spring mornings. Behind a shutter or two, a mother who was watching turned to the breakfasting family had remarked, "It's the stones for Jerges house. That will be a house built the way they should be."

Zina's father presided over every detail of the building. Selections were important. *That's what makes a house last.* Italian marble was better than Spanish. Furniture from France, rugs from Persia and Syria. The chandelier had fifteen hundred crystals, and above it on the ceiling, an artist painted fluffy white clouds on a blue background, with doves circling the Virgin Mary. *This is how a house should be built.*

Zina removes her hand from the stone of her new house. But good materials don't make a house last, she thinks. *How long did*

*we have it? Live in it? As if we hadn't learned from Nagy and Elia,
our grandparents, whose house was demolished, whose hearts were
shredded by the armies marching through. What makes a house last,
Father? You even put in a chapel, piled the blessings up from the
monks and priests and seminarians who prayed mass for us.* Prayers, stones, tiles, glass. They lost that house to debts during the
war. They moved to the basement, then to Batroun—from one shack
to another, to Marseilles, and the hotel, then the small apartment.
When they finally crossed the water, they moved again—twice in
Uniontown and finally to McClellandtown. *This house will last.*

Although it was built by hands she hadn't watched and backs of
men, bare and stretching, heads covered with rags, soaking the
sun, although she hadn't seen them passing the stones to each
other, she runs her finger along the crevices and knows the house
will last. The stones are cemented and will not collapse on themselves as in the old country, where the stones press onto each
other, the lower ones giving way until they all became a heap of
bones.

Zina steps back and examines the straight roof of the new house.
The children's bedrooms will have large windows up beside the
catalpa trees. The attic will gather old clothes, books, and school
uniforms. They will wander through this house year after year as it
fills and empties. Near it, other large houses sit, belonging to
prominent families, the realtor told Boutros. Dr. R. and Mr. and
Mrs. B. have roomy porches and yards. A shiny hedge divides the
Naders from the R's on one side, and on the other, a new gas
station is being built. *Pennzoil,* its flat sign reads. Zina's yard is
lush and not very large. At the end of it two garages can be reached

from an alley where they will put a car they share with Boutros's brother Jean. Boutros's peddling days are over. Left with the McClellandtown store, Jean needs the Ford to take his goods to the coal patches. But Boutros and Zina have their own store now on Main Street across from Feranti's Hardware Store, diagonal from the First National Bank of Masontown, Pennsylvania.

Other buildings will become available too, and they will buy those for a restaurant maybe, or a stationer, or a dress shop Zina could run. They will call them all Nader's, shorter and so much easier. And like her father. She signs her name *Mary Z. Abi-Nader* on the official papers, but her husband uses Boutros. "Why don't you use Peter, the American way?" she asks him. "Because Boutros is my name," he answers. In a letter she wrote to her sister the day after her wedding she signed, *Mrs. Peter R. Abi-Nader*— how do you like it? she asked. She whispered "Pierre" in his ear as they made love. He was so American compared to the other men in Lebanon, and he fit with her so well. Peter and Mary or Boutros and Zina—it really didn't matter now.

She lifts a box of towels and walks into the house. The furniture sits against the walls of two rooms on the first and second floors. Zina wipes out shelves and places her kitchenware in them. A door leads to a small porch and the backyard. She stops and walks into the other rooms—a dining room, a living room, a parlor. Two sets of steps to the upstairs. A large basement that is dry and heated.

She wants to have most things out of the center of the room before Camille returns the younger children. She sits with them while the two older ones are at school. Camille enjoys taking care of Zina's children. She plays and sings with them, but Zina hopes she will have children of her own soon. The operation she just had was supposed to take care of her tilted womb and make it possible for her to carry the whole nine months. They would move from McClellandtown too. But the two families would not live together again. Too much, too many.

Zina watched Jean, Camille, and Mayme move into the basement of the store when they came from Lebanon in 1938. "This is your Aunt Lily," she told her children. They looked at her bright friendly face and listened to her voice singing at them. She held each of them and covered them with kisses.

The newcomers needed to work. Boutros had inherited Shebl's territory, so Jean had to find his own. One truck, two peddlers, and a small corner of southwestern Pennsylvania. The women watched the store, and for a while, life didn't change much. Camille always wanted to go out in the truck as she had with their father. She drove the best and sold the worst.

The store's truck was designed by Shebl, and when Zina saw it for the first time in 1921, she knew her father was a genius, knew he was worth waiting for. She had thought about him all the way on the train from New York when they first came. Drifting in and out of sleep, she prayed as the train entered tunnels that went right through mountains. She and Mayme pointed at the small towns and their neat little streets. Each town seemed to have an Esso sign towering as high as the crosses of the tiny churches. But what Zina drew in her little journal were the round tall buildings that she learned later were called silos. They were shiny, like ceramics. Some had names across them, *Hillsdale, White*. She wrote these too in her little book but pronounced them *Hiyasdalee, Wheetey*. They weren't French words; neither were Harrisburg, Johnstown, or Pittsburgh that were lettered on the posts in each station.

∴ *2 5 5* ∴

The tall round buildings were clustered beside the houses or barns. She thought they might be churches or towers but saw no crosses. The tops had smooth shiny caps on them, so they couldn't be smokestacks like the ones on the boats which opened to allow the gray clouds to fume from inside. Would Shebl's house have one too? Would he have lots of land, a fence made of wood and wire, and cows roaming in a field? She watched as they stopped at each station for the word they were looking for: *Uniontown*. She knew how to pronounce that one, having heard it time after time. Her mother asked anyone who had been to the United States, "How is Uniontown?" Some knew the place, since many of the villagers went there. Others said they did not know it. Mrs. Bayly had described the green hills to her and taught Mayme to say *Penny-syl-bania*.

Zina saw Mrs. Bayly's mouth curl when Mayme repeated it in her way. Zina tried. Pen-sil-vane-e-a—a long word and a long state strung along the track. Her eyes only half opened for every sign, but her mother stayed awake most of the time. When Mayme saw that either girl had awakened, she began a string of comments and questions—about their father (do you remember him, Zina?). Mother, of course. Elias (he has the bluest eyes and reddest hair you ever saw). About America (you will start school soon).

On the train they ate in a dining room that had white cloths on each of the small tables. The waiters did not flirt with the little girls as the porters on the boats had. Zina tried to speak French to them, but they did not answer—they barely spoke at all. While Mayme counted the American money onto their little silver trays, Zina looked at the numbers—like Portuguese. In her journal, Zina drew the numbers in a line and put the Arabic symbols below.

Her mother had green paper money, but preferred the coins. Silver dollar coins were kept tied in her handkerchief inside of her blouse.

Other passengers helped them order—some spoke French; one man knew a little Arabic from the war. "Beruity?" he asked. No, no. Batroun. He had never heard of it. They finally settled on Jabali. Oh yes, they were mountain people, he told the friend who traveled with him. Jabali, Zina thought; nothing of the sort. She brushed her shoes on the backs of her shins. We have been living in France. Tell him that, Mother. They had been stylishly dressed compared to the others on the boat. Some families came from the streets it seemed.

Zina combed the front of her hair and sat back with her arms crossed. Another tall round building flashed past the window. Right before they reached Uniontown, a porter tapped Mayme on the shoulder. She hurried her daughters, pulled at their arms, straightened their dresses, and dragged them to the door of the train. First they saw a wooden platform, the sign blurred by them, then the train slowed. Zina saw faces looking up at the train; some people waved. She tried to remember her father's face. He definitely was tall and had fair hair and dark eyebrows. No, the eyebrows were her uncle's—Uncle Rachid and his solid inscrutable face. She would recognize Shebl, she was sure. The train stopped with a jolt.

Staring at the door, Mayme waited until the steps were placed. She descended, looking around her quickly at the people standing near the track, holding babies, yelling into the air, and she began to cry. She bent and kissed the ground. "This is my home. Thank you, Jesus." Camille hid behind her mother. Suddenly Mayme stopped, screamed, and flung her arms around a large man. Shouting, Camille pulled at her mother's skirt.

"Be quiet." Zina waved a hand at her.

Mayme touched Camille to shush her. "Camille," she said, "this is your father." The big fair man bent to kiss his daughter, but Lily backed away. Zina put her arms around Shebl's leg and placed her cheek against the rough gray wool of his trousers. He picked her up and kissed her cheek. *This is my father.* His face did resemble Ummi Rachid's, but it looked happier. While the family waited and puffs of steam hissed along the ground, he ordered their baggage to be taken to a car.

Zina followed Shebl while she held her crying sister's hand. The adults spoke, directed the baggage onto the top of the auto, and put the girls into the backseat. During the short ride, Zina had to lift herself up to look out the window. They stopped in front of a store with big windows. It had a sign that Zina would copy down later: *Nader's Dry Goods.* In a large front room, clothes hung from bars, fabric sat on long tables, and glass cases held white handkerchiefs and silk ties. A lady stood behind a case and bowed her head when Zina's father spoke to her. When Zina turned to show Camille a white furry hat, she couldn't find her. Camille had walked to the back of the room, where she had heard voices. Zina followed.

Camille was approaching a man in a chair reading a newspaper. He closed it as the little girl came near. *"Intee Ummi Elias?"* she asked.

That must be him, Zina thought. That's Uncle Elias. He asked Camille, "How do you know who I am?" Putting her on his lap, he kissed her on the cheek. Over the course of the next week, he told the story of how the little girl knew who he was many times.

The girls wandered around the store as the three adults talked in the back. Zina heard her mother's shrill voice in its excitement wherever she walked. She found Camille staring into a glass case. Zina stooped to see what her sister saw. "What are you looking at?"

Camille put her hand onto her reflection. "Do I look like an American?"

"I don't know. Maybe. Many are fair like you." Zina gazed at her own reflection. She had her mother's high cheekbones and her nose and mouth. But her skin was dark. The waiters on the train were darker. They were called Negroes. Pulling up her sleeve, Zina checked the dark hair on her arm.

Their mother took their hands and directed them up the stairs that led to the apartment above the store. They looked through the kitchen and the bathroom, then Elias's room, and, finally, the bedroom where Camille and Zina would sleep in one bed and their mother and father in the other. The beds were not very large. Mayme smoothed the covers and turned to her husband and smiled.

The neighbors would come that night to meet them, Shebl announced. Mayme whined, "Already? There is so much to do."

Shebl patted her shoulders, "Don't worry, don't worry." He pointed to the bathroom. "You take baths and get ready and Elias will cook tonight."

The girls waited on the cold floor while their mother untied their hair and pulled their wrinkled dresses over their heads. She stared at the tub for a moment, then ran her hand along the white edge. Camille sat on the floor and put her fingers against the clawlike feet. Mayme twisted the knobs and watched as the water poured out. She positioned each girl in the middle of the tub and washed her down, not plugging the drain. They did not sit. She powdered them with a scented talc from the store.

"What's this for?" Camille turned her head away as the fragrant dust flew.

"To make you smell pretty for the company."

Zina dressed herself and began to fix her hair. She wanted to go out and watch her father. Everything took so long. She sat on the toilet swinging her legs while Mayme combed Camille's hair. Camille did not fidget as usual. Her mouth was drawn into a little red circle, and her cheeks seemed to sag to her collar. Her mother whispered encouragingly to the little girl. "Your father loves you and is very happy to see you. Will you smile for him?" Camille did not look up from her solemn pout. Mayme sighed and buttoned up Camille's blouse.

Zina wandered out into the hall. Rolled up against one wall sat a mattress and some sheets. She sat on the bundle. A man walked in and looked down at her. "You're sitting on my bed." He smiled. She backed against the wall. He bent down toward her. "I am a friend of your father's. How do you do?" He put out his hand; Zina didn't move. Mayme and Camille stepped from the bathroom, and Mayme introduced herself to the boarder and began to talk quickly. The man nodded his head up and down. From the top of the stairs, Zina could hear Shebl's voice tunneling toward her. She descended, placing each foot carefully on the steps. Shebl was positioned in the front of the store with his arms crossed, and he spoke to a man with a green cap pulled toward his eyes. This visitor could not be Libnani. His red face spread widely, and his mouth formed a thin line—he didn't wear a suit jacket, a tie, or a white shirt. His white shirt had large spots on the belly, his pants were covered with mud at the hem, and his boots were heavy and laced down to a big round toe.

Zina tours the second floor of her new house and stops at the small bedroom. This will be her sewing room, and the bedroom next to it will be a nursery. There will be lots of light. In Abdelli, all the houses received plenty of sun. Beit Shebl had a terrace on the east and the west ends—sunrise and sunset. In Batroun when she and her sister and mother took walks to escape their little shack, she lingered in front of the large houses. One house she especially liked was shaped like a ship. Portholes dotted its facade where it faced the sea. She imagined it was Noah's Ark and had settled there rather than on Mount Ararat. Mayme told them stories of the boats and ships she had sailed on in Brazil, of the strange plants that hung over the river like waterfalls, and the trees whose roots sat exposed near the banks. She panted like the engines of the small vessels that were fed wood and kept large fires burning inside. Rocking back and forth, she pretended she was sick again as she had been on the launch up from Manaus. With her hands she drew the grandeur of the large chandeliered dining room in first class when they returned to France.

The ships they would sail on would not be one of those. No large and fancy dining rooms; instead they would eat on their beds. The crew cleaned the floors by flooding them with water, and the passengers sat up on their beds holding their children and their things while the men swished mops back and forth. Zina knew her mother appreciated this with so many people in one place, so many sick and careless with their sickness and their waste. Even the dirt floors they had lived on in Abdelli and Batroun had been swept every day. They dusted a table, if they had one, wiped the windows if they had these. Each daughter had had her duties. Zina had scrubbed, dusted, swept, washed, dried, shaken out the rugs of the big house, swept the floors of the basement and the grounds of their veranda, beat the mattresses in the shack, the sofa, couch, and dusted the table in their apartment. Each day, every day. Her mother sewed, washed clothes, ironed, cooked, and disappeared into other people's houses where she did the same.

When the family had settled themselves into that first apartment in Uniontown, her mother hung flowered curtains around each bed. The next week after the neighbors had come and gone, they walked together hand in hand toward St. John's Elementary School. Zina stood in front of the building and watched the clouds pass through the glass. She could not see inside the large windows. In the office a nun dressed in black sat at a large desk. She and Zina's father spoke in English, then she turned to each girl and addressed her. Zina didn't speak; Camille started to cry quietly and looked at her mother. After the sister spoke to Shebl, the family left, marching hand in hand the same way they had come down.

A couple on the other side of the street called over to Shebl. After he crossed to talk to them, Zina tugged on her mother's dress. "What happened, Mother?"

"You will start at the school on Monday, but Camille can't start until next year, since she doesn't know any English."

"But I don't know it either!" Zina was frightened they might have made a mistake.

"Yes." Mayme stopped. "But you are older and will learn it."

Shebl returned and shouted at Camille, "Put that down."

Camille froze, holding a half-rotten apple she had picked up from the garbage. Mayme grabbed her hand. "We have lots of food now. Don't take anything from the trash." Camille dropped the apple, still staring at Shebl.

School became Zina's secret life. Each day she walked down the hill to St. John's. Shebl's truck passed on its way to the coal-mining villages. She held on to her books tightly with one arm and waved with the other. She did learn English quickly and brought home certificates for her penmanship. She told stories of Angela and Billie.

Mayme bent to watch Zina's careful imitation of the alphabet. "What is this?"

"A *K*, Mom."

"Khy."

"Kite, kitten, words like that."

"Khy," Mayme repeated.

When Shebl converted their business from a dressmaker to a confectioner, they lost all their money, and had to move to the other end of Main Street. Uncle Elias, who had persuaded Shebl to make the change, shrugged his shoulders. So Zina changed schools. She loved the name of the new one: the Ella Peach School. It sounded like a piece of nougat. They skipped her to the third grade. She pored over *Al-Hoda*, the English-language Arabic newspaper; she read directions, packages, cans, and Elsie Dinsmore books. Late at night, her uncle, seeing her light, banged on the door. "Aren't you asleep yet? Put that book away." Zina stuffed a towel at the bottom of the door and put the lamp under the blanket. Camille's sleeping breath droned behind her in the room.

When the family moved to McClellandtown, Camille started elementary school. Both girls spoke English better than the grown-ups. But the children at school ignored them. Girls grouped together

in the play yard, and Zina and Camille stayed by the school building. Some other Lebanese girls played with the Slovaks, as Shebl
called them, but Zina read, and Camille wandered the parameters
of the fence.

Zina throws an empty box on the back porch of the new house. Not
much has changed—Adele has come home crying more than once
from going to school with the children of the Slovak people. "You
should hear what they called me today, Mother!"

She took her daughter's head in her lap. Addie's dark olive skin
was streaked with tears. Maybe the dark daughters are born first,
and the light ones are second, like Camille and Amanda, Zina's
fourth child and second daughter. Is the blood thinner, the pig-
ment weaker? Is the second daughter just a shadow of the first?
Zina's face, as she sees it in the kitchen window, is heavily powdered to a lighter shade. Rouge in careful circles dots her checks.
Camille uses nothing on her face, just a little lipstick. Her fair
skin reddens in the sun, and freckles cover her cheeks.

Zina turned quickly once when Camille chanted to the baby,
Amanda, "Are you my little girl?"

As girls the sisters had agreed that Amanda was the most beautiful name they had ever heard. Like a saint, an angel, music.
Camille stared at the girl's bed and cooed, "Are you my little girl?"
Zina's mother will live in the basement of the new house and take
care of the children. Camille and Jean lent Boutros and Zina Camille's savings as a down payment. Now that Boutros has two stores,
Jean could peddle the old territory.

Their life would be changing in no time, Zina told her mother.
We just need patience. She has been through times when the car

has been piled with merchandise, back and front. Shebl's truck had large doors that opened on each side of the truck with shelves that held notions, yarns, and tools. Below them, long drawers were filled with fabric and linens. At the top a rack ran along each side for coats and dresses that the seamstresses made in the shop. After Shebl pulled out all the doors and raised the sides, his customers could see all the merchandise. He parked across from the mines on payday, near the church on Wednesday before Christmas. They circled his goods. At the mines' entrances the sooty-faced men passed through with their new money. He stopped in his truck outside of Buckeye, Edenborn, Point Marion, Sandy Bottom, Ronco, Deep Hollow. In the summertime he put a five-gallon ice cream drum in the back and took one of his daughters with him to scoop for the children.

Zina loved to go with him. She took the money while he handed out the three yards of flannel or two bottles of tonic. Some customers didn't have money, and he accepted jars of jelly, enough chickens to have to build a coop behind his house, and a piglet that wouldn't stay penned.

In the evening Zina talked with her father. He taught her to write Arabic and French. Camille, too, sat with her pencil in hand, but she looked puzzled and bowed when her father asked her a question. "Are you lazy or just dumb?" he spit.

On Sundays they drove to Pittsburgh and Wheeling to buy from wholesalers. Arbonot and Stevens had five floors, one filled with dresses, another with coats; another with children's clothes, and men's suits, and household goods. Her heels clicked on the floor as she walked from rack to rack. While her father and Mr. Stevens talked in the office, she examined the dresses. Everything was beautiful. Her mother had picked two frocks for her and her sister. They were beautiful chiffon-covered party dresses, but they were exactly the same. "I don't want to look like her," Zina protested.

"You should feel lucky to have a sister." Her mother handed the dresses to the woman standing beside her. "Wrap these, please." Zina leaned into a rack of clothes and crossed her arms across her chest. Her mother looked through a selection of women's things. She pulled out a dark straight dress with polka dots and a simple shirtwaist. Her mother ignored Zina and held the dress up to her body. Lifting her foot, she checked where the hem fell.

"Oh, that is perfect," Shebl teased. "Have you ever thought of wearing polka dots before?"

Mayme laughed behind her hand. "How about this one?" He pulled another polka-dotted dress out, then another. He smiled broadly.

"I like them." Mayme giggled. The clerk stood behind them grinning and trying to understand what they were saying to each other.

Finally Shebl glanced toward her. "My wife, she can't resist the polka dots." The clerk moved her head in exaggerated nods. "What you really need is a coat." Shebl grabbed her around the shoulders.

"Do you suppose they have dotted ones?" Mayme asked. Shebl explained what she had said to the saleslady, who laughed. Zina approached them, but she stayed quiet until it was time to leave.

On the way home they stopped at a restaurant for sandwiches and milk. The girls did not speak in public. They laid their gloves on their purses beside them at the table. Although the waiter bent to Camille asking her what she wanted to drink, her father ordered everything. She stared at the man until Shebl said, "Bring them milk."

Down the road from the store, Miss Littlefield opened her dancing studio, and since the girls were being raised as little ladies, they would take lessons, Mayme said. She made them black bloomers and bought the required shoes. Zina and Camille stood in line with the other girls and imitated their gestures. A leg in front, back, around, they thought they might knot themselves. The teacher shouted instructions while the sisters tried to understand the English. Sometimes she spoke in French. After the second class they didn't return.

Mayme understood her daughters' problem. She had spent weeks trying to talk to Shebl's saleswomen. At first she tried to be friendly, and then she noticed they were stealing merchandise—panties in a purse, a blouse stuffed into the bloomers. Shebl was away all the time on peddling trips, so it was up to her to try and stop them. At first she spoke the words she knew, slowly. She watched carefully, then grabbed their hands, looked in their purses. They ignored her and laughed to each other, walking out and letting the screen door swing.

When Shebl returned he stroked his wife's shoulders and promised to take care of it. Zina glanced up from her reading and watched them talking. She remembered his voice bellowing across the hall in the harra, and her mother's frightened face as Shebl grabbed Mayme by the shoulders. Zina had rolled over in her bed, had tried not to hear. What had he wanted then?

Zina bent her head to her work and discovered she had used Arabic symbols in her arithmetic problems. She erased furiously.

Her uncle walked in with two friends behind him. He announced they would be their new boarders. Her parents shook the men's hands.

Mayme and Camille began to prepare diner. Zina wondered if these were paying guests or not. The men's voices rose from the back of the store. When the store was transformed into a confectionery, the staff had been cut in half. Along the walls where the bolts of fabric had been they placed tables with marble tops. The eighteen-foot-long fountain reached midway down the store. Wrought-iron chairs with curly backs circled petite round tables. Elias made all the candy himself. Sometimes he bought old candy from Kresge's and recooked it and made little squares that he wrapped in cellophane.

Business did not improve. Zina's father spent weeks away selling on the road. Zina and Annie Esper walked to school daily, and she spent the nights helping her mother or doing homework. The house was very quiet. Elias sewed costumes and suits to sell on consignment at stores in town. One Sunday Shebl took everyone in the truck and he pulled into a dirt lot near Edenborn in a town called McClellandtown. A stone foundation had been built in front of a small hill. Trees surrounded the building and a narrow footpath led to a small pond.

"This is where our new store will be," Shebl announced.

The family stared at the hole in the ground. It was larger than the Uniontown swimming pool, Zina thought. What kind of house could fill this hole?

In less than a month they moved to a large windy flat building on the same spot. Camille and Zina walked from one end to the other. They listened to their shoes on the linoleum. In the back was a bedroom for them and one for their parents, a living room, and a kitchen, but no bathroom. Only a spigot brought water into a barrel in the kitchen.

The store was a general store with candy, clothes, and kitchen-ware—everything the neighbors needed. In front Shebl put up a Standard sign and pumped gasoline into trucks and cars that pulled into the lot. Camille washed the glass cases with vinegar and water. Zina folded caps and pushed them inside one another. Green-and-white-striped towels stood in columns on a wooden table, cans of Carnation milk formed a red wall with white flowers. Each day after school the sisters wandered through the shelves, straightening, folding, and cleaning.

In the morning they climbed a long high hill and descended to a blond-brick township school below. All kinds of children attended it—many traveled more than the two miles Camille and Zina walked. Before a clerk was hired, the girls missed many days while they helped. Zina hid a book under a pile of shirts.

The front door slams and voices come from the living room. Zina drops a stack of dishtowels onto a box and walks through the small archway. Camille is surveying the boxes, and Zina's two youngest children stick their faces into what they can reach.

"Is it three o'clock already?" Zina lifts Amanda onto her hip.

"Mm-hm," Camille says, leaning against a mattress placed against a wall. "I am worn out."

"Did you fuss for your Aunt Lily?"

Amy shakes her head and her braids fly back and forth.

"No, no, they were good. They even helped in the store," Camille says.

"I sweeped." Georgie pulls a book from a box and opens it

to the middle. Zina takes it from him and places it on the table.

Putting Amy down, she takes her by the hand to the stairs. "Your bedrooms will be up there." She points, and they look up the long staircase.

"I want to see," George announces and starts to climb the stairs. Amy follows, taking one step with both feet.

"George, take your sister's hand and make sure she doesn't fall."

He stops at a middle step and waits. When Zina returns to the living room, Camille is leaning with her eyes shut.

"Are you sick or something?" Zina asks. She has thought that Camille might be one of those people who imagines a disease every day. My back, my feet, my head.

"No, my muscles are tired, that's all. There's so much to do in the store to get ready. I get tired, that's all."

"I know what you mean." She turns. "Well, I have to get some work done before Addie and Junior get back. They are in the store with their father. You know they walk to school now."

"Yes, you told me." Camille follows her sister into the kitchen. "Jean went up to Boutros's with the car; he needs to borrow the book for the citizenship class."

Zina pulls the dishes from a box and unwraps them and places them on the counter. Camille starts the water and puts her hand under it.

"Do you have something to plug the sink with? Is there soap?"

Her sister picks up a box and lifts it to the counter; she searches it until she finds a box of soap. "Here." She thrusts it toward Camille, then picks up a rubber stopper. "Put this in there." She points to the drain.

"I know." Camille wiggles the plug into the hole and shakes the powder into the water. Zina carefully unwraps cups, saucers, and glasses. Boutros took his citizenship a few years before. It was easy for him. He tries to fit in—learned English, drives a car, joined the fire department and the Chamber of Commerce. When she met him, she wrote to her sister that he was disappointing, but later she regretted that and said so. *Gee, he's so sweet and lovable. I'm certain you are going to like him. He's all-American. He can dance, I don't have to teach him. He makes love perfectly, I don't have to teach him. He adores me, I don't have to teach him. I teach him nothing because he's fully equipped.*

First impressions are deceiving, she wrote to Camille when her sister was in Lebanon. She hated Beirut when she first arrived. The whole country looked like a pile of rocks to her. She expected something more sophisticated. *We reached Beirut Thursday night at seven but were not allowed to go ashore until Friday at about nine. Beirut was so disappointing. I expected sidewalks and nice ships and soon was set back in my thoughts. Really Masontown is a lot nicer.*

She had always wanted to live in Masontown. It was just the right size and had a long row of businesses on Main Street. Zina had heard about a women's business organization, and she would join that. The women in the stores in town like her and are very polite, but they speak loudly to her husband and ask him to repeat what he says.

Her sister slides a rag over the dishes and talks about how they were starting to put electricity in Abdelli. They didn't have telephones yet, but they were waiting for water lines. Zina glances at her sister. Camille is barely over five foot two inches. Maybe she'll start to wear a straighter-cut dress as Zina recommends, but Camille doesn't care enough about clothes. She puts on the same flowered shirtwaist day after day.

The sisters are four years apart, and Zina wonders how crucial these four years are. Her sister is careless. Zina checks the glasses before she places them on the shelves. Once Zina overheard Jean tell his wife, "I like you in an apron." Camille laughed. Always a little tomboy. No wonder their father depended on Zina to see that her sister's purse and shoes, gloves and hat matched.

"Lily, remember when Dad was studying for citizenship?"

"Mm-hm. I tell Jean that story all the time." She turns to her sister and lowers her voice. "What is the capital of the United States of America?"

"Edenborn," Zina responds. They laugh. "Just because he made all his money there, he thought it was the center of the universe."

"It was." Camille catches her breath. "Of course it's not as funny as Jean taking his driver's test."

Camille tells the same story over and over when it comes to her father. She was the one who went back to Lebanon with him, who saw him die. Once Camille told her that Shebl had seen his death twice. Once he was climbing a mountainside that had a burning bush at the top. He stood and Jesus appeared to him. He watched the form flicker before him. The figure waved his hand at Shebl. "Go back, go back, it's not your time."

Darling Daddy, How much shall I tell you I miss my dad? I can't tell. You and mother are never out of my mind. I miss your arms around me and the sweet kisses you used to give me. But Papa, I have such a sweet man, he almost takes your place.

"He knew when it was his time, though," Camille continued. "In his dream he saw the lights of the hospital shining over his body. People whispered goodbyes to him; someone was crying and he saw Jesus." He died the next week.

Zina wishes she had been with her father, but she saw him die herself so many times. When she was three she had crept down the stairs of the harra to where she had heard voices and cries. Through a small crack in the door, she saw Shebl lying on a long wooden table. A man held an iron rod in a fire, then raised it. Zina had seen pictures of Michael the Archangel with his fiery sword. The man placed the rod on her father's stomach. Shebl screamed and kicked his legs. Zina gasped and put her hands over her mouth. Someone grabbed her from behind and she screamed. "What are you doing here?" her mother asked.

"What are they doing to father?" she cried.

Taking her hand, Mayme led her back up the stairs. "He always has stomachaches, bad stomachaches. That is how they are cured." He shrieks in her sleep and in her mother's sleep. Her mother twitches and mumbles, "Shebl, Naum." In the middle of the night Mayme sits on the edge of her bed reciting the rosary, saying her Kyrie. The front of her scarf becomes damp against her forehead and she cries the rhythm of a train.

When she first came to the McClellandtown house, Zina had to sit with her children when they were frightened by her mother's noises. But then it became the way they teased her. Like her English. She handed Zina two dimes. "Buy the kids some bop."

Junior responded, "Can we have it with banunzi? Addie, what kind of bop do you want? Orange bop?" They laughed together, holding each other's arms and bending. Mayme pinched Junior's neck until he yelled, "Hey!" Finally, Zina intervened. Later they sat with her while she told stories. "The Treasure of the Bike" or "The Lost Tiger." Zina crocheted under a lamp in the corner. Mayme had not told her and Camille stories like that. She related times in Brazil, repeated the tragedy of her brother's death, the misfortune of Elia and Nagy, but never a fairy tale. She listened quietly to her mother's voice dramatizing the various roles.

Zina dries the dishes and places them on the shelf while Camille twirls a towel inside the glasses. Everyone knows the story of the driving test. "Maybe if Jean had let me finish teaching him how to drive, he wouldn't have had such difficulty. But he was a terrible student and I am a good driver, but maybe not a good teacher."

Oh yes, the license story. Camille remembers everything Jean said. "When the officer asked, 'What do you mean by pedestrian?' he answered, 'People or dogs crossing the street.' "

But what happened next wasn't as funny, although when Jean tells it, everyone laughs. "I passed my oral test and he assigned a state cop to give me a driving test. When the cop picked up my papers, I heard a guy say, 'This cop is a meany, he won't pass anyone.' We walked to the car and he looked the car over, kicked the license plate with his feet. He came to me and said, 'Go and straighten the license plate.' We fixed the plate and then we all took our seats. He said, 'Start the car.' I turned the key and stepped on the accelerator and it didn't make a sound. The state cop got up, and he slammed the door and disappeared without saying a word."

The story goes on with a dead battery, a crook of a mechanic, Jean's backing up over the grass, not stopping at a stop sign, and passing the test anyway. When it is told, Boutros adds his part and both men laugh until they cry into their handkerchiefs. One party after another. "Have you heard this story?" Zina brings coffee to their company on trays and serves them quietly while everyone shakes with laughter. Smoke circles around the parlor and glasses ring as they are placed on the glass tables.

Parties stabilized the McClellandtown house. Shebl had many friends whom she, Mayme, and Camille served. In and out, the neighbors, people from the church and friends of her uncle. During prohibition, Uncle Elias had a thirty-eighth birthday party for himself. The singing was loud and the party crowded; political arguments ricocheted against the walls. Someone from next door called the police. When they drove up, the liquor was poured down the sink or down throats. Zina heard commotion from her bed. She had had cramps all day and hadn't come down to dinner or the festivities afterward. Suddenly the police burst into her room. "Is this girl drunk?" one asked. Mayme screamed at them and pushed them out through the door.

"Will you have dinner with us?" Camille wipes her hands on the dishtowel after everything is put away.

Zina looks at her a moment, then picks up the empty carton. "No, I think it would be nice to be here tonight. The children have to get used to the house."

"I think they will love it. It's so big, and they will get to have their own rooms. Children like to have rooms to themselves."

Zina put the boxes out on the porch and came back in. "I think the girls will have the one just over the living room, and the boys the next one. We'll be at the other end of the hall."

"Will you put a nursery in, or just put the new baby with you?"

"I don't know." Zina strokes her stomach with her hand. *Best friends.* As children they played together much as her own children do. The Esper girls, Nora, all had similarly strict parents. When the families got together, the girls walked through the woods behind

the house, Camille chewed on grass; Jeannette and Annie held
hands. Zina led them through Neff's Woods to a blueberry patch.
They filled their hands and mouths with the fruit, knowing that the
stain would get them all beatings.

"We're going to get killed." Jeannette had tried to wipe Annie's
smeared mouth with her hand.

"Let's not go back," Zina said. She looked at the hill in front of
them. They could wade through the creek and swim to France.

Every May the Naders closed the store early for devotion to Mary.
Dressed in bright dresses and woven crowns of wildflowers, Zina
and Camille held bouquets to place at the Virgin's feet. Each wanted
to lead the procession and competed for the honor. They recited
novenas at a shrine Shebl built in the back of the store. While they
prayed, the neighbors beat on the door. Children wanted candy;
someone needed gas. But they never opened the door or turned
toward it. They stayed on their knees with their fingers pointed
straight toward heaven.

Zina's children sing together, especially Junior and Addie. They
rock the glider back and forth, singing "Row, row, row," in rounds.
While Zina sweeps the living room, she listens to the squeak of the
glider. She pauses for a moment, then opens the door. "Quiet now.
I'm going to put Rachid to bed." They look up at her. Addie locks
her mouth with an imaginary key.

At the top of the stairs, Zina holds the baby. The long hallway
is covered with a gray flowered carpet. She strolls down to the east
end, peeking into the boys' and girls' rooms to see if everything is
in order. "No fights today, please; company will be coming for

Labor Day dinner." Mayme sits in the sewing room crocheting a blanket. "Very pretty, Mom." Zina stands in the doorway.

"It's for the new baby." Mayme lifts a pale blue corner. She places it on the table. "Here, let me put him to sleep; I can stay with him."

"Thanks, Mom." Now Mayme, not Camille, takes care of her children.

Zina, pregnant again, hopes her sister has her own child soon. *That house killed my son.* She hears her sister's voice as it told her the story of her baby's birth in Abdelli. The first night she returned, Camille sat at the kitchen table, poking the cloth with a knife. "I need an operation to have more children." And their mother's voice, scratchy and low, saying, "After we came here to live with your father, I became pregnant again." Her daughters looked at her in startled silence. "It may have been a son, I don't know." She straightened out a folded napkin. "I went to visit Labibi at the hospital and fell on the ice. I lost the baby right there. I never did tell your father."

Someone made tea, someone walked in from another room, and the women, the mother and her daughters, gossiped about the village.

Except for Addie, born in the old country, the births of Zina's children were easy. Poor Addie—crying so hard, crying to eat, her tiny head became soaked with tears. Her face was like a newly born lamb's, pointed and tiny.

Elmaz walked the village looking for the wet nurse. Boutros sped to Batroun to buy a "swinging bottle," and Zina pushed on her breasts, waiting for the milk to rise to feed her daughter. It took three days. From that day on, she dripped with milk, slept in it, dabbed in from inside her clothing. *You will love being an aunt,* she wrote after the birth of Adele in the old country.

"You have wonderful, beautiful children," Camille told her.

Zina returns to the kitchen and takes out her cold nut roll dough. As she rolls it on a board, her shoulder cracks. She pauses and wiggles her shoulders around. "Addie," she calls, "do you want to cut out some cookies?"

The screen door slams and her little girl rushes into the kitchen. Zina carries the board covered with dough to the kitchen table. Addie scoots onto the chair, and Zina hands her a cutter. Her daughter pushes circles into the dough. Zina was happy to have a daughter as her first child even though she knows a son would have been better, but the attitude in the village has changed since her own birth. (Lucky to be alive.) Boutros and his family circled her bed and gazed at her dark daughter. Very small. *Best friends.*

Addie is obedient, just as Zina was, always at her mother's side, listening to her mother's voice, moving her hands as her mother moves hers. Folding the end of the dough, Zina rolls it as tight as a stumpy cigar. Would Addie push a basin under Zina if she were tied to the wall? Would she carry her waste, wash her clothes, care for her, as Zina did for Mayme?

Zina's kitchen is floored in white linoleum. (Why did we sweep floors made of dirt?) The cupboards are filled with dishes with red flowers around the edges. (Eat it, before it gets dirty.) The children sleep on soft mattresses with piles of pastel blankets. (Her sister leaned against her and breathed; Zina could not rest.) They own a Ford. (Mother, my feet are burning.)

Camille walks into the house from the back porch. Zina stands at the stove stirring the rice, then places a cover on it.

"It's a hot day," Camille says.

"Do you think it's too humid to set up outside?" Zina turns toward her and kisses her cheeks. She hears the children running and screaming in the yard. Boutros and Jean are tying the grapevine arbor in front of the garages.

"No." Camille walks into the dining room and living room. "The house looks wonderful; you've done quite a bit of work." Boutros wired it himself, removed the doors between the main rooms, and laid carpets. Zina pauses by the archway. Yes, it does look nice—white flowered curtains, a round chandelier. She has plans. Her sister is staring at a photograph of their parents together. Her mother has her mouth pulled tightly, and her father's glance looks distant.

Zina stands behind her. "I just got it framed."

"It looks wonderful. When I have a house, I will have walls and walls of photographs like royalty and their portraits of ancestors. Each of my children will be placed where I can see them all the time." Camille's voice is cracking. Her face is damp.

"Are you all right?"

"I'm pregnant." She smiles.

Zina raises her hands to the sky and then clasps them around her sister. "I am so happy. Did you tell Mother?"

"Not yet."

"Well, go."

Camille goes out the back door.

Zina feels serene, relieved, and surprised at this news. Sometimes what is real is unbelievable to her. On the S.S. *Sinaira*, the ship that took her back to Lebanon, she couldn't believe that a moonlit night could be the same as what was written in books. She wrote to her sister: *November 13, 1931. . . . Every night we have a dance. I dance sometimes, but I sure do miss my sweetheart. I have not the heart to dance. I was thinking of you last night, Sis. The night was simply wonderful. I often read of these wonderful moonlit nights but could hardly believe that it was true. I saw the moon overhead. I saw the beautiful smooth sea with the lights of the moon flickering here and there. I could not believe the beauty.*

Zina lifts the pot lid and steam rises to her face. Another daughter or another son. She scrapes the rice onto a platter and picks up another. As she walks onto the porch, she sees her mother dressed in polka dots and her sister in a slim rose-colored dress hugging.

◆

T w o S o n s

◆

C a m i l l e

1947

When **J e a n t e l l s** the story of how the scorpion was sewn into his nose, the scar itself wiggles. As he speaks, the black line that winds a path along the length of his nose dances. *They took*, he says, *the hair right from the horse's tail and put it into a carpet needle this big—he raises an index finger—and mended me right there on the stones, where I had fallen. I tossed like a fish thrown up onto the beach. My hair was long, and it fell into my mouth and in their way. Godfather sewed and Mother brushed back* *the strands so he wouldn't weave them right into my nose or now I would have whiskers like a cat.* His shoulders rise and fall and the others around the dinner table join him in laughter. As he speaks, the scorpion moves and his eyes fill with tears.

Camille can't remember from what he fell—was it the roof of his mother's house in Abdelli? As a small girl, she could see Jean's family *harra* from her father's house on the hill. Its large stone porch opened onto the rest of the village as if all should stop there in homage. Or had he fallen from the steps that connected the high roads and the low ones? Or was it from those blond walls piled high with stones that divided the properties? She gets the stories of children confused. One falls and cries *Mommy, my knee,* another wanders away from where she stands talking and runs into the street; another is sewn up by careless old men who are nearly blind, leaving his nose crooked with a creature crawling on it. When he sleeps she looks over at the nose and imagines something is written on it.

Now the scorpion on Jean's nose is not moving. Sitting on their stuffed flowered chair in the New Castle apartment, he is staring at the rug. A spot is worn through near the coffee table, but that is not what Jean sees—not the rug, not the chipped leg of the table, and not Camille. He rises for the sixth time and goes into Roger's bedroom. Camille follows. Jean's whole face stays in profile to Camille as she enters the boy's room. He stares into the crib at the child. His nose is completely still. A crying man will shake the end of his nose or squeeze it with his finger and thumb to clear it out when he thinks no one is looking. Camille has not often seen men cry. When her father was near death, he said he was ready; yet his face paled when he looked at Mayme, his eyes swelled, and he held his nose pinched between his fingers, then covered his face with a pressed white handkerchief.

Jean stands beside the bed in a chenille robe; the lower pockets sag with dampened hankies. His nose is dripping and he grasps a trembling rosary—castanets, worry beads, die rattling in a rough palm. His neck strains, his arms curl down. "There is nothing more we can do; take the boy home," a doctor told him, and he told Camille.

Camille and Jean do not turn to each other nor against each other. When Boutros died ten hours after his birth back in the old country, Camille was kept away from him. They told her his head was soft; they told her he didn't have fingernails. She lay in bed while Jean whispered that the boy's eyes were blue. Camille clutched her stomach and cried.

Later a doctor in Lebanon told her that an operation would be the answer to everything and that she shouldn't try to carry another child without it. But they only do it in America, he added. *America*, she whispered to Jean as they walked along the roads. When he stopped and studied his thriving tobacco fields, she cried, "You can lay one field of corn in Pennsylvania over this entire village." She wanted him to see the hills around McClellandtown, Pennsylvania, where her father had a store. In the spring most of the farmers rode giant wheeled machines that tilled the earth. Some stood behind handles with blades that turned it over and over. Others led stocky horses along the curve of the hillside. While she described it, the strong scent from the orchards in the valley below rose up to him and the morning light warmed the translucent leaves.

In 1934 when Camille drove to New York City to deliver Zina to her ship, she crossed Pennsylvania from west to east. Along the road, carriages of the Amish farmers slowed the traffic. She peeked into the black shells to see the bearded men, the women with the pinned hair, wearing long dresses and no rouge. Their daughters wore bonnets; the sons had black hats like their father's. *All their fields are worked by hand,* she read to her mother from a sheet a paper in a restaurant. The truth is, other customers said, the Amish were quite rich and didn't want to share with others; that's why they had their own schools. Camille looked at the faces of the woman and her two sons who sat in the carriage outside the café. She did not move, did not talk, but only stared at the door her husband had gone through. Camille tried to imitate her, to let her hazel eyes dim to dark gray, to let her cheeks pale. This is the face she thought of after Boutros died. That was the face she wanted to show her mother-in-law. Camille wanted that woman's mask.

After the baby's death, Jean agreed they should go and take Mayme back to America. He left the fields he had worked the last three years—the blossoming fig trees, the beans snaking along the ground, the tomatoes wrapped against branches used for stakes. And he left his mother and father, saying he would return soon.

A few months later in an office with yellow walls, Dr. Larkins said to them, "Afterward you can have children." But her mother warned, the operation was trick or magic. Camille knew nothing about it, but she trusted the doctor and his sure language, she trusted the hospital's confident maneuvers, and the swift routines of the nurses.

When Camille awoke from the operation, she tried to imagine what was different in her, what made it possible for her to suddenly hold a child inside of her womb. Her stomach pulled with pain. Placing her hand on it, she found a thick bandage. She did not lift her head to look around. What now? Although the stiff sheets were folded up under her chin, her skin felt cold, and she wanted to wrap herself up, but she did not move.

The room was lit by midafternoon sun. She turned toward the window—the other bed had a crumple of white sheets on the top. On the table beside it a pitcher held roses and leaves. Camille rose to look out the window. Outside the road going east to Uniontown, not west to McClellandtown, was dotted with cars. She flopped onto the mattress and felt under her pillow to find her rosary. The operation hadn't worked. Where was the celebration? Her body ached. She did not feel a gush of newness or the heavy breasts of pregnancy. Why wasn't Jean with her? She blessed herself with the silver crucifix and began her prayers. When her eyes started to close, she fluttered her lids and forced them open. She was afraid to sleep in case Jean came and went away.

After two months in this country, Jean had learned English, obtained his driver's license, and established his selling territory. Out in the hills of Greene County, he bumped along the dirt roads in the 1934 Ford piled with clothes in the back, fabric in the front, and dishes in the trunk. He tried to ride with the windows closed, but the heat overcame him. Jean liked to stay clean and carried a jar of soapy water and a washcloth. He wiped his face and hands before he approached a house or a station. Camille had shown him every road she knew from West Virginia to Pittsburgh.

He watched silently as they followed the Monongahela River up Route 88. Across the railroad tracks, the mills and mines filled the air with smoke and dust. He read the signs: Carmichaels, Millsboro, Fredricktown, Marianna, and Centerville. They jogged down washboard roads that had no route number to the villages with the slate-gray houses that looked exactly the same and connected at one wall. Coal miners' homes did not appear on maps. Jean drew blue arcs on lined paper: Dry Tavern, Rices Landing, Ronco, Crucible, and Nemacolin. They stopped by Hamilton Creek and ate spinach pies.

After a day on the road, they returned to the McClellandtown store, and Camille fed Zina's children their suppers. Jean discussed with his brother a corner where all the miners from Buckeye and Nemacolin passed after the three-o'clock shift change. He might set up the goods there on the paydays. Their voices hummed below a crying child's, a scolding mother's, a tired aunt's. Noisily descending to their room, Camille hoped Jean would follow her. Because the basement had no heat, she could not wait and soon had to return to the kitchen and stare at the stove until it was time for bed. She put children to sleep, sorted grape leaves, and washed dishes. They bought a bedroom set with a vanity and a large mirror to brighten the basement. But it did not help. Camille washed the posts and headboards, wiped the mirror, and shook the rugs.

The day after the operation, Camille listened to her roommate, Connie Mae Kelley, breathe in the next bed. She wrote only two lines in her diary. The sky was overcast and the air was humid. The Allegheny Mountains had blue mist around them. Wheels squeaked down the hall and a small whir filled the air. Connie was awake and smiling. Connie offered a *Woman's Day Magazine* to Camille. "Would you like to read this?"

After dinner Camille asked if she could call home. The nurse brought a wheelchair to take her to the phone in the middle of the floor. As they traveled down the corridor, she glimpsed other patients in their rooms lying in tilted beds. Some had visitors around them. An orderly passed with a basket of flowers. At the high desk the nurse pulled the telephone and clicked it. "What is your number?" She handed Camille the receiver. The phone clicked and rumbled, and Zina answered in a groggy voice.

"Where is everyone?" Camille cried. She tried to cover her face.

"Oh, Lily, everyone is sick," Zina whispered. "They are all in bed. Even Jean didn't go selling today."

"I am nauseous," Camille said, glancing up at the woman standing beside her.

Back in her room, Camille lay against her pillows. The door was left slightly ajar and she saw the hospital personnel as they walked down the hall. Many doctors came in and examined her. She tried to remember each of their names to put in her diary: Dr. Larkins, Dr. McHugh, Dr. Hogdson, Dr. McLaney. "Do not try to conceive too soon," Dr. Larkins announced in front of them. They circled her bed and their silver stethoscopes hung as they bent to listen. Camille stared at an empty chair. The doctors talked among themselves, pressed her stomach, looked under the adhesive, and walked through the door. A wall of white.

The hospital room did not become dark. From morning to afternoon, to evening to night, a gray lingered like an eternal dusk. She held the *Woman's Day* above her, but her arms were tired; she could not sit up for very long. The pages fell to the center, and she dropped the magazine. Connie Mae Kelley talked about Ireland. "The green hills there are like the green hills here." While a nurse pricked Camille's hips with needles, she smiled and spoke pleasantly to her back. She felt the point enter her skin and the vial empty inside of her. "Try to sit up and eat," she told her as she wrote in a notebook. The food sat on a tray with legs. "They'll take it away if you don't."

"Do you have any children now?" Connie asked.

Camille stared at the ceiling, pale green paint, veined and peeling. "I had one once for ten hours. I carried another for two months. But now I can have as many as I want."

She will tell Jean that when he comes to visit. She will tell him that she shouldn't conceive too soon, that they could have as many as they wanted; that she would fill the house with lovely children. Will Jean see the puffiness around Camille's face, will he detect the heaviness in her stomach? Looking into a hand mirror, she combed her hair and tried to dot her face with rouge.

Jean arrived at her door that night wearing a suit the color of wheat. Unlike the other men who went to their church, Jean often wore light suits and tilted his hat over one eye. Mayme said that without his ring, he would look like a bachelor. When the couple walked alone through downtown Uniontown on Sunday, Camille put her arm through the crook of her husband's elbow. She imitated the women in high heels in Beirut who walked along the sea. They pointed their toes and put each foot down daintily in front of the other. Their dresses swished around their hips. Zina walked this way too. Even when families were together and children pulled at their arms. Zina stood upright, her face perfectly powdered, her hair tamed and curled, swiveling her hips.

As he paused at the door of the hospital room, his lean body hid inside his baggy suit. His face was narrow and sharp and the scorpion darkened. He spoke English to her, and his accent gave the words a strange stage quality, a ringing. Mayme followed Jean into the room and sat on her daughter's bed.

Finally they had come. Camille knew she should be happy and put on a good face, but she only could cry. "You took so long," she wailed.

In the McClellandtown days, as they talk of them now, the farmers made less than a dollar a day. They reminded each other of this fact when business was slow. Jean found ways to buy on credit, pay it quickly, and buy more. He designed a new life plan: to stay for only ten years and return to Lebanon with the money to start a new business. She didn't remind him of this when he allowed unending credit on the neighbors' accounts. It didn't hurt them very much.

When Zina and her family moved out of McClellandtown into the large house in Masontown, handiwork filled Camille's evenings; Jean read books and newspapers, and texts from classes he took at the YMCA in Uniontown. She did not miss her sister's children crowded at the kitchen table. She did not miss Jean's and Boutros's return from the selling trips when they talked alone about their adventures until bed.

Even though the store was empty Jean and Camille imagined themselves lucky. To rebuild the business they first sold merchandise from a small table and one showcase. Then it grew as if they had power. They added merchandise and had to hire two other women to wait on customers. A neighbor lady helped Camille clean and an old man swept the grounds around the store. Why did it all seem so easy in McClellandtown?

Their house began to collect odd pieces of new furniture. Camille favored flowers on the couches and curtains. She bought a sewing machine with *Singer* swirled on its black enamel top and pressed into the iron curves of the treadle. Like everyone in the village, they bought an insurance policy from a German who visited each house with a little book that he kept the accounts in. He sold a whole life policy that would be worth one thousand dollars. When he came to the store, he lingered. Jean leaned against the glass counter and listened to the salesman as he stood in the middle of the floor. He quoted the book of Revelations without moving. He talked about the war—talk that worried everyone. The United States would enter the war, he said, to save the Lion of England and the Lady France from the great bird. And help the Jews who would go to gather in Palestine. His voice was hard and loud. He never shook hands with Jean. When he left, he waved after turning his back.

Camille knew their life had finally begun when she became pregnant. Jean, convinced he did not belong with merchandise, took more courses: he tried welding, photography, and law. The couple was constantly coming and going—to see friends and relatives, to work in the church, to attend socials, and to buy merchandise. Camille carried her child for the full term with little pain.

When the time came to deliver, the Metropolitan Life Insurance Company sent a doctor and a nurse to her home. Elias, their son, was brought into the world above Nader's Dry Goods Store in McClellandtown, Pennsylvania. After Elias's birth, Camille rested from years and years of being tired. Zina had recently had her fifth baby, so she became Elias's wet nurse for the first two days. Kissing her son, Camille passed him to her sister. She fluttered her eyelids and surrendered to sleep.

When did it happen? When did she hear the scream? Zina's

voice called, "Jean!" And her screaming lashed around the house and into the room. Camille grabbed her chest and pushed herself up. In the living room Zina stood with Elias in her hands and her blouse open. His face had turned blue and he gasped for breath. His mouth stayed opened, crying without making any noise. The door of the store banged and Jean's feet stomped the steps to the living room. Mayme pushed on Camille's arms. "Go back to bed." Camille leaned against the couch, reaching for her son, but Jean and Zina wrapped him in a blanket and left.

Camille lingered at the window shivering. The car spun away from her toward Uniontown. The silence of the house seemed louder than the screams that left her. Camille tiptoed toward her bed and slipped her feet into her shoes. Dropping the keys into the pocket, she walked out into the drive. She would follow them somehow. Across the road three boys ran through the ditch calling one another girls' names. She tightened her coat and leaned against the screen door.

When the phone rang Camille pulled on the knob. The door seemed to stick and she yanked it, nearly sending herself into the gravel. Zina was calling from the hospital, and her breath puffed each word. "They are transferring blood from Jean to the baby; he will be all right, they said. They didn't even test to see if their blood would match. They put him right to sleep." She didn't stay on the phone. It clicked and Camille was sure the baby had died, would die, would not come home.

Jean returned that evening and took her to see their son. Elias stayed in the hospital for weeks drinking from bottles. The crib they placed him in was small, and he was swaddled as if he were a caterpillar in a cocoon she remembered from the grammar school science books—silvery shells that the caterpillars made.

After Elias was brought home, she kept him in the store with her all day. He lay in the bassinet in the back of the store. Months later he crawled on the red rug that ran from the shoes up front to the candy. Eventually he stood with his hands pressed against the glass and talked to his reflection. Camille heard his squeaks as she spun the handle on their wooden cash register.

On Jean's thirty-third birthday, Camille gave him a present of his second living son. She had said countless novenas in the nine months and credited at least two saints for the healthy child. They named him Roger, for roji—*"hope"* in Arabic. Two sons and there would be more is what she told Zina one Sunday as she threw an oilcloth across a wooden table in Gaston Park. Camille kissed the baby and handed him to Mayme, then set the dishes, three on each side, and paper napkins. Elias tossed a small multicolored ball back and forth with his cousins. Addie and Amy, Zina's daughters, rocked on a seesaw, occasionally banging the ground with their seats.

Many of the men in the town were drafted, leaving their women standing on porches even after they were gone. Because fathers did not have to go to war, there was something else they would have to do. Jean did not know what. The insurance salesman disappeared. The neighbors decided the insurance man was a German spy. His distance, they thought, was very strange. Jean shook his head at that idea.

War can be good for the economy but not for business, Jean said to Boutros. A new road was being built that would detour the traffic away from McClellandtown. Business would definitely drop. Drivers would no longer see their gas sign from the highway. Jean considered his growing family and proposed peddling again.

Boutros said he should wait.

While the children played on the swings, they sang Arabic hymns. The squeaks of the chains accompanied their voices. For a moment the adults became quiet. Boutros and Jean paused in their back-gammon game. Zina stopped her needle in the air. Mayme rested the baby against her shoulder, and Camille put her hands in the pockets of her apron. Back and forth, up and down, squeaking and banging, the song twisted through the park. When it ended, the children giggled and shouted to one another. Camille glanced around her. Other families played baseball; a woman bounced a baby up and down on her knee and smoked a cigarette. She surveyed the adults at her table. Jean shook dice in a black velvet cup and let them tumble on the mosaic backgammon table. Tablecloths draped Zina's knees. A colorful swan covered her foot. Roger reached his hand out toward his father's nose. Jean lifted his face toward the child, and for one moment that was brief and possibly imagined, tears cradled in his eyes.

Camille is in the eighth month of a hard pregnancy. Now she is so big she wears a housecoat and Jean's felt slippers. Roger is back from the hospital, and Dr. Skerrish says nothing can be done. They should have stayed in McClellandtown, where it was safe; where Elias was born quietly in her bedroom with a doctor, nurse, her mother, and sister.

Jean was not sent to Europe to join the war, but to Elwood City to work in a defense factory. Again the store was emptied and this time sold. The family moved up the Monongahela and Ohio rivers to New Castle, right into their uncle's parish house. Because he was sick with pneumonia, Uncle Elias needed them to take care of him until he recovered. Camille didn't like the idea of living in the rectory of St. John's Maronite Roman Catholic Church, but the family came first. She made Jean agree they would move into an apartment as soon as their uncle was well. The boys needed room to play—something priests' houses were not constructed for. She hadn't imagined their days sitting at the kitchen table waiting for their uncle's guests to leave. The boys wiggled and whimpered. The hum of adult voices silenced them until they could go into the living room.

Suddenly caring for a sick priest included cleaning the church and preparing the hall for weddings and baptisms. Camille and Jean stood at the sink in the morning passing dishes to each other. He worked the graveyard shift at the factory. Two sons, a new store, service in the church, and a new business during the day. The store they rented was one-fourth the size of the McClellandtown store. On Sunday afternoons Jean drove to Pittsburgh to the wholesalers, who he hoped would remember their good payment record. He filled the car with shoes and dresses. Although the sign in front of the store said *Nader's* in red paint, Jean and Camille called it the Long Avenue store. Jean became foreman in the shop almost immediately.

Although Uncle Elias regained his strength, he had become accustomed to Camille's hand guiding the domestic life of his parish house. When they moved, he did not hire a housekeeper. Each step, every candlestick continued to feel the persistence of her cloths. Her knees hardened like the marble she scrubbed.

At lunchtime she and the boys walked down the block from the new apartment to take Jean some food at the store. Lifting Roger high, he landed him on a chair the shoe customers used. Elias pressed the buttons on the cash register and listened to the bell ring as the drawer swung open. Placing a dresser cloth on a small table, Camille set Jean's lunch on china plates. Before Easter Jean snapped a picture of them in front of the store. The large window reflected Jean holding the camera. Elias and Roger strained at Camille's arms. She looked as if she would burst through the surface of the photograph. Her face glowed, and despite the boys' clinging to her, she cocked one hip. Camille and Jean were never their real ages, only younger and often older.

When Roger's throat became sore, Camille did not worry too much. She gave him anise tea and crackers, but he stopped eating and he stopped drinking, and he began to lose weight. The doctor said the boy would be fine soon. But he wasn't. For weeks he couldn't talk and a fever simmered on his pale face. Camille checked his temperature each day by kissing his forehead, and each day he was hot and couldn't eat. "He needs a new doctor." Her uncle and husband agreed.

Dr. Skirrish ordered immediate hospitalization for the boy. He also examined Camille and found that she was pregnant. Something grew in each of them, she thought. The word *tumor* loomed large as if it had a power of its own. She had read about plagues in high school and knew this was how they happened: one day everyone went about their business in an ordinary way—eating, shopping, working; the next day thousands died. This plague, condensed and concentrated, lodged in the lung of her child.

When Jean returned from the first day at the hospital, he did not face her. "There is a malignant tumor in his lung." She felt a jolt. Their uncle rushed to bless Roger. "Perhaps he can live on one lung," Dr. Skirrish hoped.

A beetle had begun to eat away at Camille's leaf of a heart, and she needed it. She needed it badly. She looked across the tiny apartment and everything seemed darker and lonelier. Everyone disappeared and the furniture vanished and a mist rested in her eyes. Finally she rose from the couch, left her husband explaining the doctor's words to their uncle. In the boys' rooms, Elias slept. By his bed, she listened to his breathing. When in her life did it happen that the small rhythms became the most important things of all?—Elias's breathing, her uncle's exhaling nose as he napped on the couch, Roger's chest rise and fall—a fluttering bird inside of him? She hears her own heart when she rests in the afternoon and imagines the house moves with her as if it were one of the great ships that brought her to this country.

When the boy does not recover, when both his lungs block, Jean tells her the luck was an illusion—something he does not need to say again. When he comes from Roger's room his face is frozen in a downward glance. He sits. Camille touches his arm. "He won't eat," Jean says. She swallows a pocket of tears and watches Jean. She wants to apologize. Roger was born on his birthday. He has told everyone this—a story to be told over and over. Like all the rest. Camille rises from the table and collapses on the couch. She knows she will never breathe normally again.

Before Jean comes home from the store that night, Camille tells her uncle she is frightened. She works in his rectory slowly cleaning glass and wood. When she tires, she sneaks into the church through the altar doorway. She stands in the middle of the altar and tries to lower her body in a small genuflect. Her knees wobble and she backs up until she reaches the communion rail. Her legs release until they land on the red leather cushion lining the rim.

Camille plans to say a whole rosary, one for Roger, maybe another for Elias; perhaps a third for the new baby. During Holy Week the statues are covered with purple shrouds. On the other side of the stained-glass picture of Michael the Archangel, a bug crawls. The low sun exaggerates its size a little and its wings cast a lacy spot on Saint Michael's gown. Camille watches its path up to the angel's face and then it flies away. She feels very hot in the empty church. When she turns back to the altar her head begins to reel; she sees nothing but a haze of purple, as if the statues have lifted from their pedestals and floated together. She drops the rosary onto the altar. *Oh, Mary, have mercy and save my son.* She leans, dropping her head against the iron, and groping for a handkerchief to dry her face. She feels ashamed and conspicuous in the empty quiet room.

At night Jean wears a T-shirt over his face when he goes to sleep. It's a habit from Brazil, he told her one summer night in Lebanon. They covered their faces because of the heat, the bugs, you understand. It does not get dark enough for him, she thinks, and not silent enough. The gas hisses, the crickets rattle, a dog barks at a door down the street. His body tosses in the blankets and he throws them off, but he keeps his face covered with the white shirt. The last spring storm frosts the streets with trails of frozen snow. It will melt by afternoon, and the daffodils across the street will spring up as if nothing had happened.

Camille knows what it is to have her heart tear. There may be nothing left. The family is frozen in their waiting. Only the baby inside of her pulses and shifts against whatever seems to be inevitable. Jean reminisces. His voice pricks her skin. "When Roger and Elias walked together and Elias wandered away, it was the little one who stopped. He shouted at his big brother, 'Elias, come and walk with me.' He waited until his brother's foot was up against his own. They walked step by step, matching strides."

Camille makes bread and sinks her hands into a cushion of dough. Keep busy, she had read in a book. But she too remembers the women in the line at Joseph's supermarket turning to her and to the boys dressed like little sailors. The women always said, "What beautiful boys." Her sons held her hands, one on each side. They stayed by her skirt until Elias took the groceries and Roger ran to open the door.

She finds it almost impossible to drop to her knees and beg, but she lets herself fall in front of a large stuffed chair. She leans over into the seat and rests her arms. Everything has large flowers on it—the curtains, the chair, the rug. They blur over one another. Elias stands beside her. A rosary is woven through her fingers, but she does not move it. She thinks prayers, but does not open her lips. She puts an arm around Elias and he steps toward her large body.

Maybe the luck was an illusion; Jean could be right. They sit across the table from each other and speak less. Jean loses weight, lots of it. Camille is frightened and finds it hard to breathe. Elias does not know what is happening to his brother. Roger does not speak to him, and he was taken from his bed to a hospital. When he came back, he was smaller. Like a new baby, Elias says. And he sleeps all the time. Elias watches him. He sits in a large wooden chair by his brother's bed. He holds a toy dog. "Roger," he whispers.

Camille hopes Roger does not hear him. Camille hopes Roger is sleeping. Jean's face no longer looks sad. It is torn. It knows terror. She checks her own face and wonders about age. Jean's body is strong, like a teenager's, and his shoulders are very broad. When he drove to Pittsburgh every day to visit Roger in the special children's hospital, his face became steadily older and thinner. Fourteen weeks of traveling back and forth. And if Roger was awake when it was time to leave, he whispered, "Daddy, don't leave me; I need you." Jean came home and sat far from the light.

Camille told him about the clerk who was stealing clothes from the store, exposed her fears of the maid who slipped money from the bureau drawer. She wanted to lay her head on his chest and listen to the way his heart was beating, to be certain.

Jean came to earth with Halley's Comet—the tenth day of the tenth month of the tenth year of the twentieth century. "Isn't that blessed?" he asked. And here is his son. A special one, born on his birthday in the middle of a world war. Blessed, *roji*, hope.

Roger's breathing has nearly stopped, and Jean gathers him in his arms in the morning and takes him to the hospital. Again Camille, imprisoned by glass and immobility, watches the car's bumper bounce down the hill. No one is left in the house. When Elias gets home from school, she will call someone to take her to the hospital. Who will close the store for the night? The clerk answers the phone. "Yes, Mrs. Nader," she drawls. "I'll put everything away. Sorry about the boy."

Camille pulls the sheets from Roger's bed and drops them in the basket with the other laundry. She could try to make it ordinary— bake bread, write letters, clean—but she feels very tired. The baby inside of her wiggles, and she rests against a wall. When Roger was born, she insisted on having him in the hospital, remembering Elias's blue face and Zina's scream. All her children would be born with every possible thing around them to make them live. Every penny would be saved for that purpose. There they know about life. He was a perfectly healthy child.

They use names from the past that become new here. Elias, the oldest son, has a name that must be used, for the uncles and grand- fathers before him. The second, Roji, *hope*, became Roger in America. Do you spell it with a *d?* people ask. No, just Roger. Roji, now "the sick one," lies like a bouquet of irises in Jean's arms. He holds the child out to Camille, *ya rouhie*, my spirit.

Children are so small. Inside of her, he weighed so much, but after he was born, she cradled him in one arm. Now dying flowers before her cannot be reborn, not by prayer, another doctor, glasses of ginger ale, or cold T-shirts held against his head. She rocked him inside her arms, pushed him against her. Held him tightly, and in the darkness, she tried to press him back into her womb. Camille won't be so careless with the baby inside her now. He will be born and he will live; so will Roger, Roji.

Roger has died. Camille is two weeks and two floors away. The cries from the babies in the nursery jar Camille's sleep. Like sirens they screech, and she tries to jump, except that she feels heavy, worn. Her father envisioned the hospital lights flashing above him before he died. As Camille was wheeled to surgery, she closed her eyes, but the light moved across her eyelids. No darkness in the hospital. When Jean sits on the edge of her bed, she climbs up his arms and falls against her pillow. "Did you see him?"

"He's a big boy. How do you feel?"

"My back hurts, of course." Camille shares a room with other mothers who are also having babies. The beds in the two rows are filled and face each other. She thinks of Marseilles. Her husband tells her the story of the maid. He has decided not to prosecute.

"Seven hundred dollars is a great deal of money."

"I know, but it is not enough. I went to the alderman and he checked with the police. She has a record. She stole from a doctor, I called him too. He was very angry; he thought I should have her put away for life."

"I wonder what kind of woman would do that." Camille remembers the lemons in Batroun. Would they have stolen more if they needed to? But it is not the same with lemons.

"When I talked to Simons . . ."

"The judge?"

Jean nods. "He said I could bring a complaint and she would go to jail and her son would be taken from her." Jean stands and looks across the room. "Maybe she just wanted to better things for herself and her son."

Camille doesn't argue. She thinks of her mother, his mother, herself, her sister, Yousef's wife, the woman on the boat whose boy used their slop jar, of Roger, and of the new baby.

"The boy looks healthy." Jean says. "His head is very big."

He is a little yellow and the doctor said he might have jaundice, but she doesn't tell Jean. When she looked at him in the bassinet, she thought how square everything in a hospital was. The bodies are lumpy and out of place on the long straight mattresses; the babies are undergrown seeds rattling in their pods. Roger's body became so small, he nearly disappeared in the sheets. She held up his head and tried to get him to eat. "I can't, Mommy. I can't. His head weighed an enormous amount in her hand and it became heavier and heavier. Finally, she noticed his eyes were closed.

She screamed for the nurse. A smell she didn't know soaked the air. She dropped his head but didn't remove her hand from behind it. *Roji, Roji.*

"He's an angel now," she told his brother.

All night they sat in the church basement with the small body in a shiny white casket. She knew she couldn't go to the funeral; she could barely walk. So she sat the night through. She did not promise a new brother to Elias. She crushed a rosary against his fist and told him to pray.

Jean clears his throat. "This one is Junior, isn't he?"

"Yes, of course." The luck is gone. They knew this would be their last child, even before the doctor told them so. She spelled carefully on the form: *Jean Rachid Abinader, Jr.*

"Good." He sits back on the bed. When they spent each night in Children's Hospital with Roger, they were in the children's ward. Around them, other parents had children there too. They were dying. She hadn't thought of that before. She surveys the ward. The woman across from her went into labor just a few hours before. The women on either side have already given birth. One is going home today.

"Johnny, how's Elias?" She holds his sleeve.

"He's fine. Your mother is with him. He has been asking for his brother."

The room is very quiet, and from the hall the cries of a baby filter into the room. "What do you tell him?"

"That his brother is gone, but another is coming soon."

"Does he understand?"

"I don't think so."

"What can you do?"

"I tell him to pray."

Camille leans her head against the pillow. Jean stands again, then he walks out to take another look at his new son.